THE BEST OF GLUYAS WILLIAMS

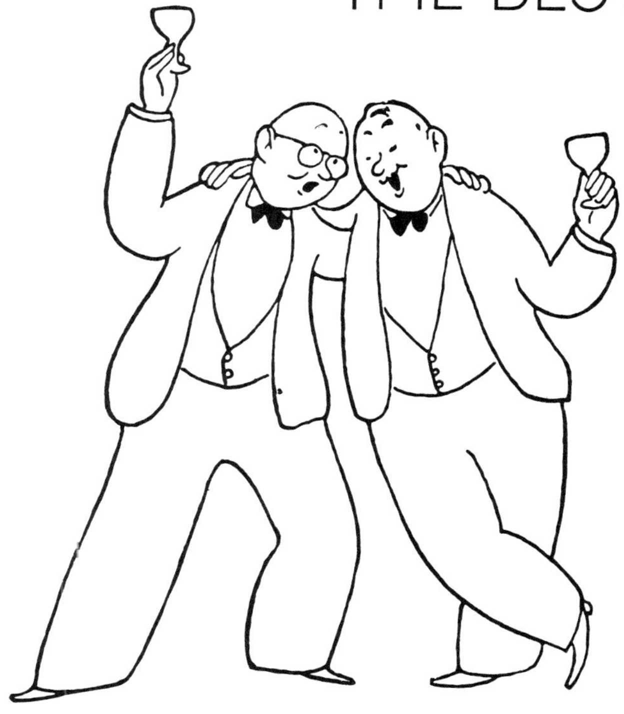

WITH A FOREWORD BY
CHARLES DANA GIBSON

AND A PREFACE BY
ROBERT BENCHLEY

DOVER PUBLICATIONS, INC.
NEW YORK

Published in Canada by General Publishing Company, Ltd., 30 Lesmill Road, Don Mills, Toronto, Ontario.

Published in the United Kingdom by Constable and Company, Ltd., 10 Orange Street, London WC 2.

The Best of Gluyas Williams, first published by Dover Publications, Inc., in 1971, is a new selection of the artist's work. All drawings originally appeared in *Life* or *The New Yorker* and most also appeared in the collections published by Doubleday, Doran & Co., Inc.: *The Gluyas Williams Book* (1929) and *Fellow Citizens* (1940).

The Foreword by Charles Dana Gibson and the Preface by Robert Benchley are reprinted from *The Gluyas Williams Book.*

International Standard Book Number: 0-486-22737-5
Library of Congress Catalog Card Number: 73-177890

Manufactured in the United Sates of America
Dover Publications, Inc.
180 Varick Street
New York, N.Y. 10014

FOREWORD BY CHARLES DANA GIBSON

No book was ever in less need of a foreword.

But I gladly write this for the satisfaction it gives me to say behind Gluyas Williams' back the things that his modesty has kept me from saying to his face.

We can all find ourselves between these covers—and with what charm and skill it is all done!

All forewords give a full description of just how the author produces his effects and gets his results. In this case I wish I knew. I doubt if Gluyas Williams knows. Perhaps only the Creator of all things knows.

At any rate, here are the matchless drawings. I don't know just how much credit should go to Gluyas. He is industrious—but that also may be a gift from the same source. His life is ideally happy—but, again, he doesn't deserve, by any means, all the credit for that.

So never mind guessing how he does it. Let us stop this interruption and thank the Creator of all good things for Gluyas Williams, who knows us so well.

This modest genius—and loyal friend.

PREFACE BY ROBERT BENCHLEY

When I was a candidate for the Harvard *Lampoon* I was under the sanguine impression that I could draw. I used to go around to the *Lampoon* office three evenings a week bearing little sketches in which I felt that I had caught something of the lighter side of Harvard life (being a freshman, I still thought that Harvard life *had* a lighter side) and I used to stand in line with the other candidates waiting to show my contributions to the editors. Most of the editors kept their derbies on and none of them ever laughed.

There was one, however, who made things as easy as possible for me. He was the *Ibis*, or head of the "art end," and his name was Williams. While he could not conscientiously applaud my technique as an artist (I had evolved a certain "wash" process, consisting of covering those lines of which I was not quite sure with a wet, black substance) he frequently engaged me in conversation about the condition of the Cambridge streets and my progress in my lessons. I was always glad when I saw Williams standing at the head of the line to take in contributions, for I knew that, regardless of the merit of my particular chiaroscuro, he would be nice about it and reduce the humiliation to a minimum.

One night Williams took me aside. I had just submitted a drawing showing two ladies (more or less in the manner of George Belcher) standing in an areaway by a large garbage can. The taller and more striking of the two ladies was saying: "Ain't it offal, Mable?" (a *cliche* of the period, and suggested, I may say, by one of my room-mates). I had a feeling that it was rather good.

When Williams took me aside I experienced a strange elation. Perhaps I was to be given an assignment to draw a centre page for the Yale Game Number. But the *Ibis* had other plans for me. In his quiet, tactful way he said: "Why don't you go in for writing, Benchley? We have several very good drawing men in the competition, but we need writing men." I thanked him, and went in for writing.

Thus, had it not been for Gluyas Williams, I should to-day probably be earning thousands of dollars as an artist.

But this friendly attitude on Williams' part has extended through all the intervening years. When first I had had enough stuff published to get together in a book, he consented to illustrate it. He has illustrated my books ever since, and I am violating no trade secret when I say that he has done it at considerable expense to himself. (Illustrating books isn't a bonanza, especially when you happen to have a daily syndicate and all the commercial work you can handle at the same time.) And I am also violating no trade secret, nor am I indulging in mock modesty, when I say that Williams' illustrations have sold more books than my text matter. I need only quote from the publisher's blurb on the jacket of one of them: "Even if you don't like the book, there are always the Gluyas Williams illustrations to look at."

There is only one drawback in having been Mr. Williams' model for so many pictures. After years of capturing those particular facial characteristics of which my mother is so fond, he has quite unconsciously taken to putting me into *all* his drawings, commercial and otherwise, as the typical American Sap. I glance at an advertisement for McCreery's and see myself, laden with bundles, illustrating the sales point that even the dullest of customers receives consideration in that store. My friends point out to me that I have been caught to the life in a Williams drawing showing the delight with which dear old Uncle Tasker will receive a dressing gown for Christmas. When people come to me and say: "I saw your picture in *Vanity Fair* to-day," I know instinctively that it was not among those nominated for the Hall of Fame but in the back of the book among the advertisements typifying the sort of men to whom a Bates umbrella or a pair of Goodyear rubbers will be an ornament. Not only in his advertising drawings but in those amazing full pages in *The New Yorker* and *Cosmopolitan* where the face of Mr. Mencken's *Boobus Americanus* is called for, mine is the face.

Thus, through his conscientious attempt to illustrate my books faithfully, Mr. Williams has made me his lay figure, and owing to the enormous popularity of his drawings, I am fast losing all personal identity and becoming a type, like the Gibson Girl.

However, if this is to be my path to fame, I am content. There could be no surer or more permanent way of going down to posterity. For while there are other artists who have caught something of the American scene, and other artists who can draw well, I know of no other artist who combines, as Williams does, the sure insight into the common mind and a technique which might well be turned to more important things—if there *were* things more important. I believe that Williams' drawings will be preserved for expert contemplations both as data on the manners and customs of our day and as graceful and important examples of its art.

I only wish that by writing something for the front of Gluyas Williams' book I might do as much for it as he has done for mine by drawing in them. Even if I were to make a house-to-house canvass to sell it, I could not help him as much as he has helped me. My only consolation is that he really needs no help.

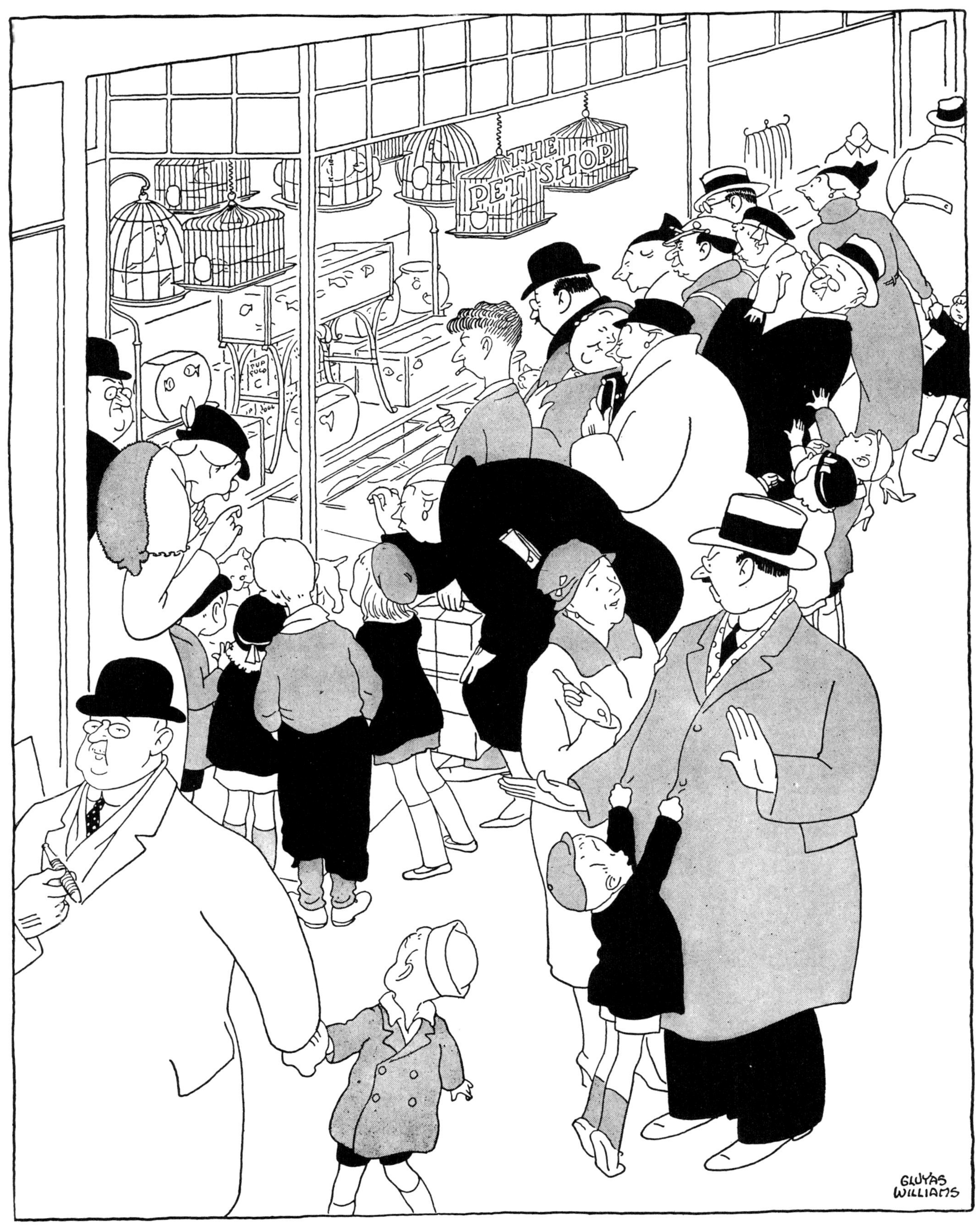

THE PET SHOP

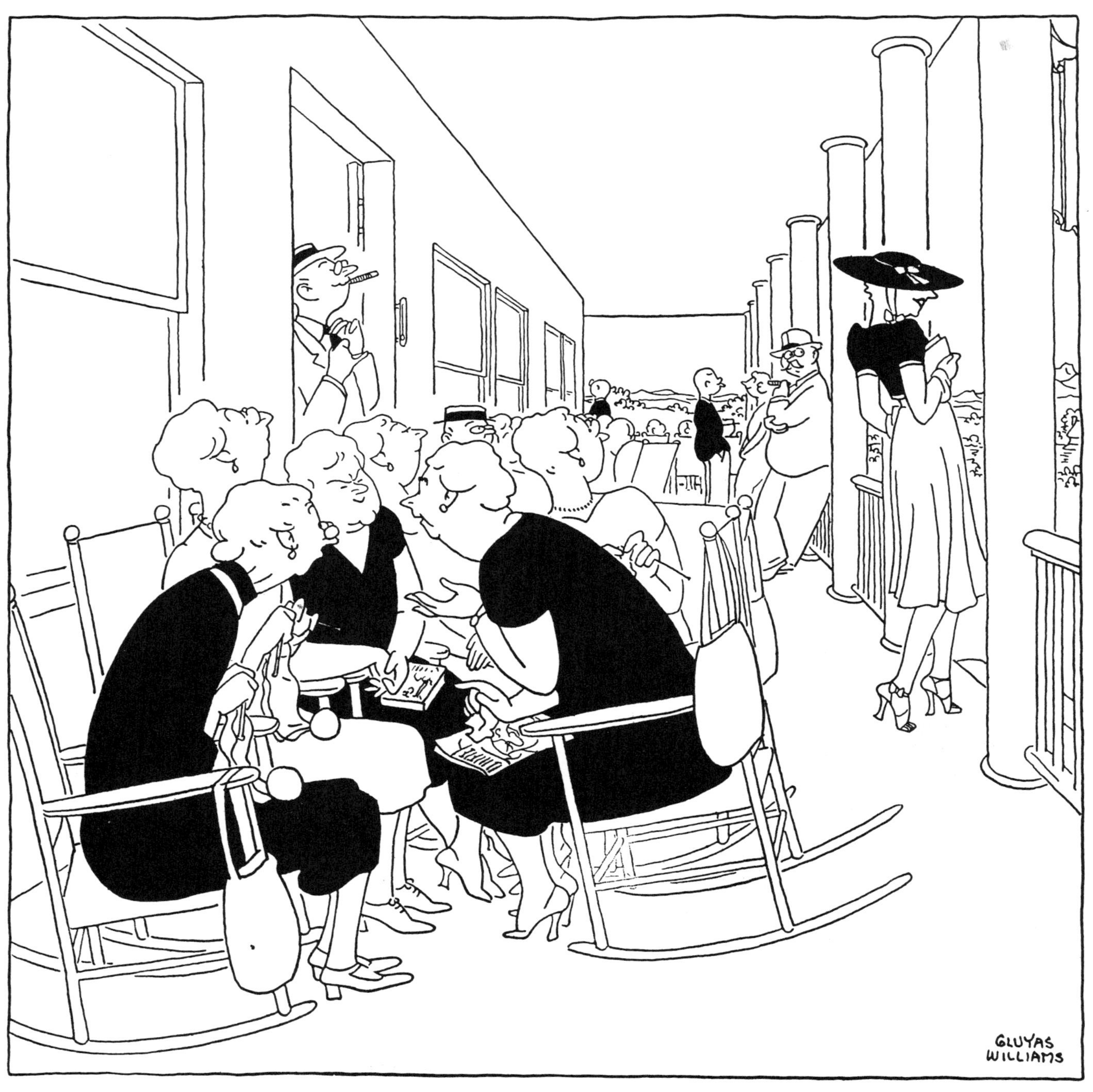

RACONTEURS

"The minute I saw on the register that she came from Council Bluffs, I was positive she must be the woman my sister has been writing about, because she fits to a T. Married a boy about ten years younger than herself, and he died, though there didn't seem to be anything particularly wrong with him, and within a year she married a man my sister says she had been carrying on with all along, and, if you'll believe it, then she . . ."

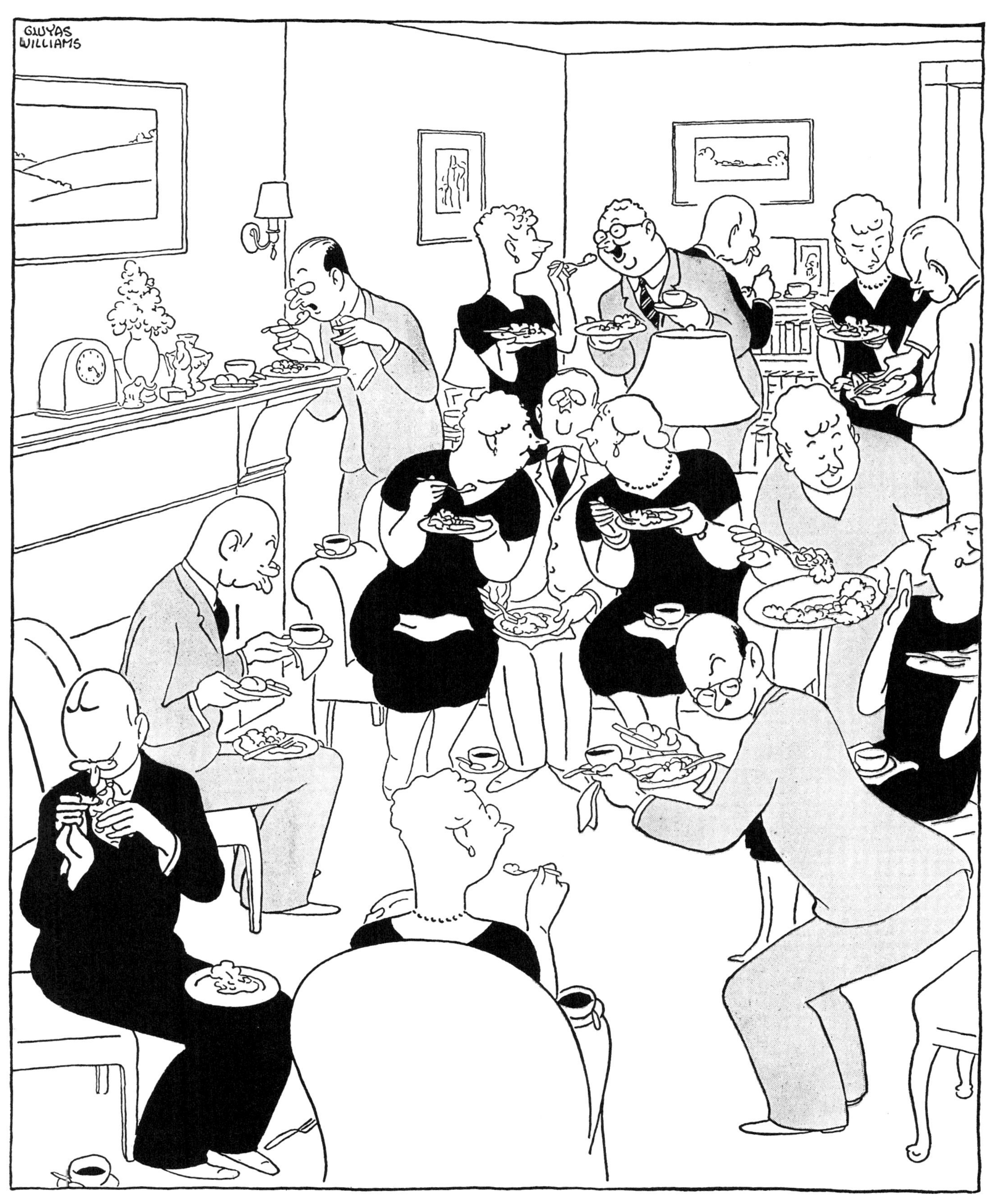

THE INNER MAN

Buffet Supper

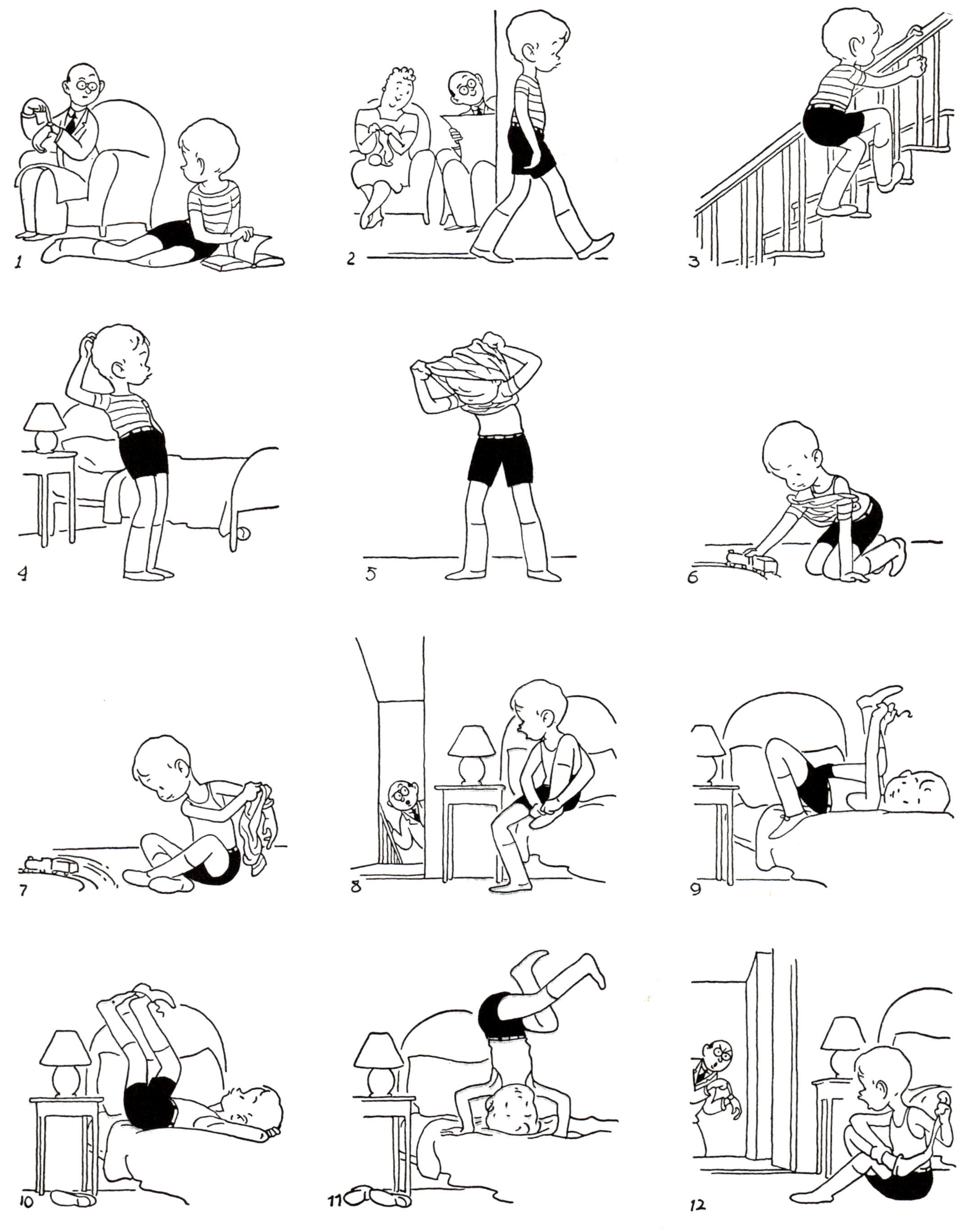

AND SO

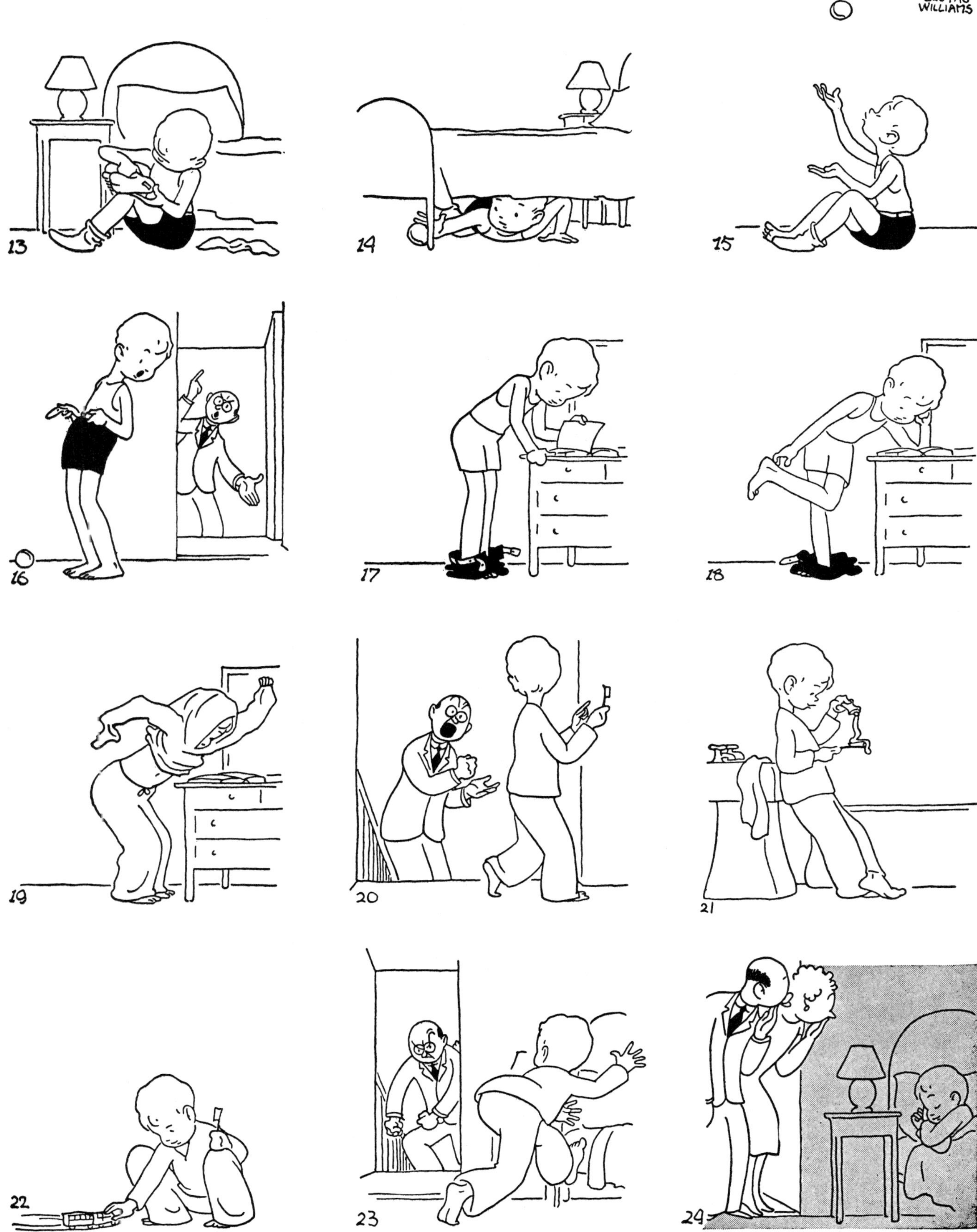

O BED

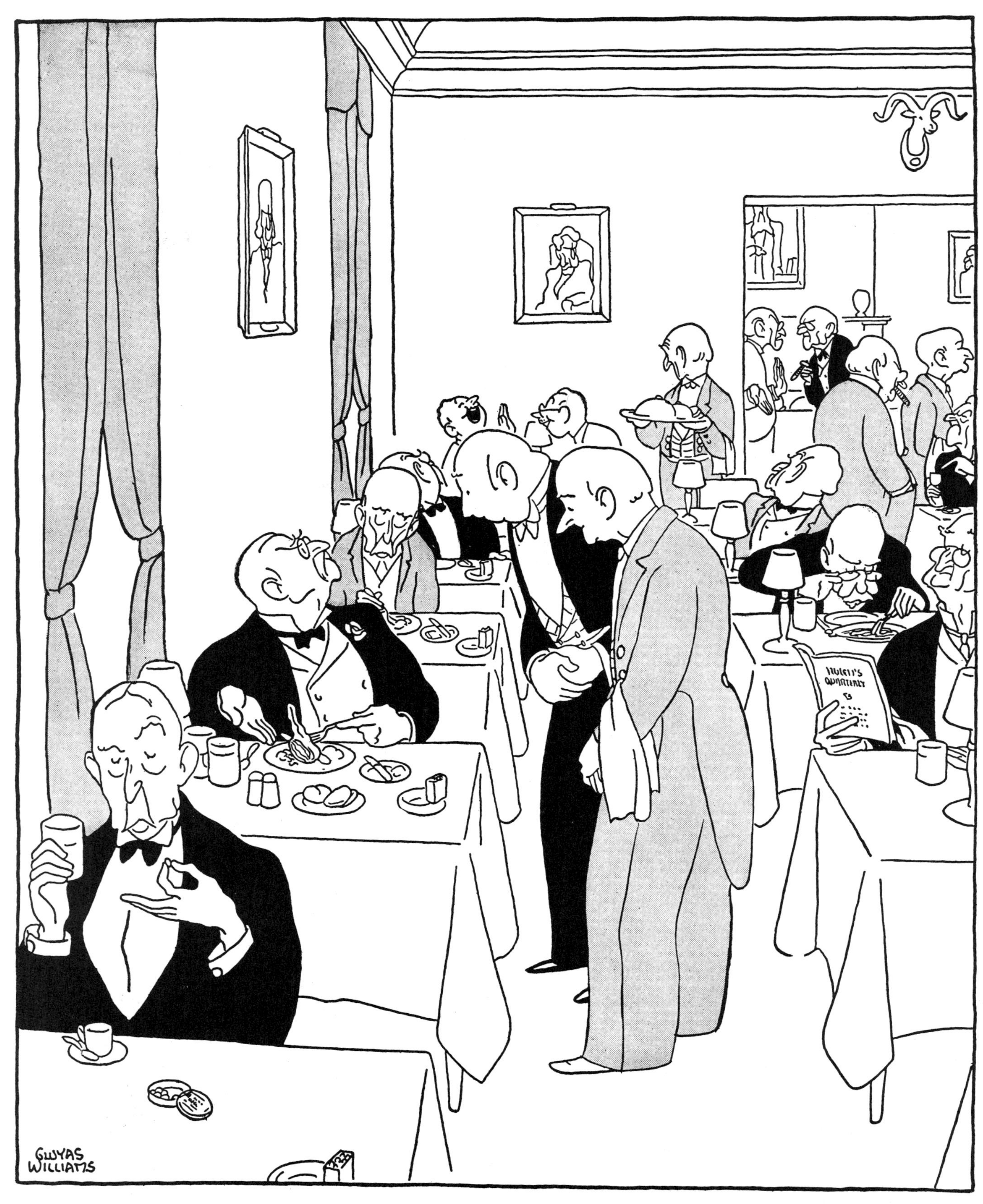

THE INNER MAN

Dinner at the Club

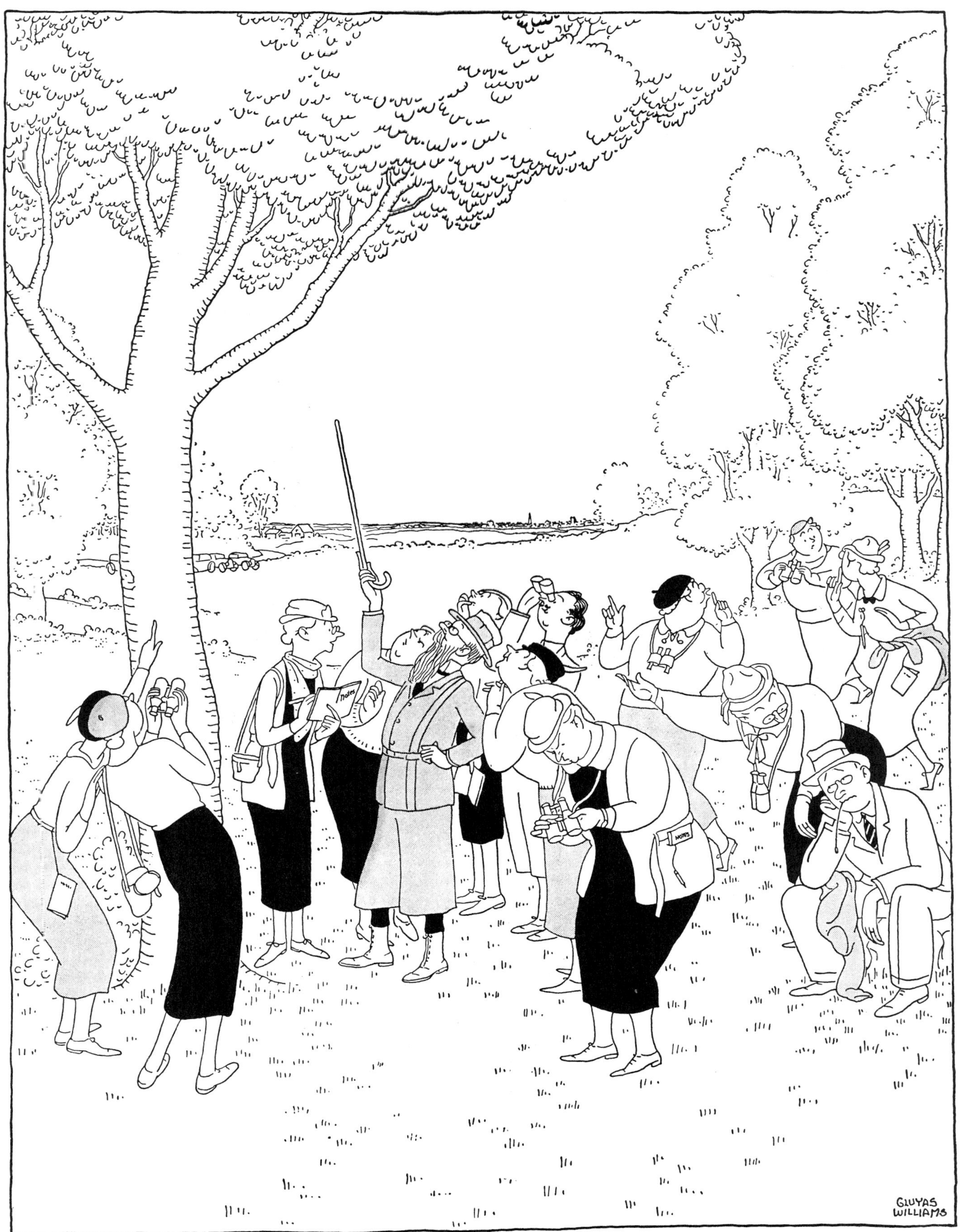

CLUB LIFE IN AMERICA

The Audubon Bird Walkers Add a Scarlet Tanager to Their List

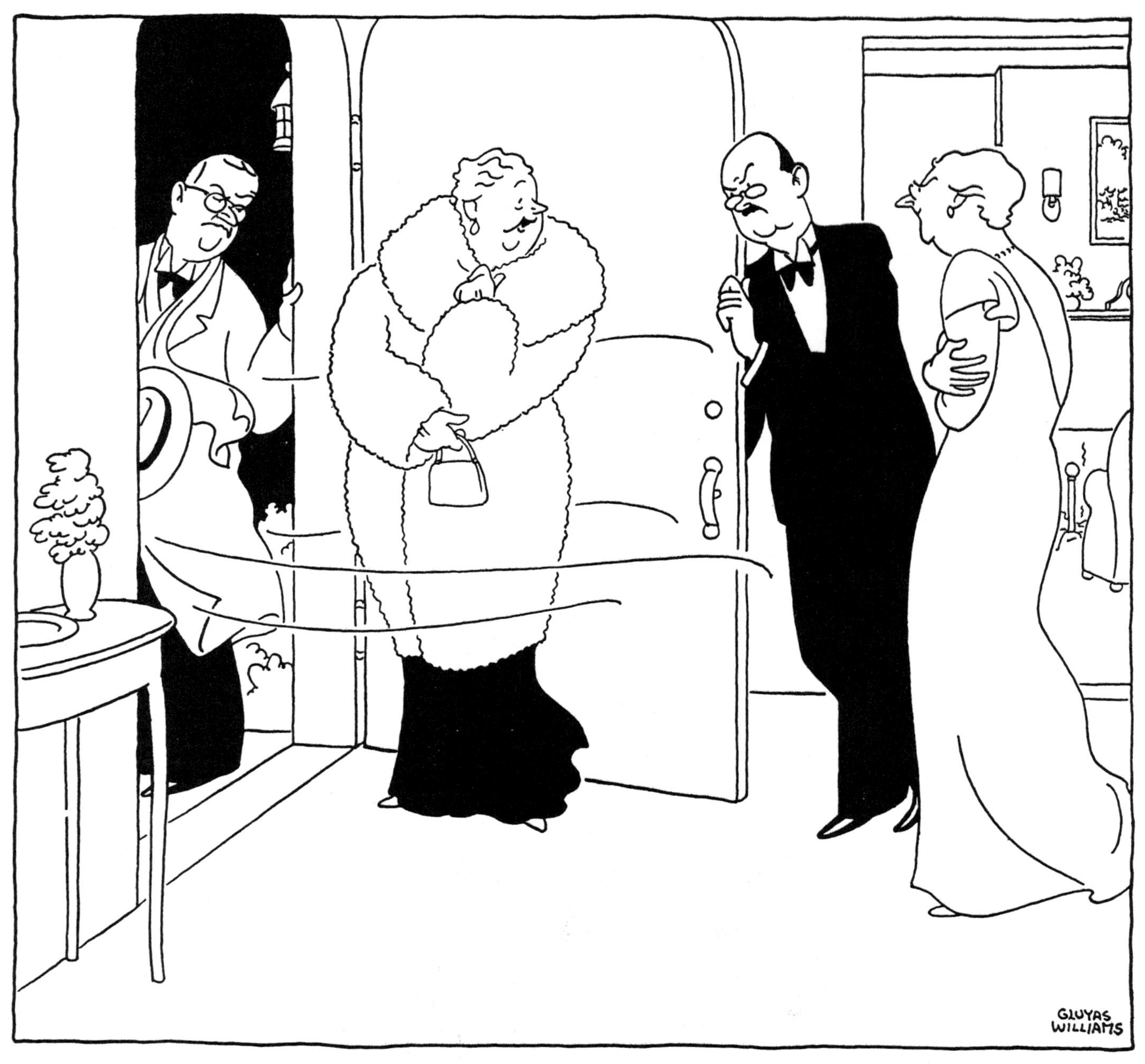

RACONTEURS

"Well, good night again—this time we really are *off. You know, Wallace scolds me. He says I never think of things I want to say until I have my wraps on and have said good night. Just last evening we got roped in for bridge at the Northrops', and you know how Wallace loathes bridge, though I must say he's a lamb about playing, but anyway I tried to break away early, and we got all ready to go, and . . ."*

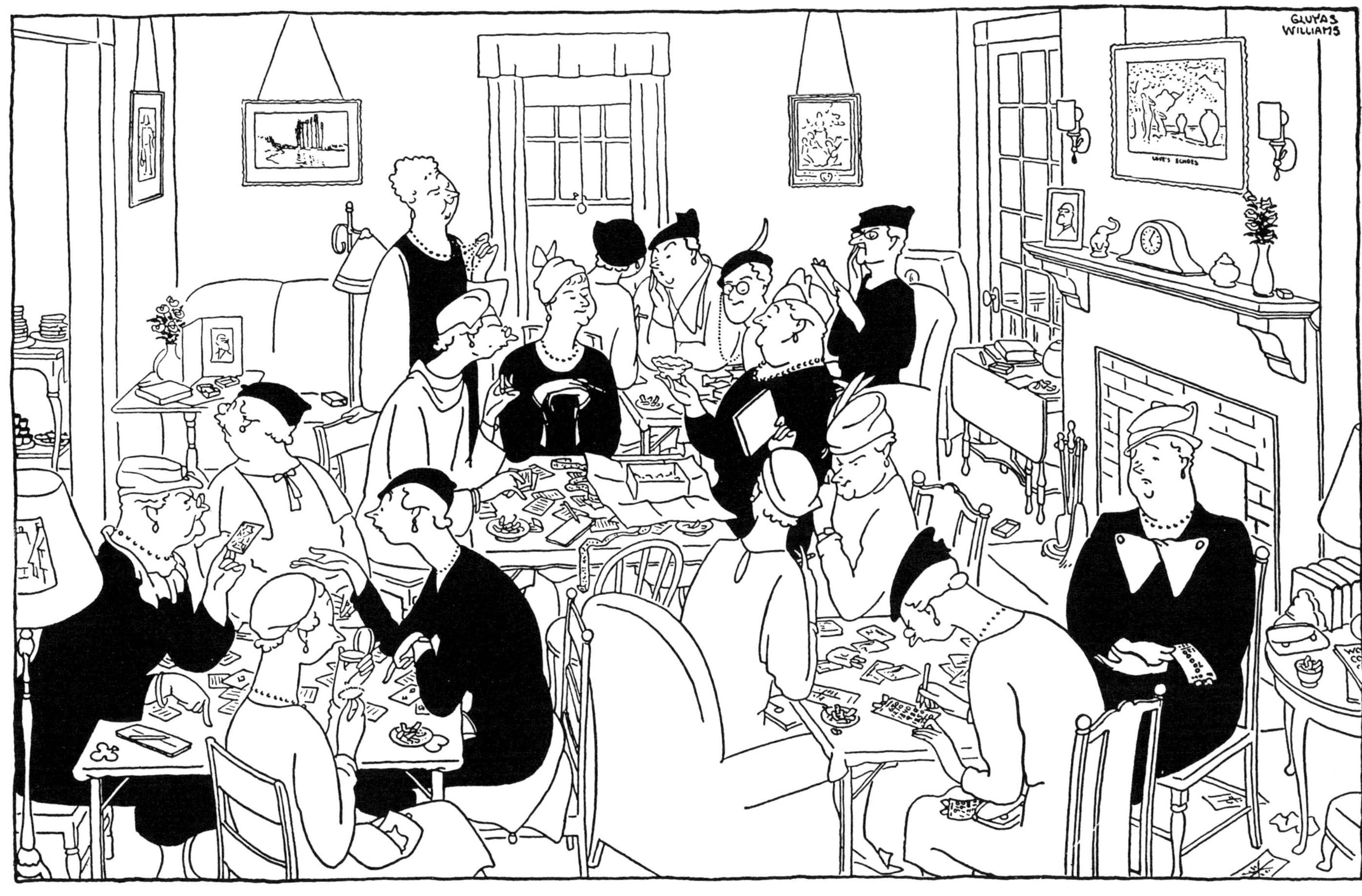

CLUB LIFE IN AMERICA

The Hostess of the Tuesday Afternooners Awards the Bridge Prize

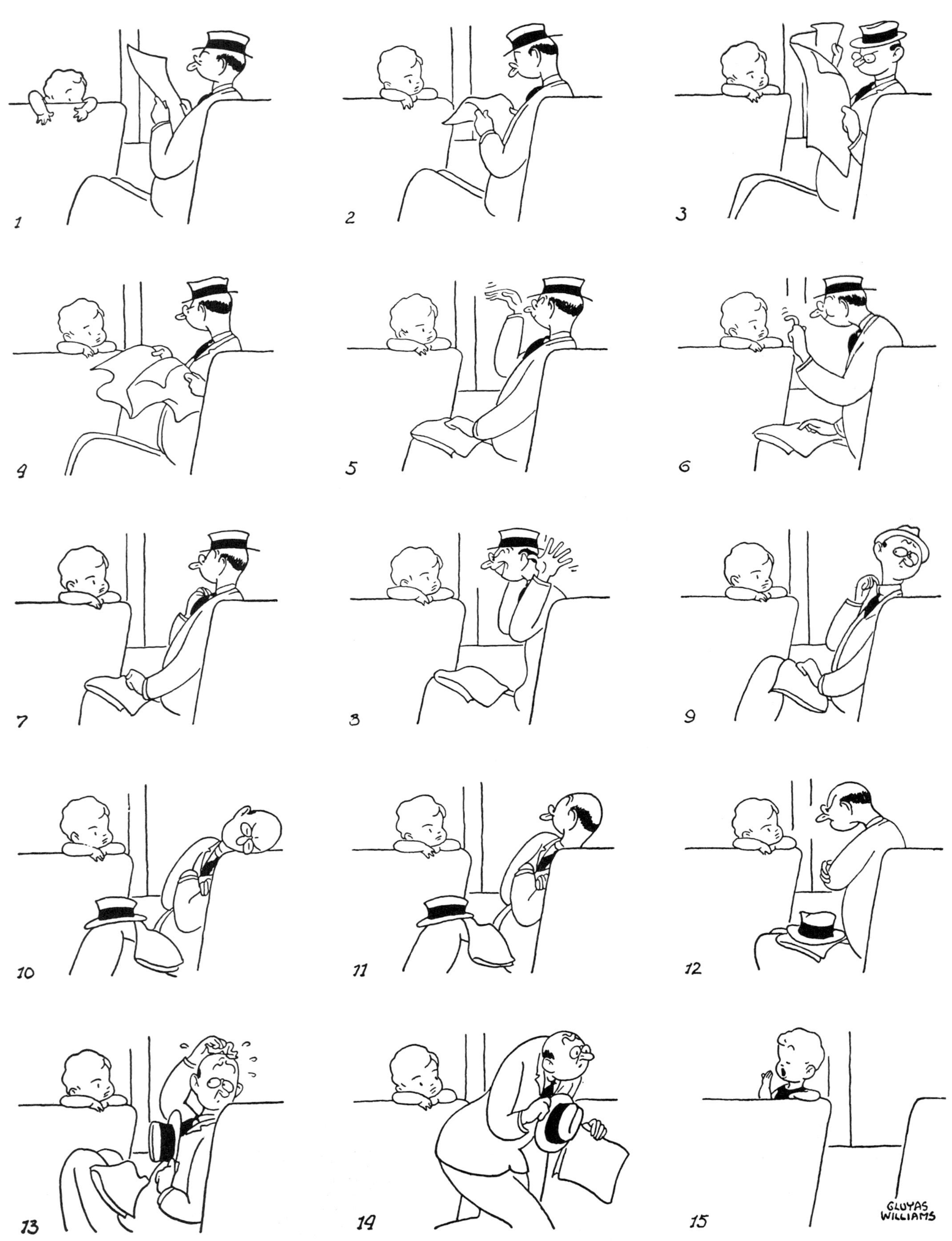

THE CHILD IN THE SEAT AHEAD

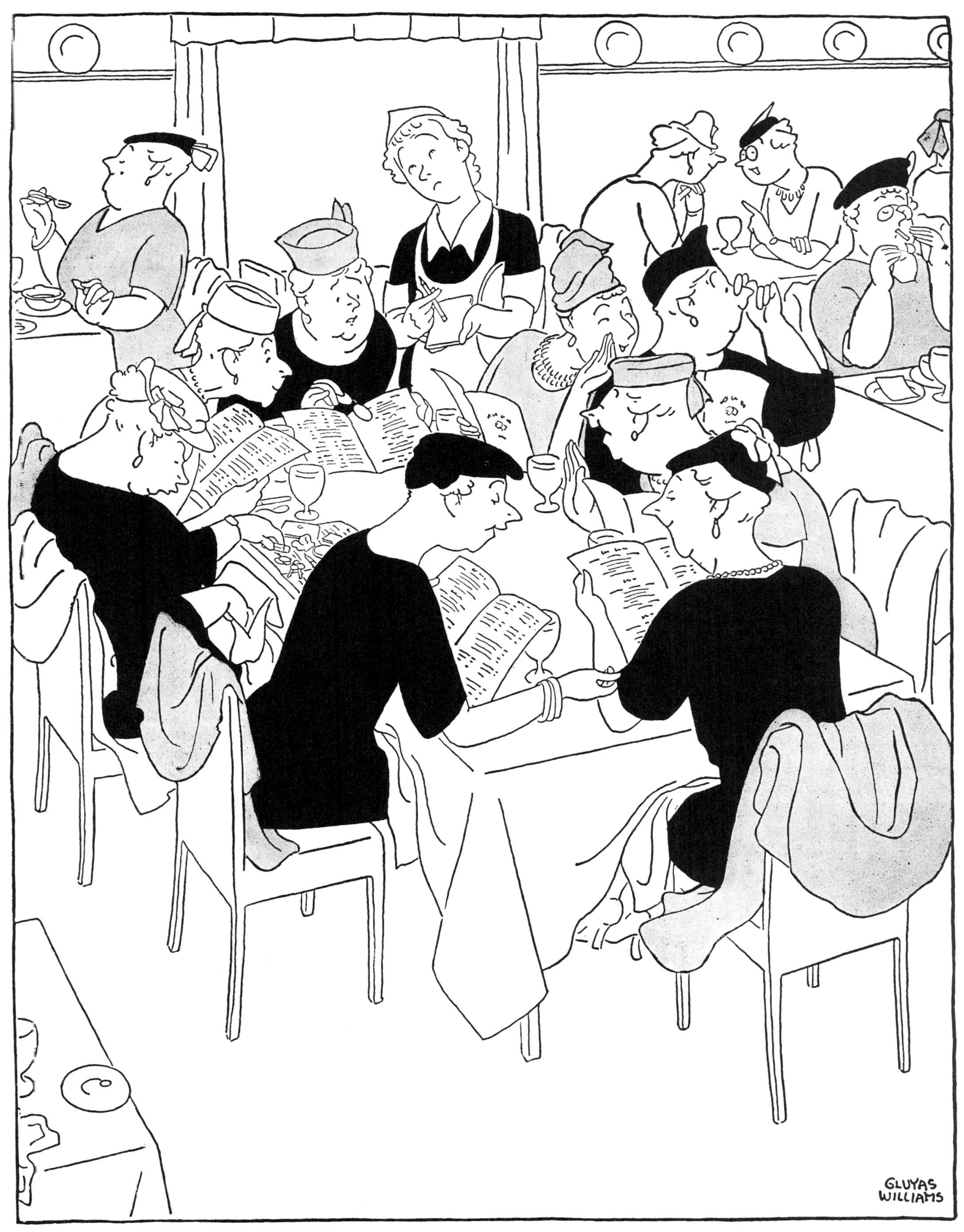

THE INNER MAN

Ordering

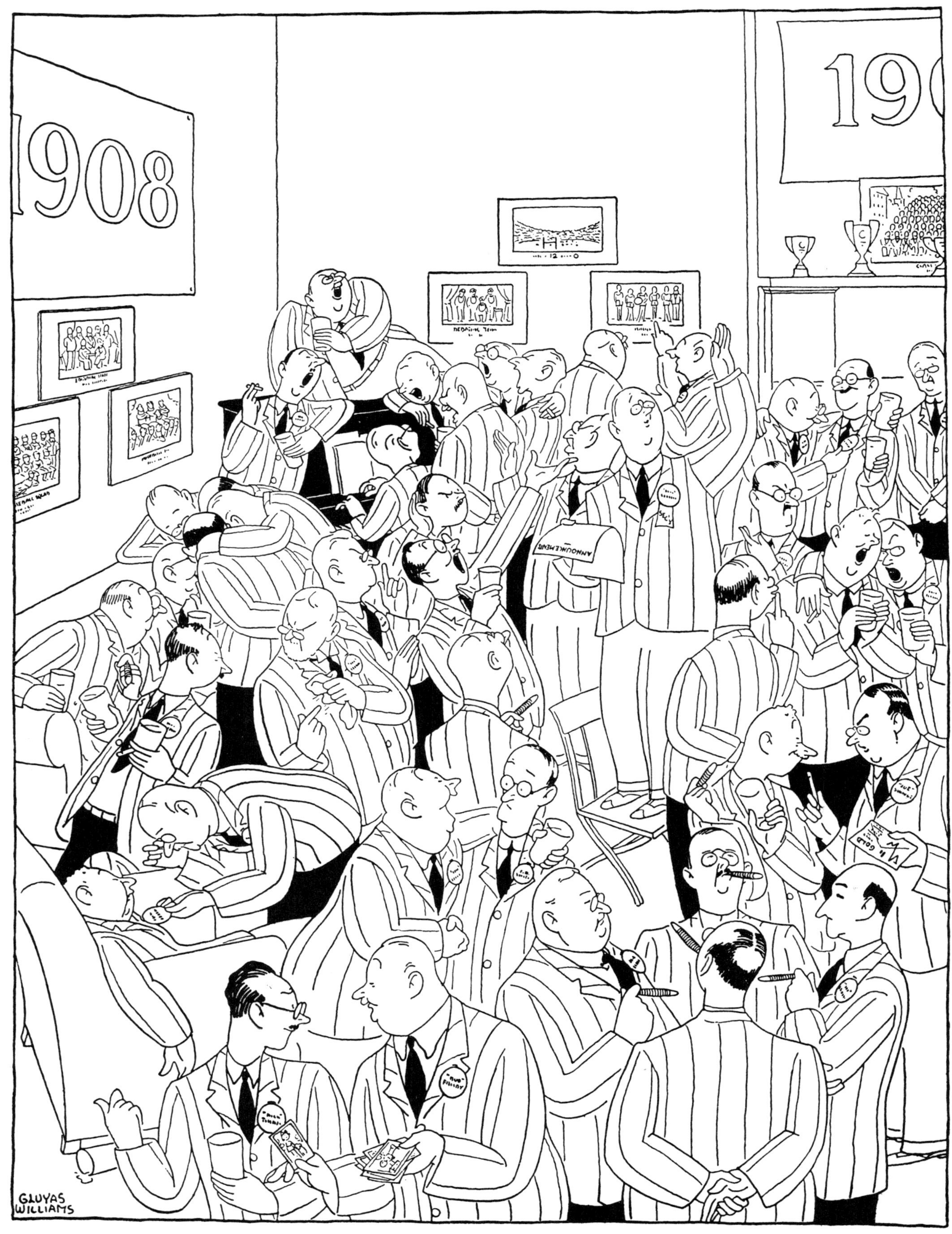

CLASS REUNION

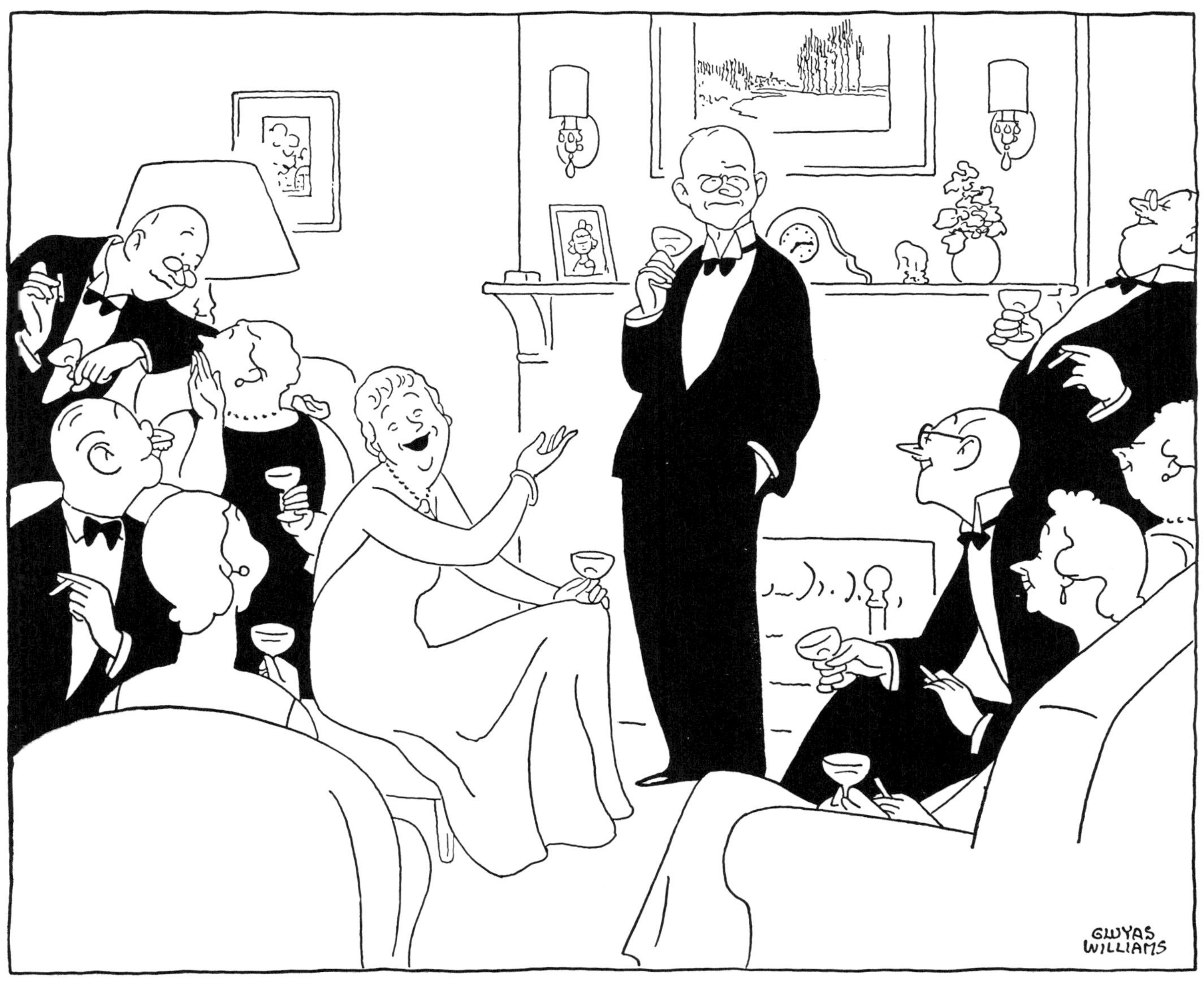

RACONTEURS

"Honestly, you would have died laughing at Joe. Give him two cocktails and he thinks he's Sir Walter Raleigh. Well, when this woman at the next table drops her bag, up jumps Joe, and you know how clumsy he is anyway, and . . ."

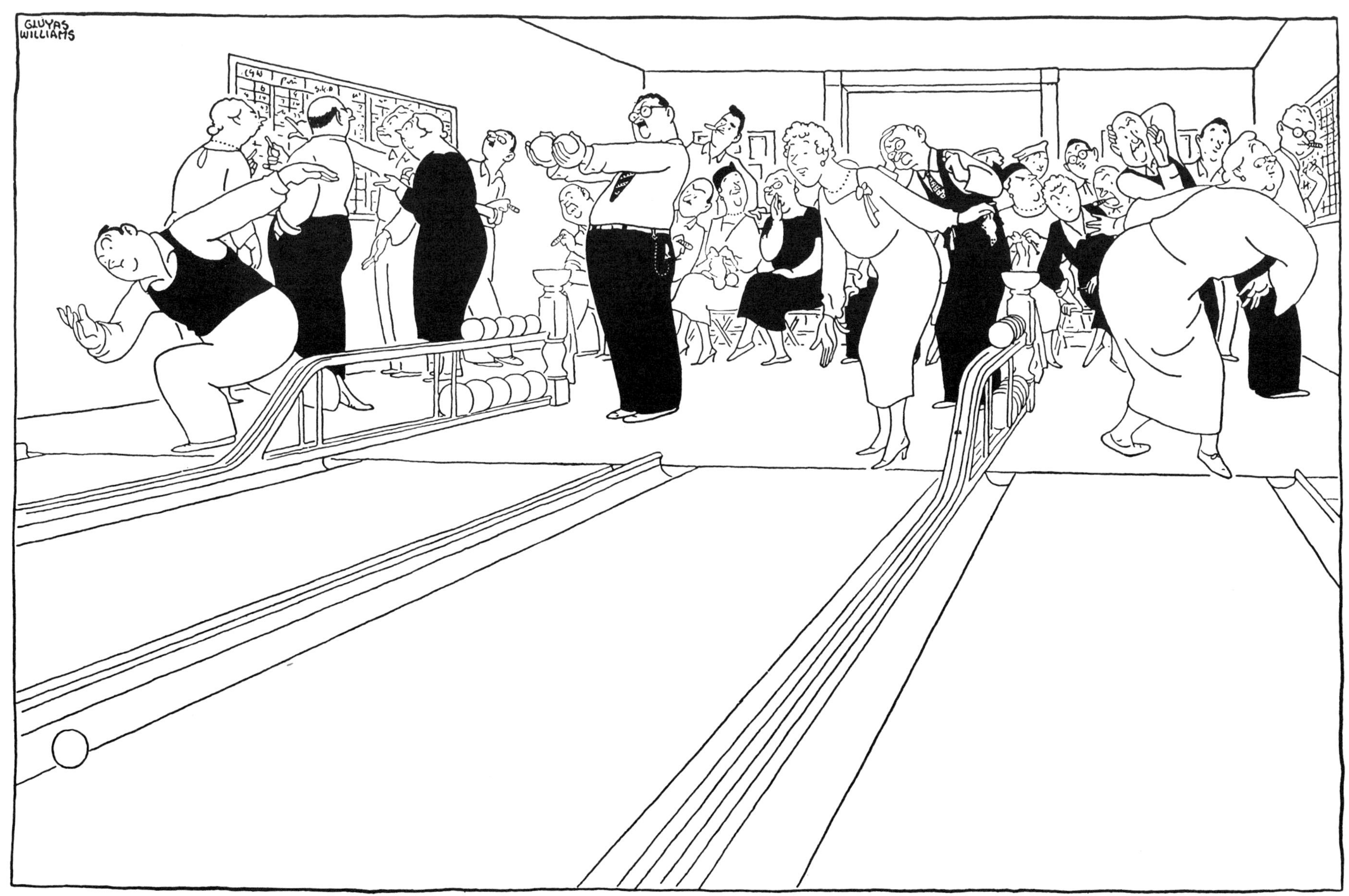

CLUB LIFE IN AMERICA

The Candle Pinners Roll for the Mixed Doubles Cup

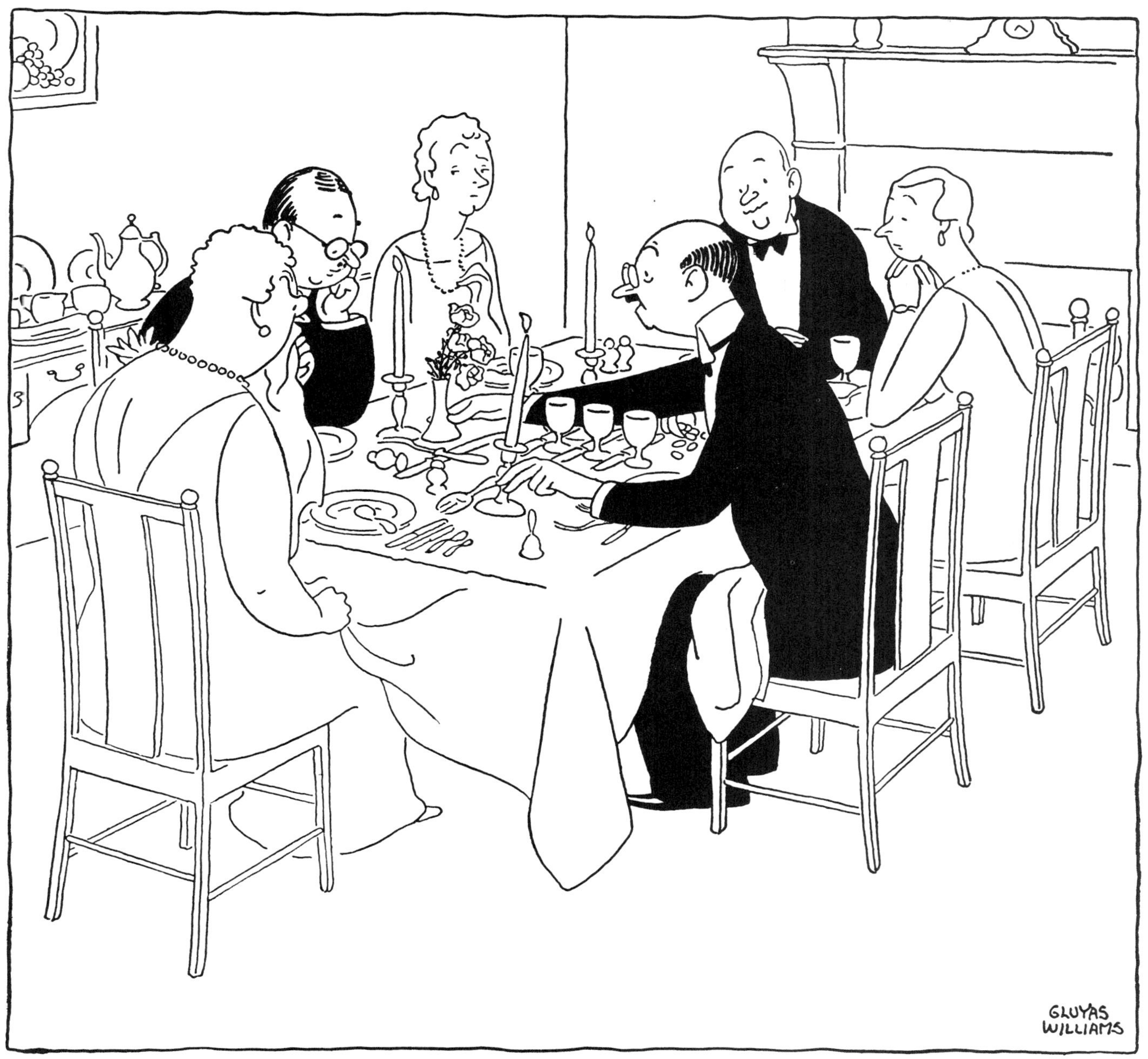

RACONTEURS

"Now I want you to see just how it happened, because it shows how careful you have to be. There was I, at the intersection, with this fellow in the Packard right behind me, and over here, backing out of a driveway, is the delivery truck. Well, this fellow . . ."

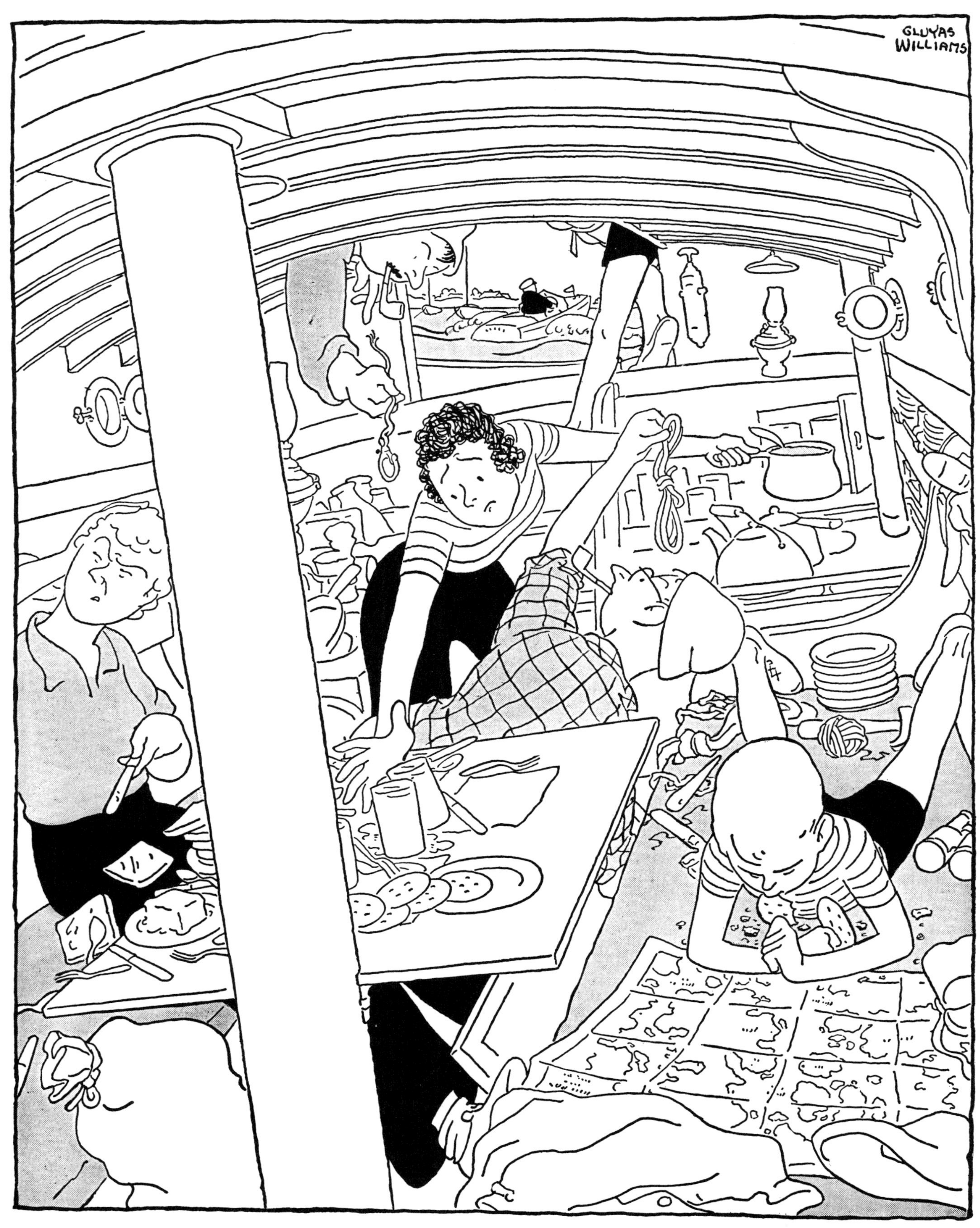

THE INNER MAN

Snug Harbor

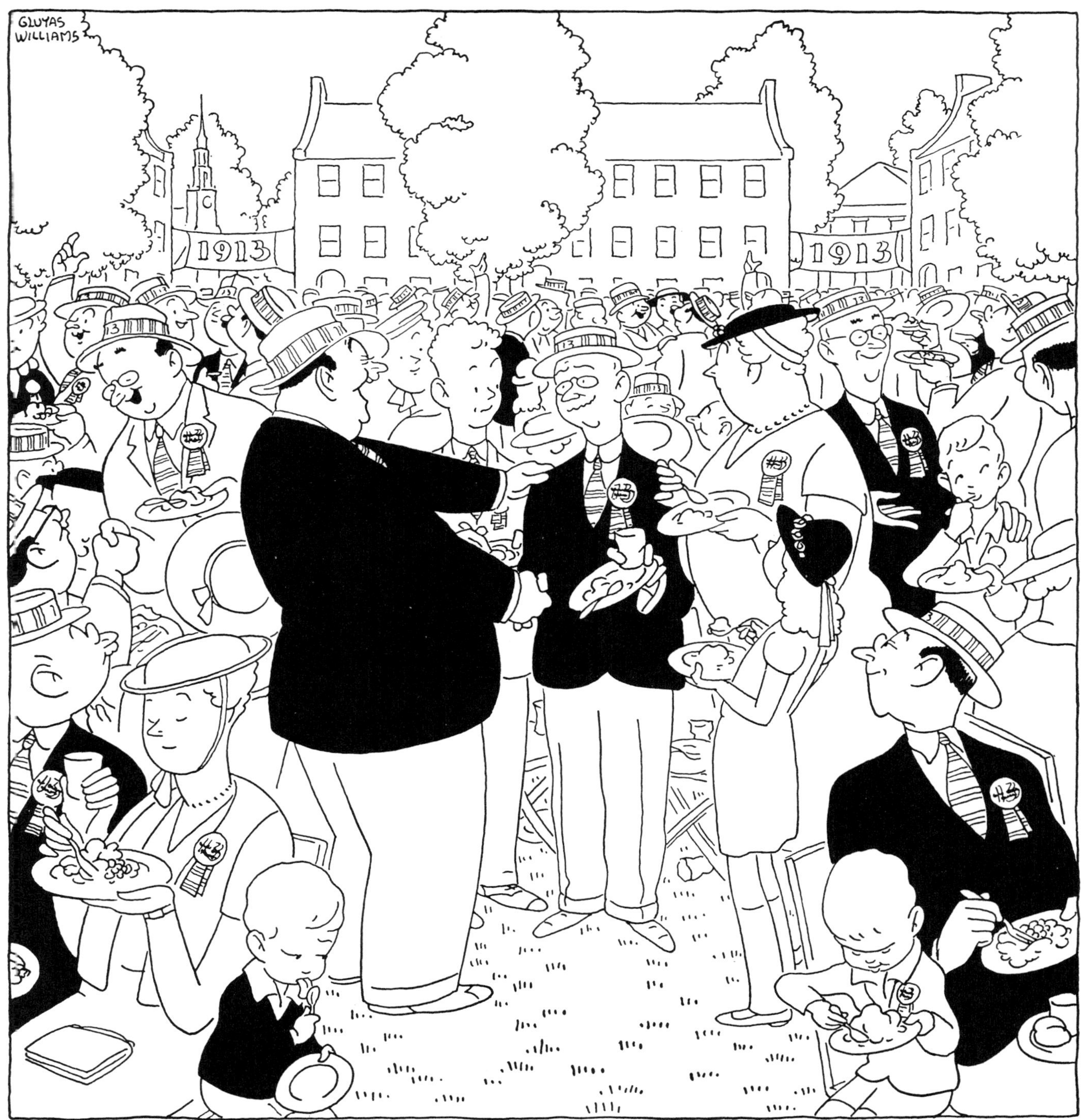

RACONTEURS

"Many's the time, Mrs Willis, this rascal of yours had to put me to bed, and—ha-ha—if it isn't giving him away, vice versa. What a time we used to have, you old scoundrel! Remember the night you decided to start training to swim the Channel by diving into the fountain in your dress suit, and . . ."

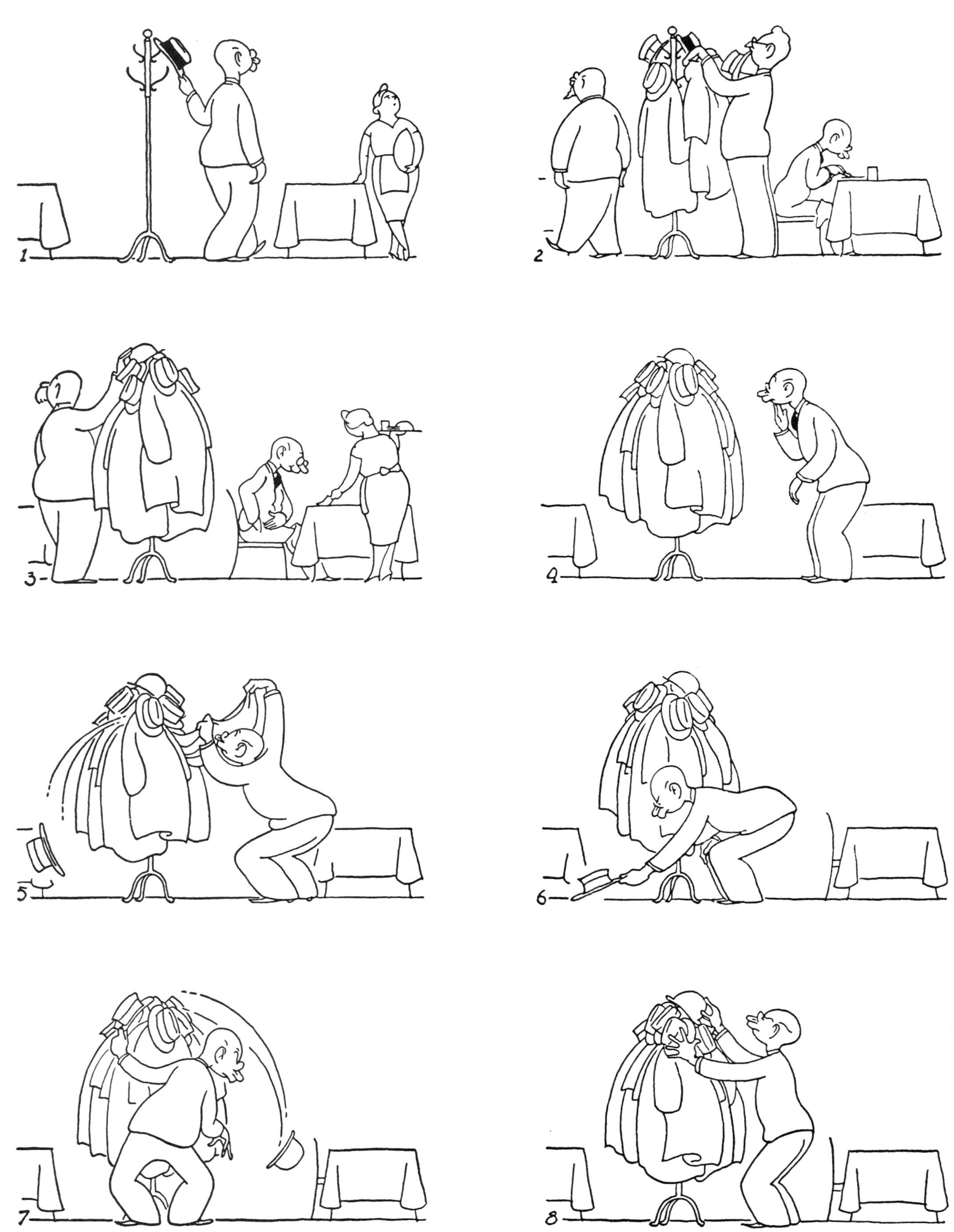

THE HAT RACK (I)

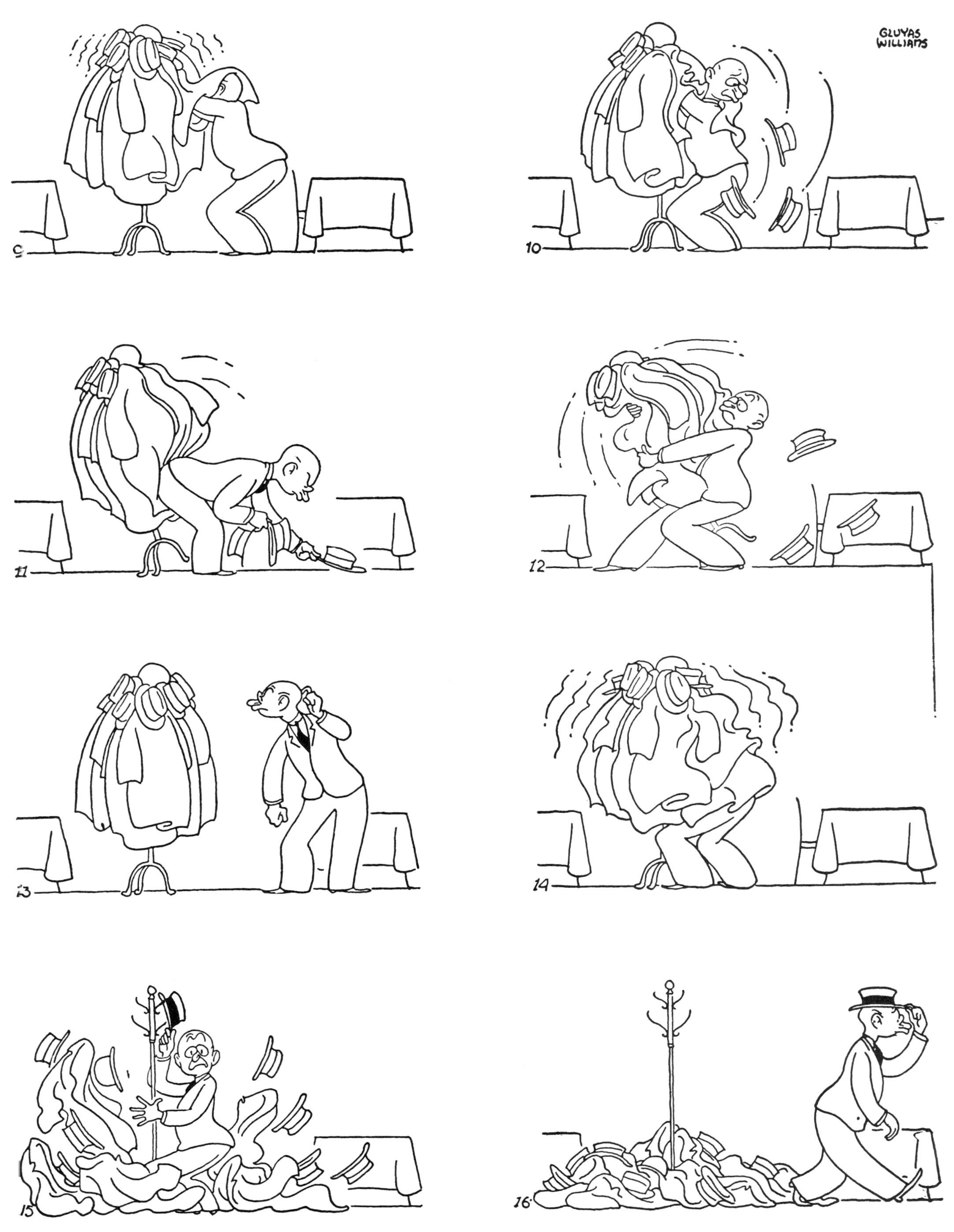

THE HAT RACK (II)

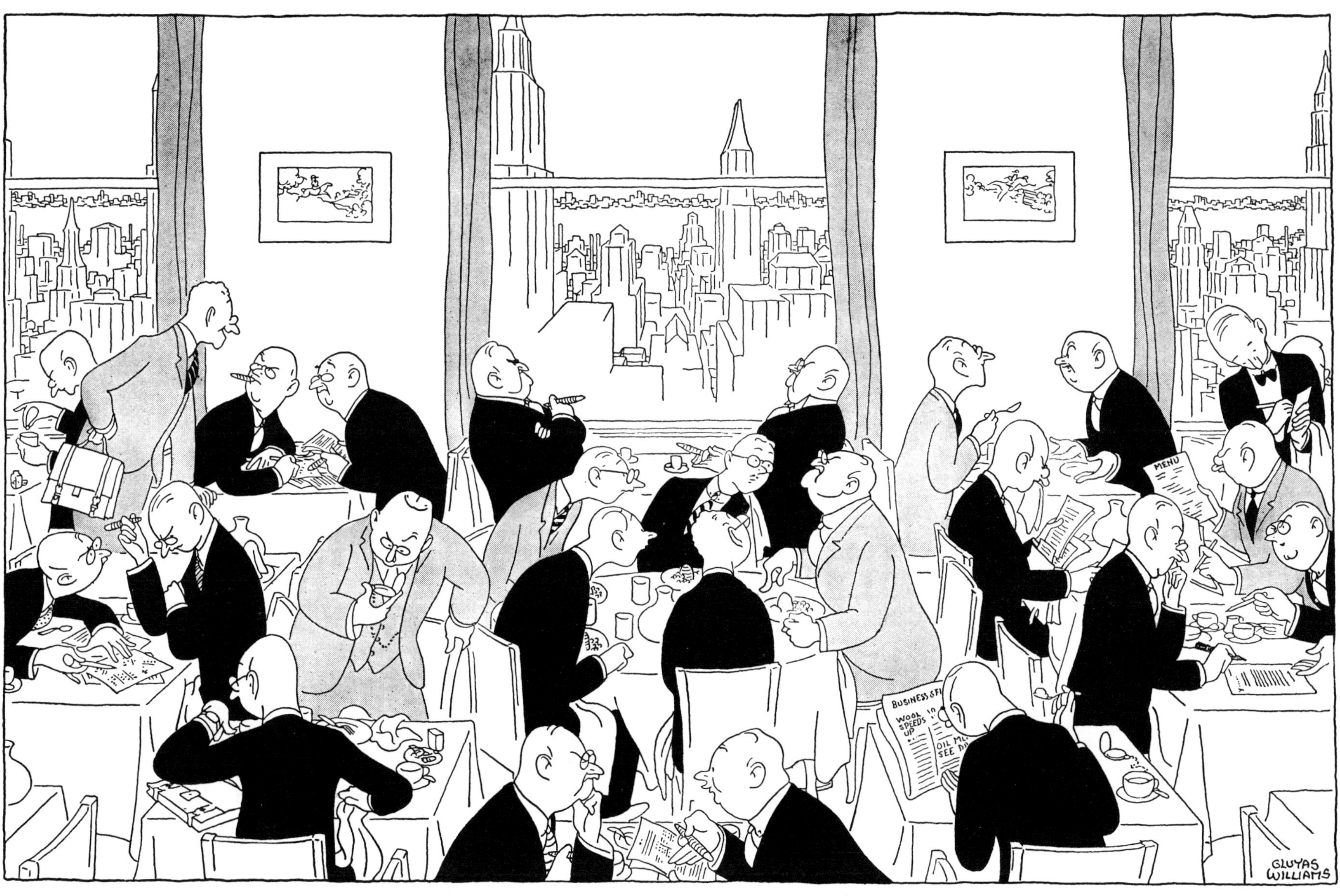

CLUB LIFE IN AMERICA

The Downtown Businessmen Relax at Midday

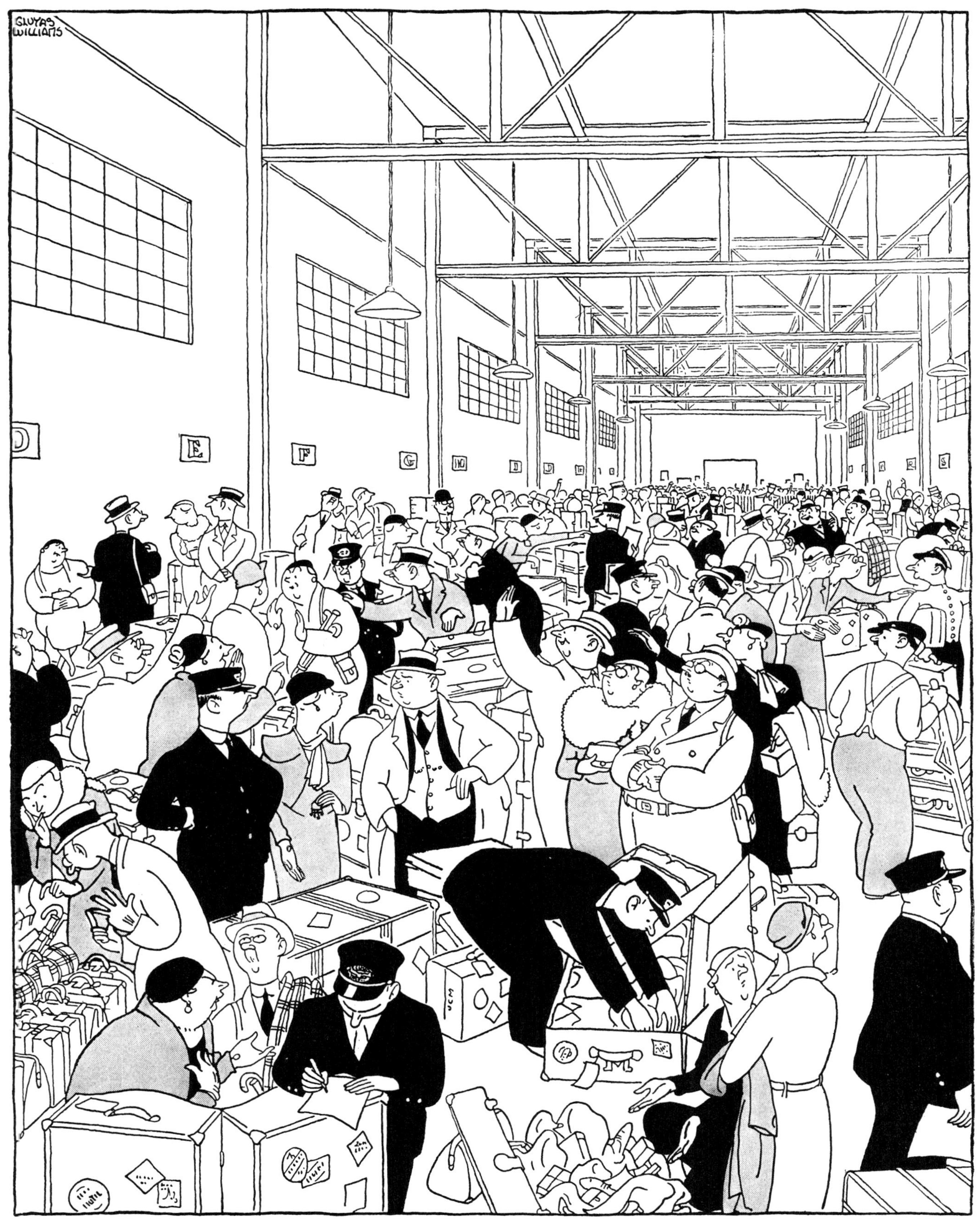

THE CUSTOMS

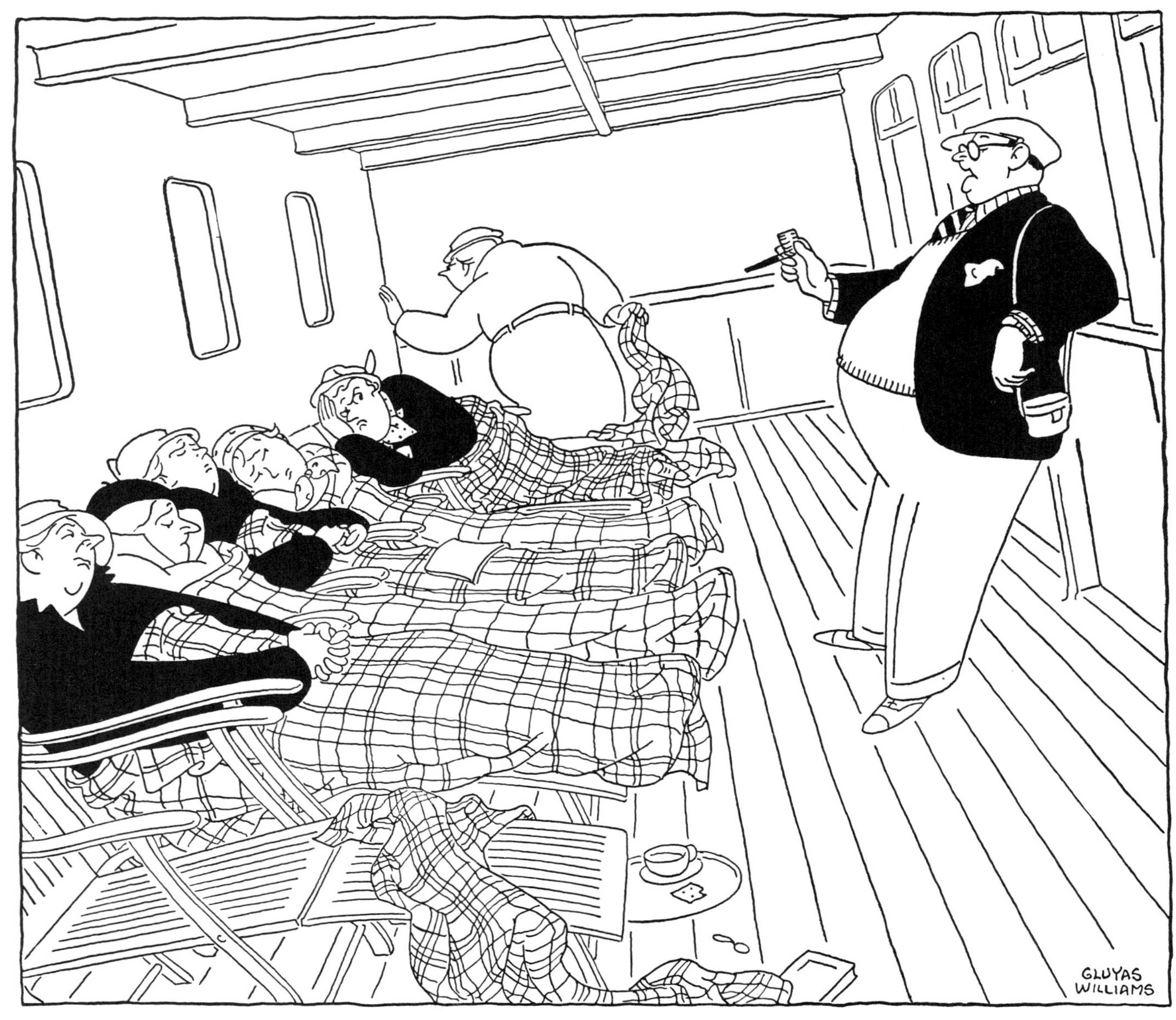

RACONTEURS

"It's none of my business, ladies, but you're making a mistake not to eat. Keep the stomach busy is what I say, and I've crossed seven times and never missed a meal. Now here's what I do. I always keep something in the cabin, some dates or perhaps some bananas, to eat when I get up. Then for breakfast I'll have . . ."

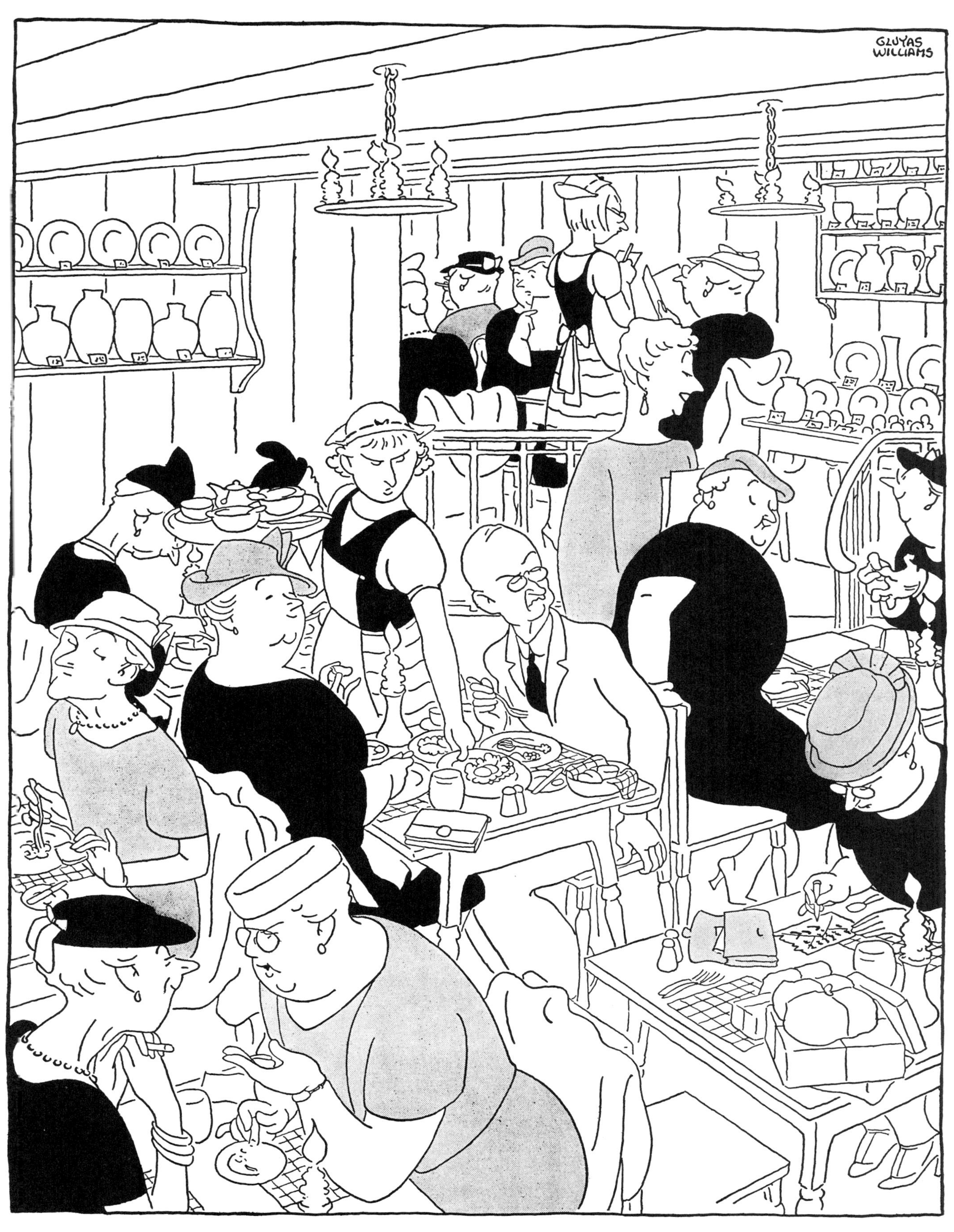

THE INNER MAN

Tearoom

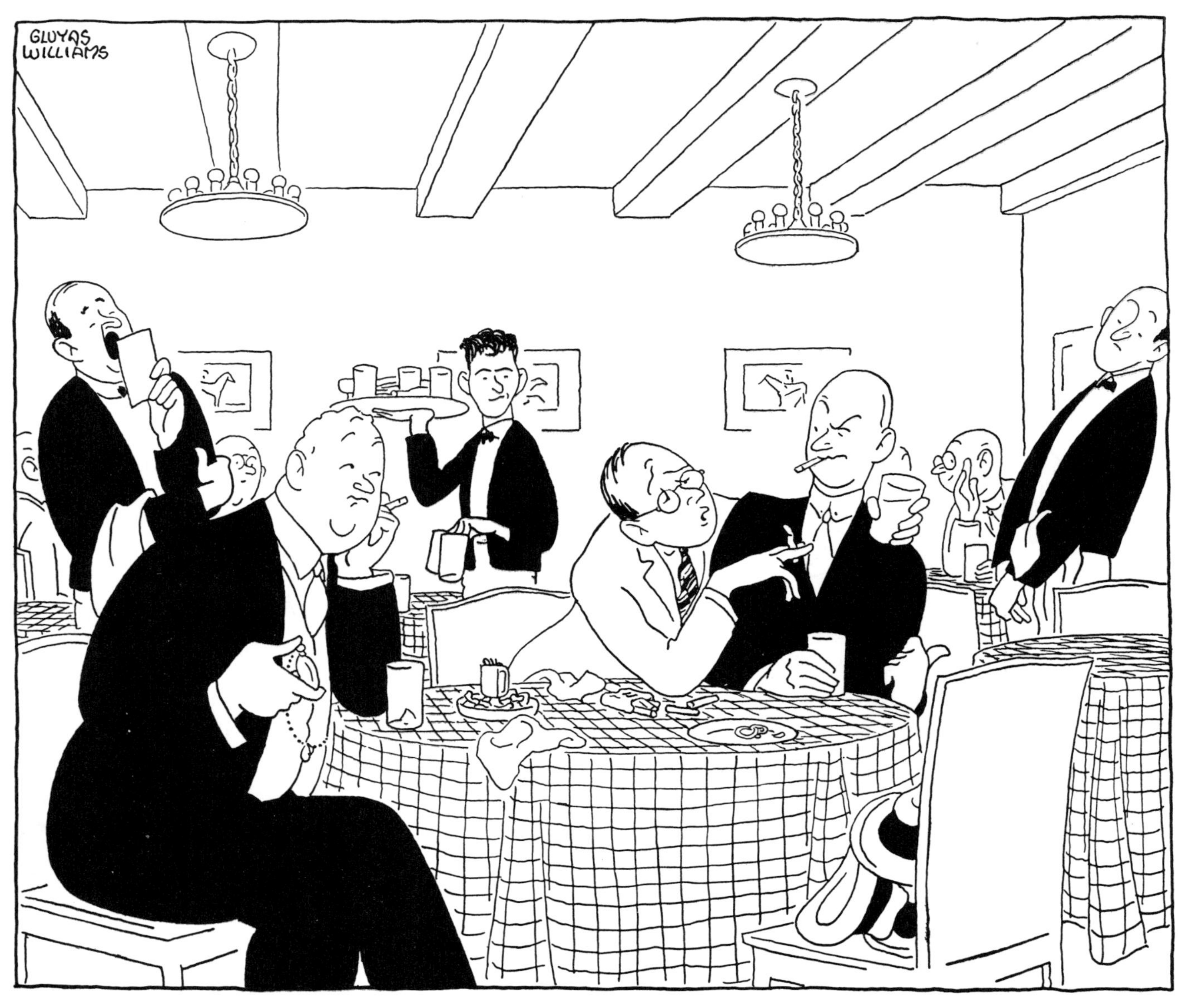

RACONTEURS

"I'm only telling you this, Joe, because you and this other gentleman here are the only friends I have in the whole wide world. Let's see . . . where was I? Oh yes, so when I got home, Joe, she had gone, packed up and gone, and the puppy was the only friend I had in the whole wide world. So then, Joe, I . . ."

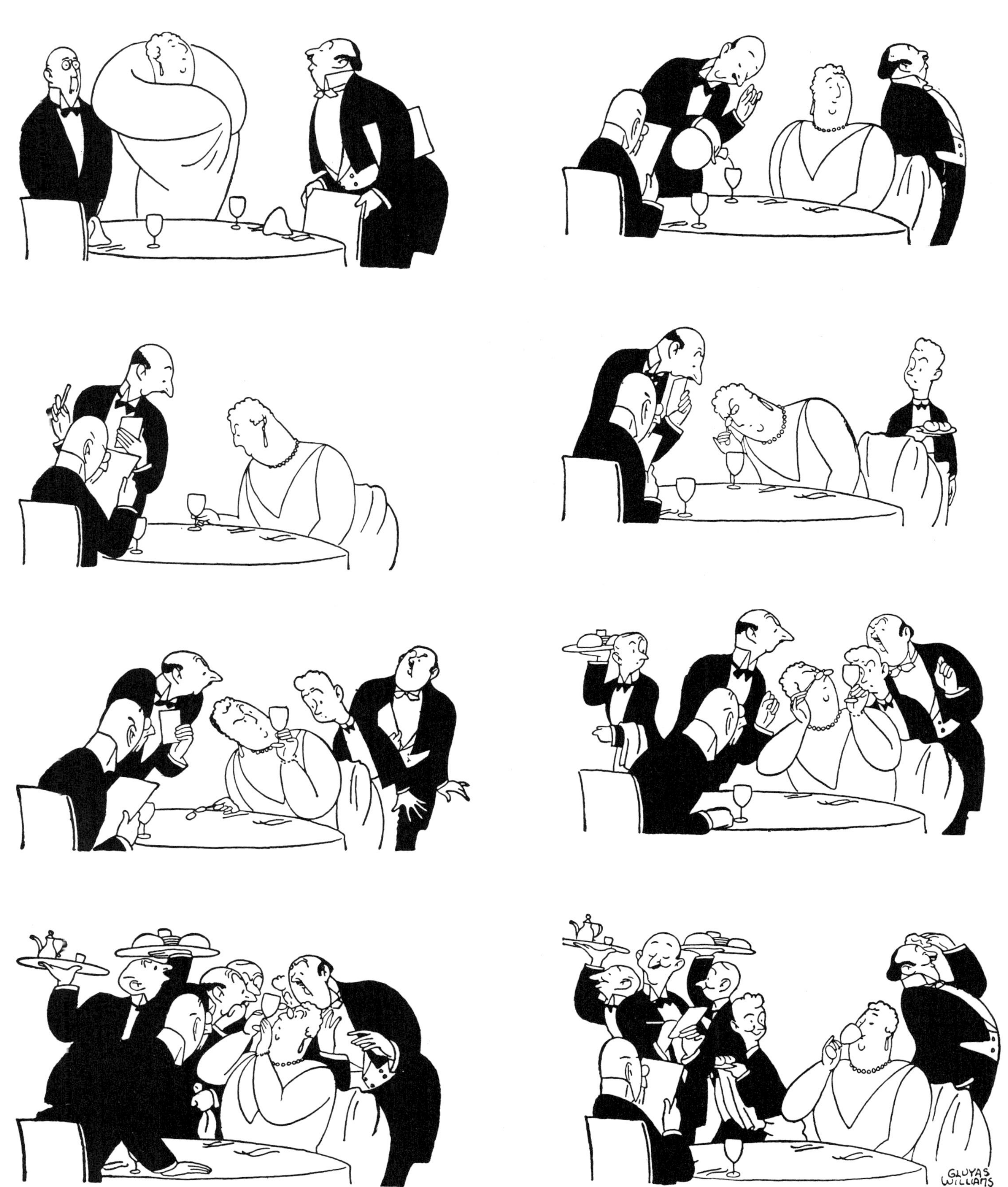

THE WOMAN WHO SUSPECTS ALL RESTAURANT GLASSES

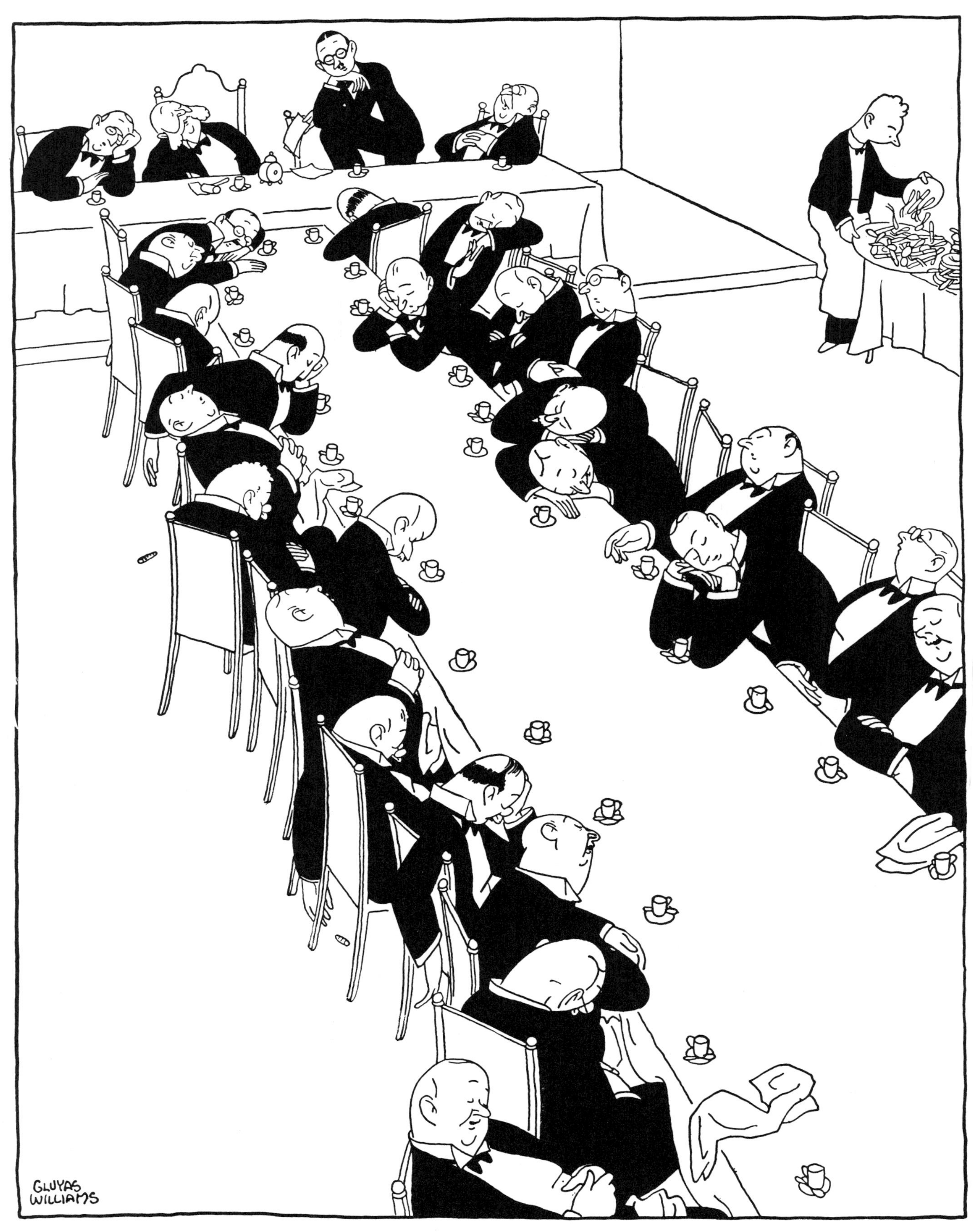

ANNUAL BANQUET OF THE SANKA COFFEE COMPANY

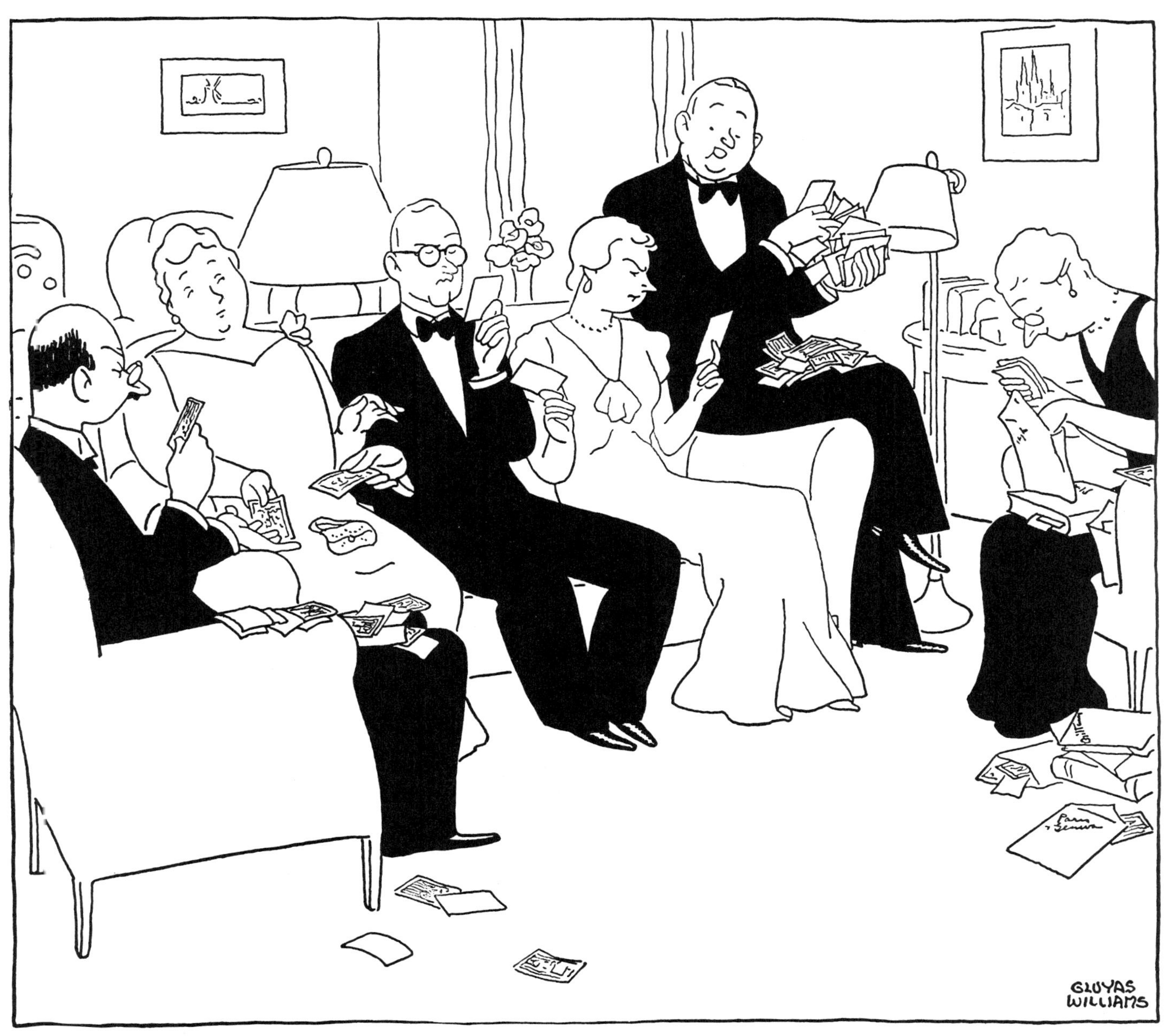

RACONTEURS

"We stayed there four days and then took a funny little boat over to Brindisi. That's the boat. The couple standing by the rail are a Mr and Mrs Mortimer, but I've got a better one of them here somewhere. . . . Well, I'll find it later. From Brindisi, we . . ."

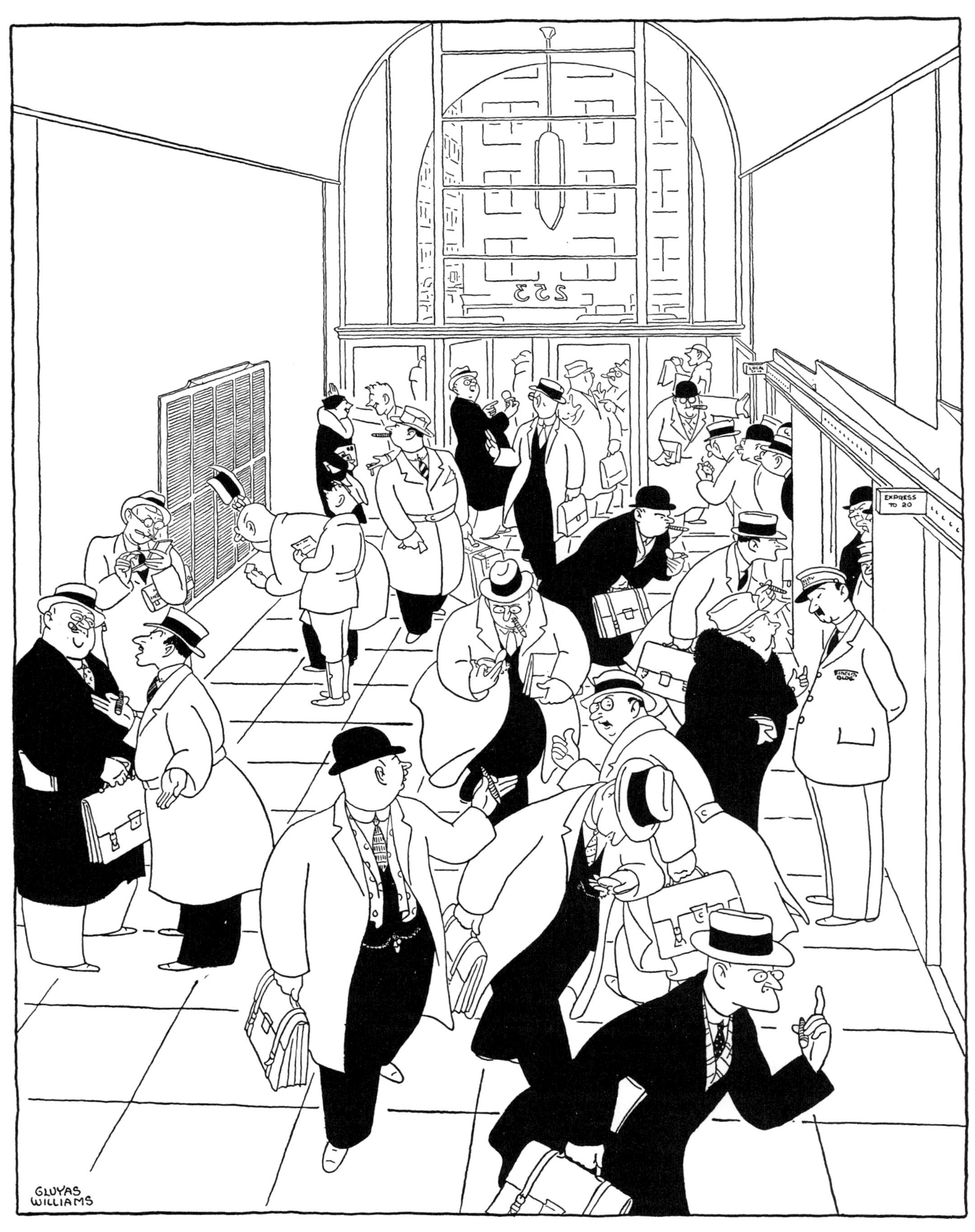

OFFICE BUILDING LOBBY

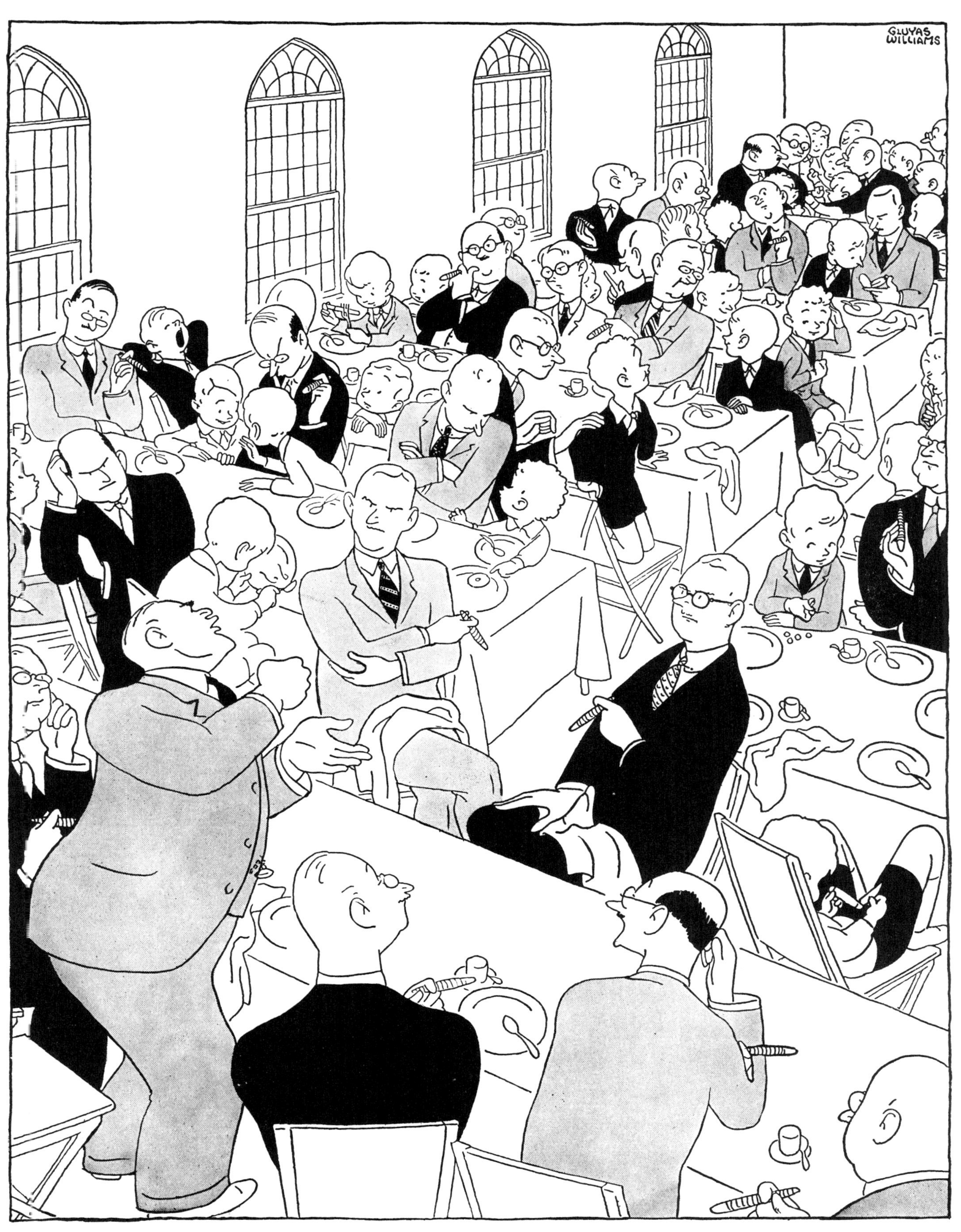

CLUB LIFE IN AMERICA

The Boys Get a Talk on "Playing the Game" at Fathers' and Sons' Night at the Men's Club

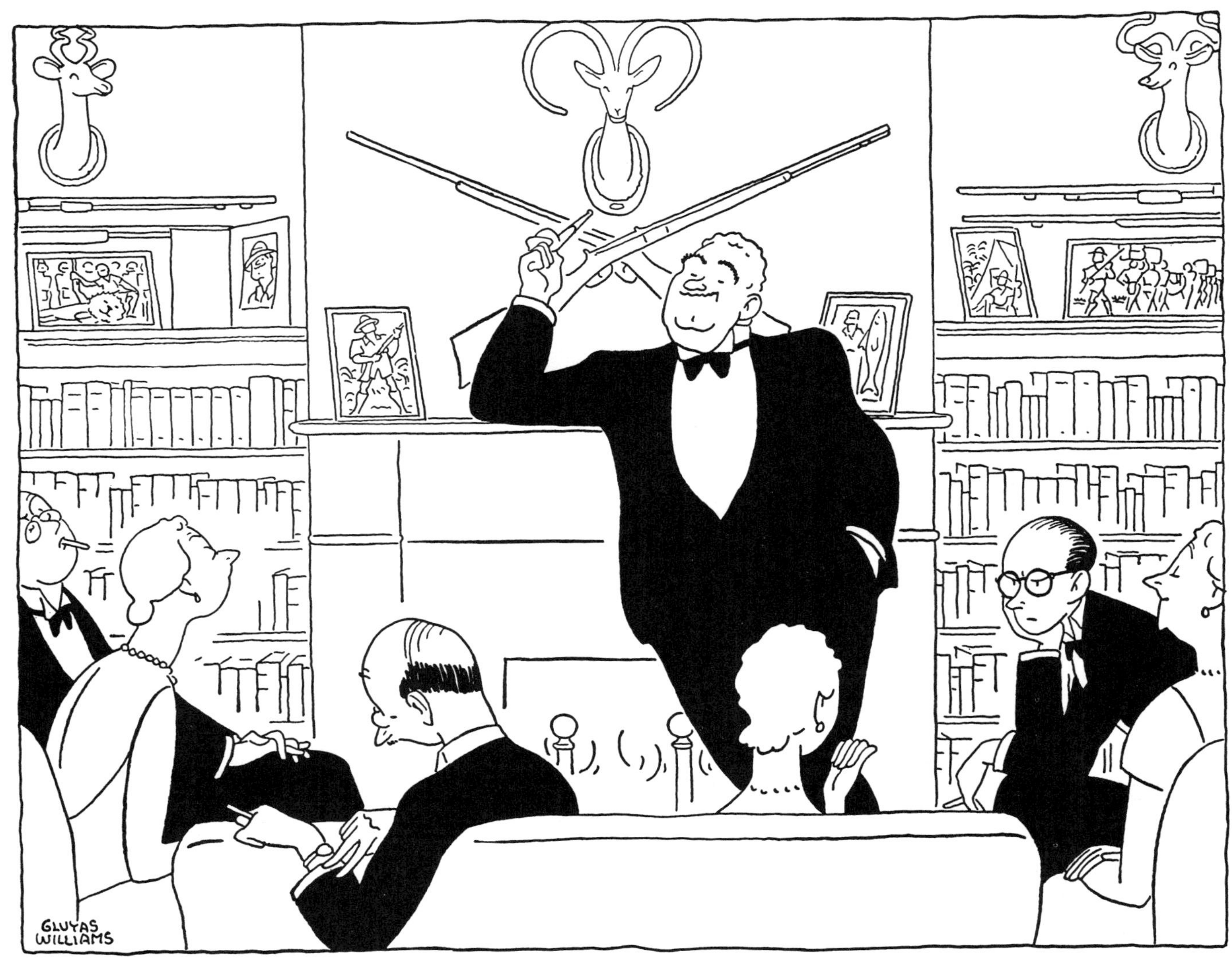

RACONTEURS

"And another bit of capital sport was the time I bagged this fellow here. That was in '25 and we had been trekking for days . . ."

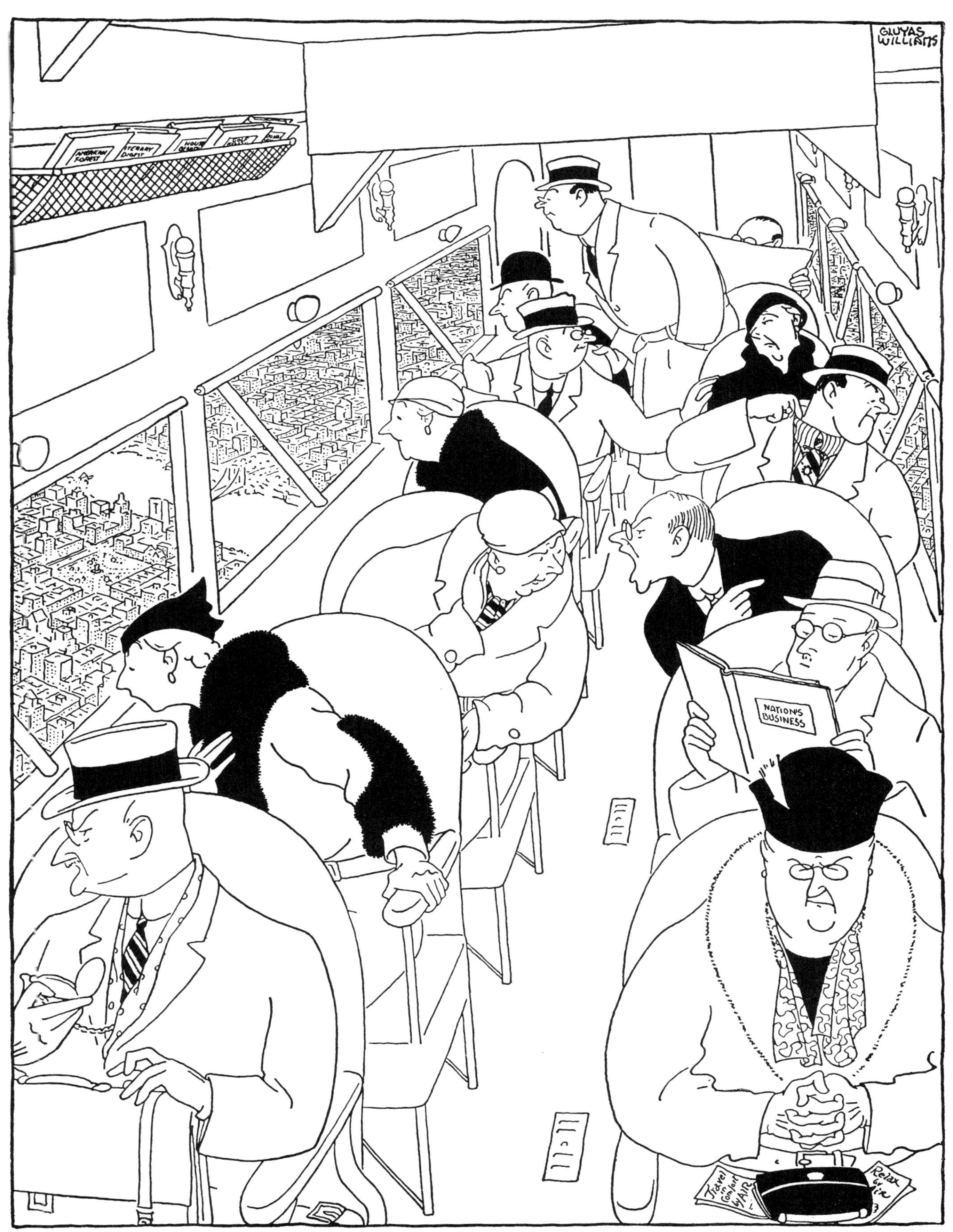

ARRIVAL BY AIR

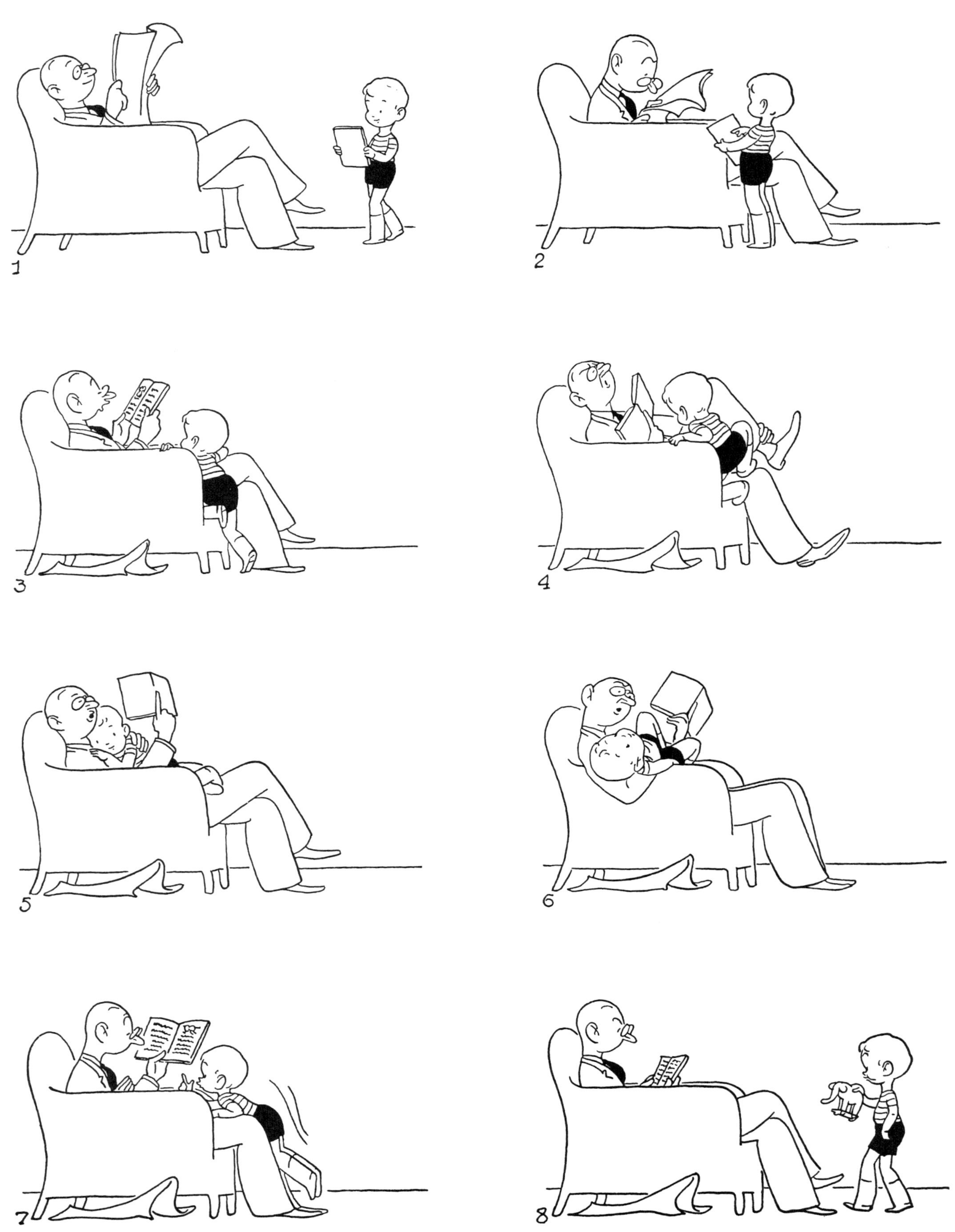

READING ALOUD (I)

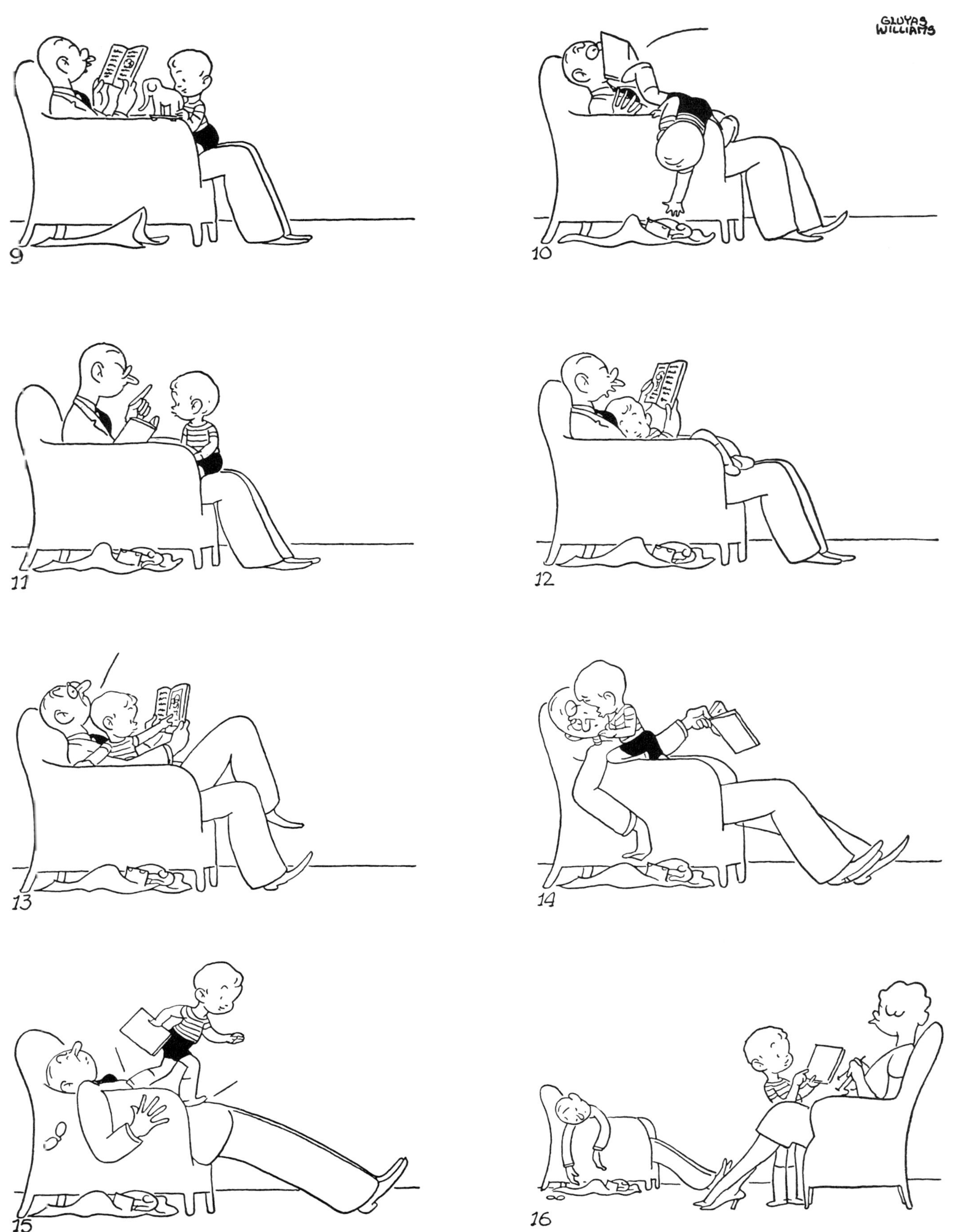

READING ALOUD (II)

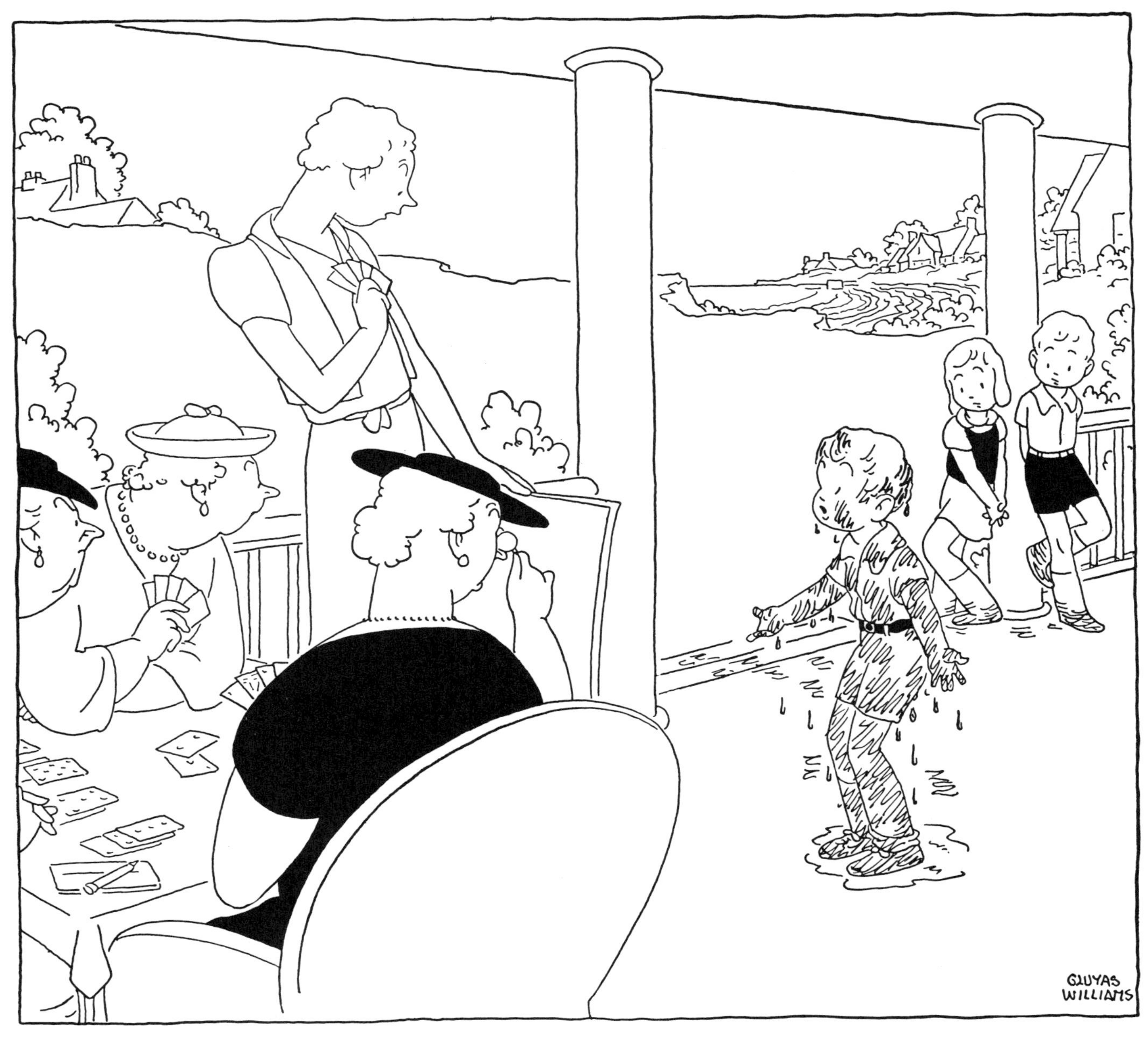

RACONTEURS

"You see, Mummy, our ball was out there in the mud and I knew you wouldn't want me to wade out to get it, but then some fierce creatures came dashing out of the bushes, and I think they were wolves, and there was a beautiful bird on the beach and probably his wing was broken, and I thought if I had my ball to throw at the wolves they wouldn't hurt the bird, and so . . ."

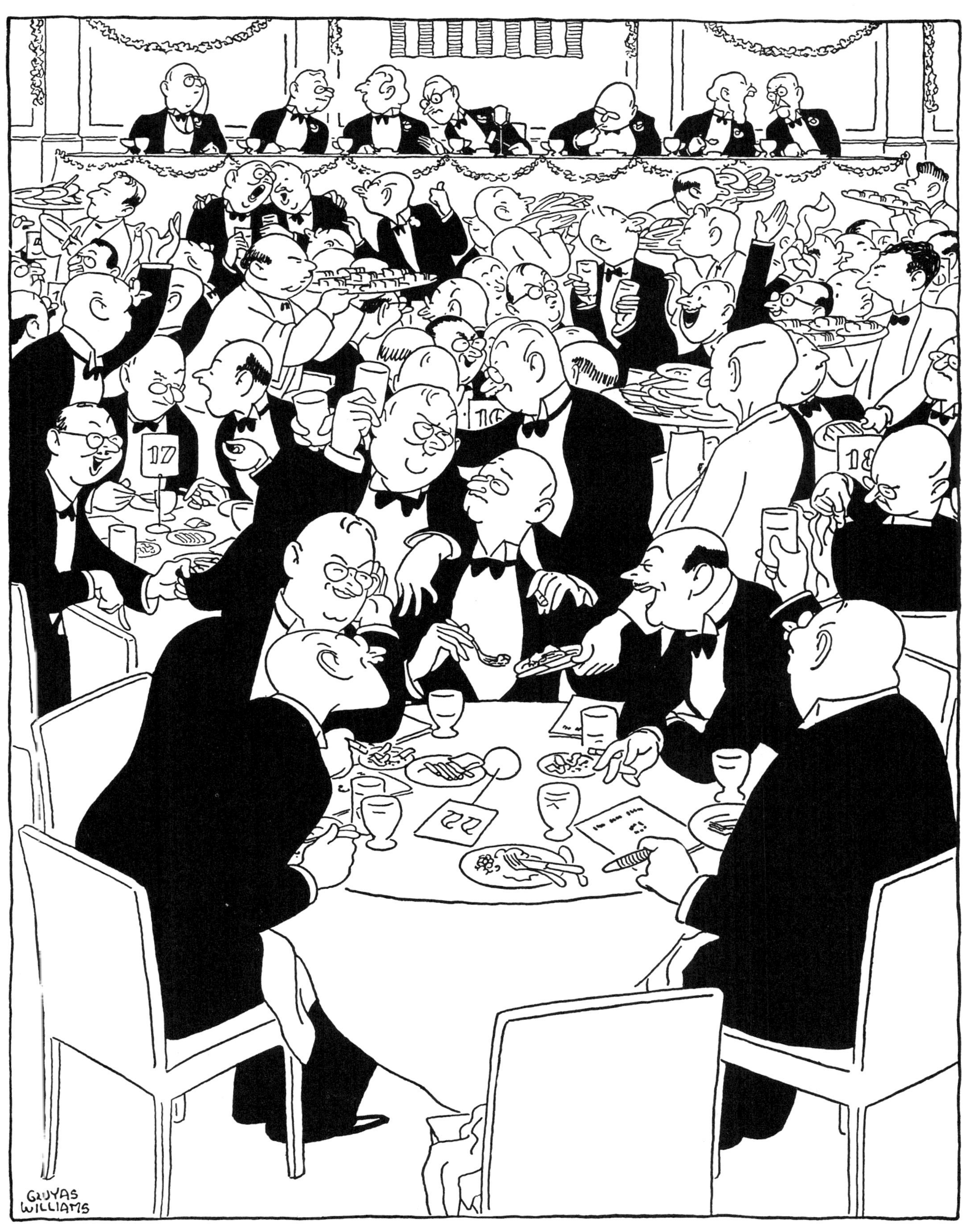

THE INNER MAN

Annual Dinner

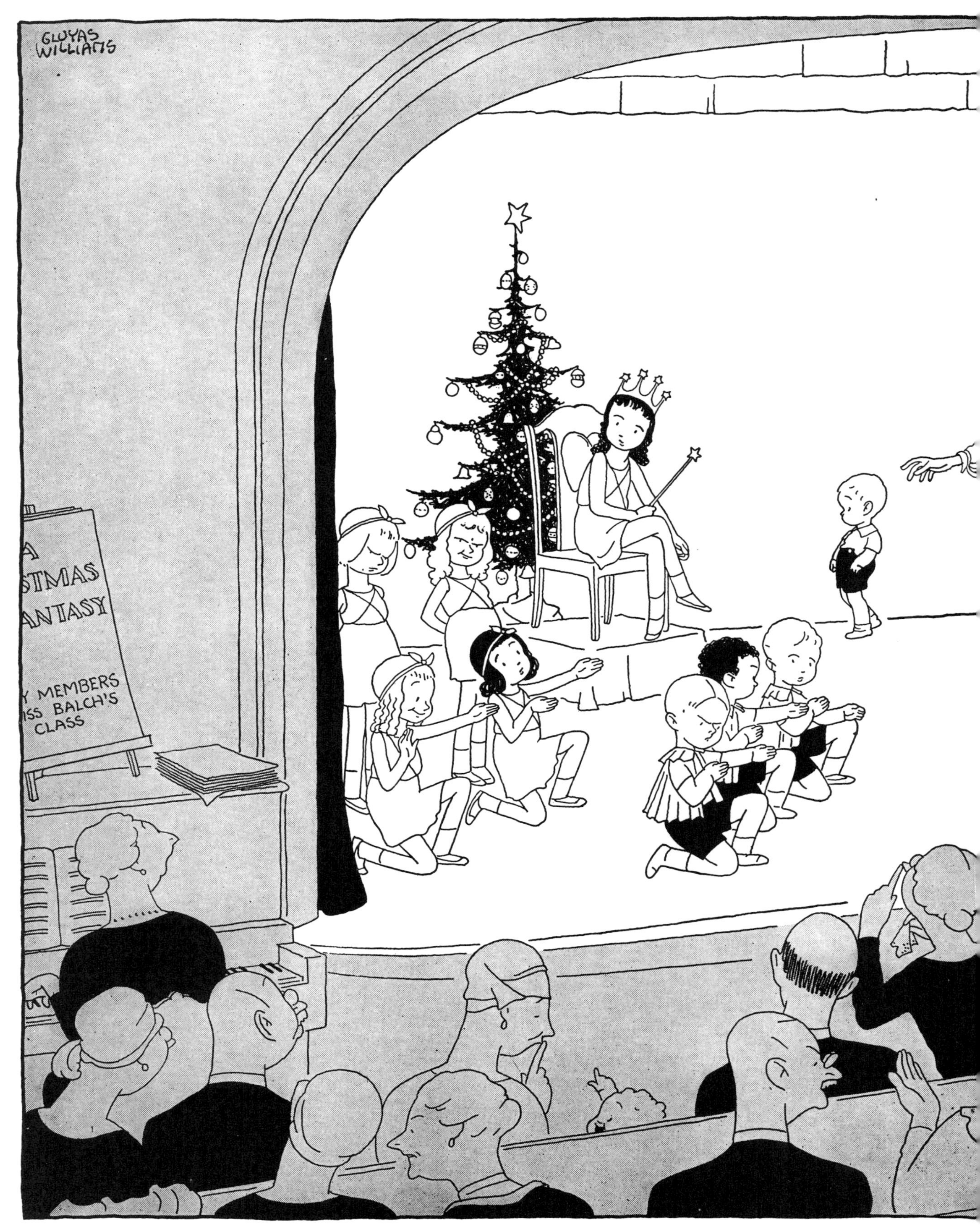

THE SUNDAY

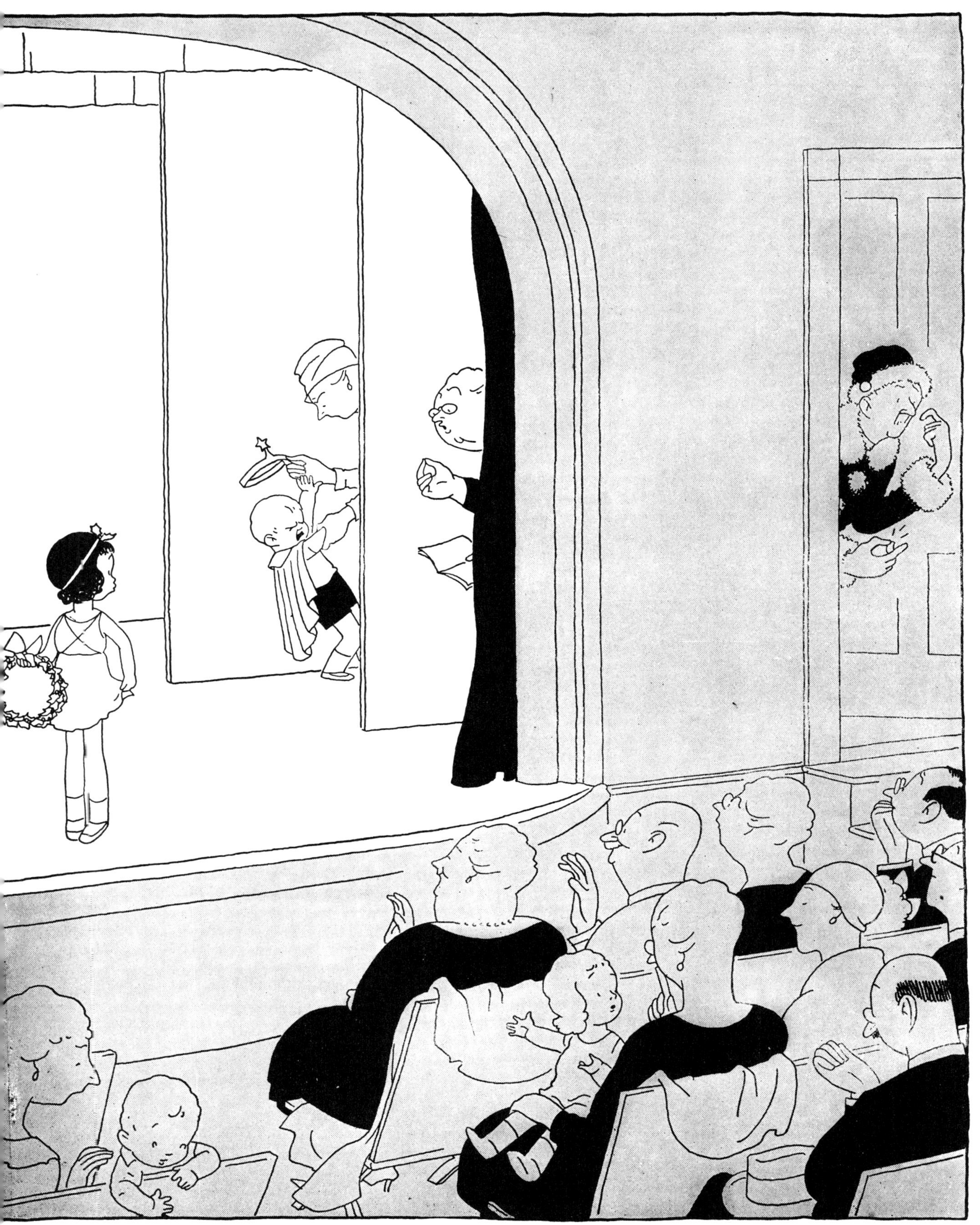

SCHOOL PLAY

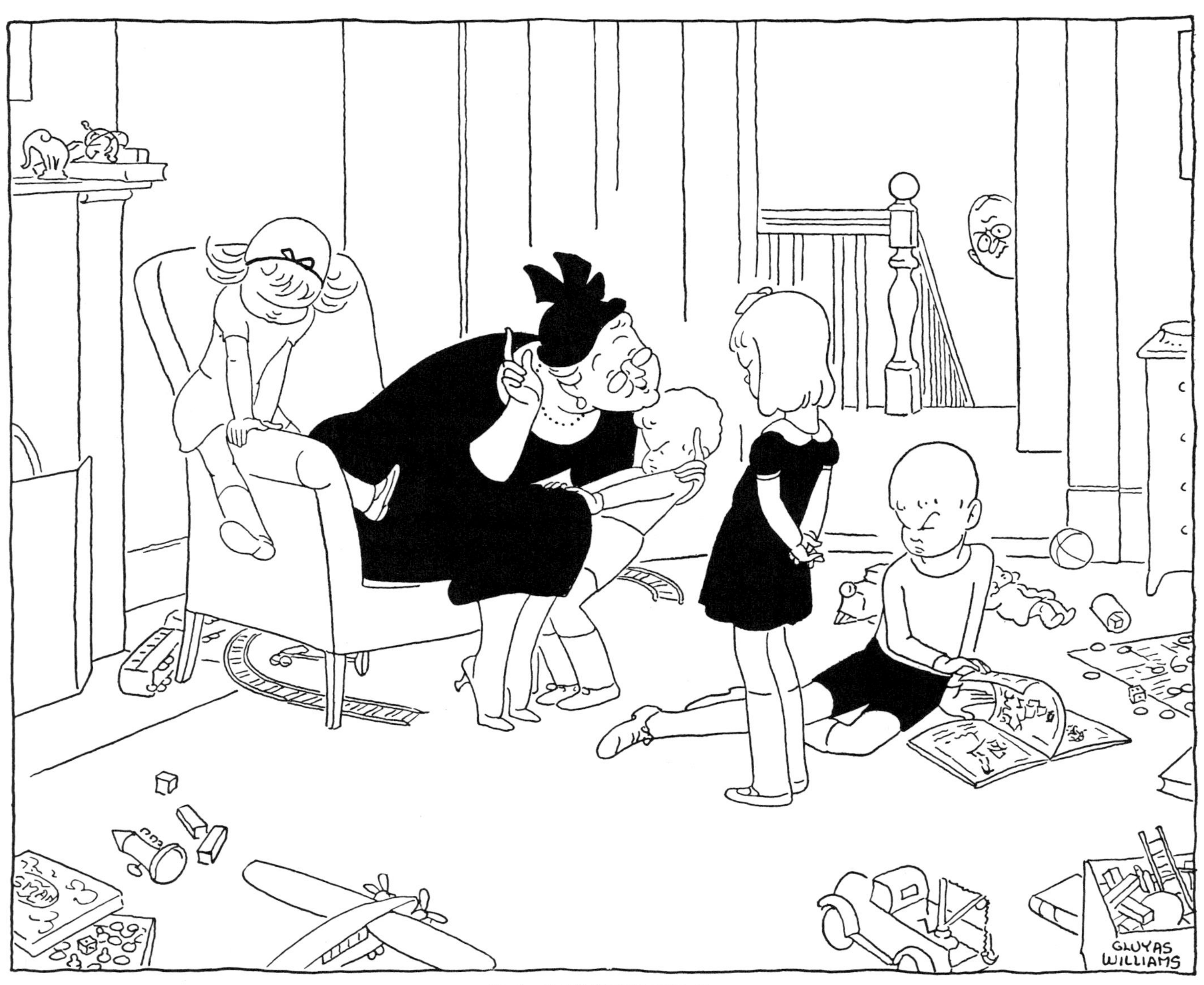

RACONTEURS

"And what do you think? Way up there at the very tippy-top of the tree was little Mr Bobolink, singing just as if his little heart would break. And just then . . ."

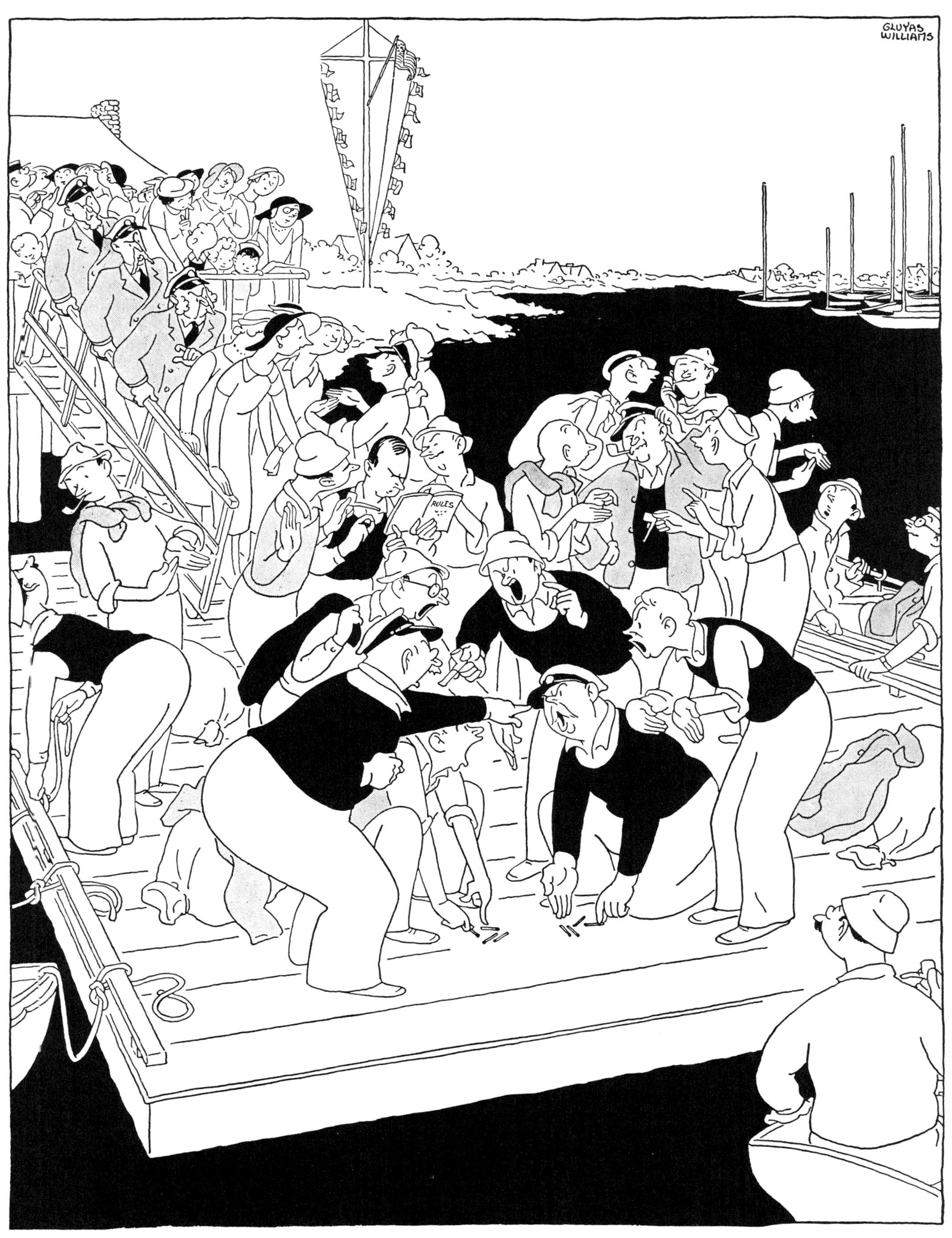

CLUB LIFE IN AMERICA

A Protest Enlivens Regatta Day

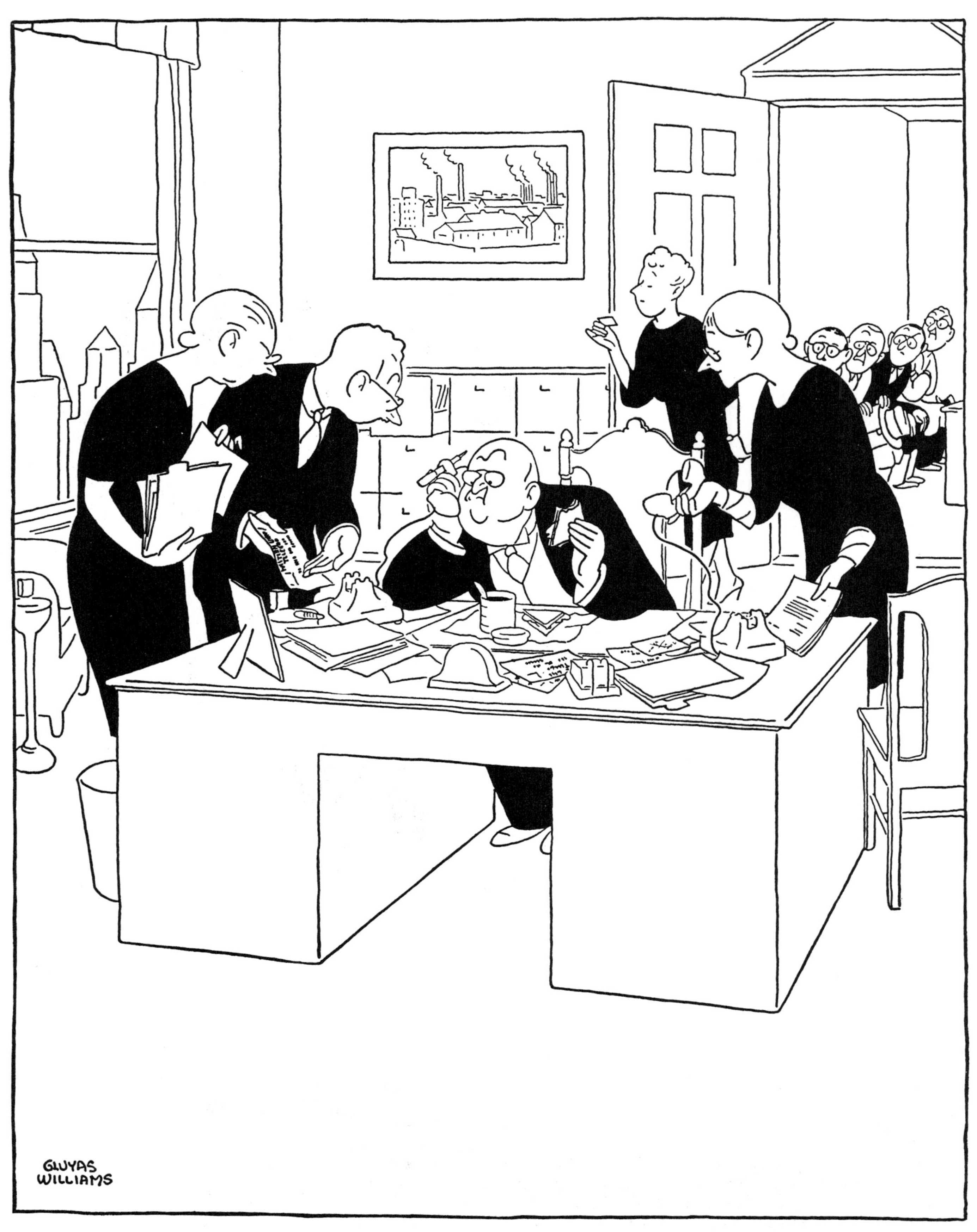

THE INNER MAN

High-Pressure Lunch

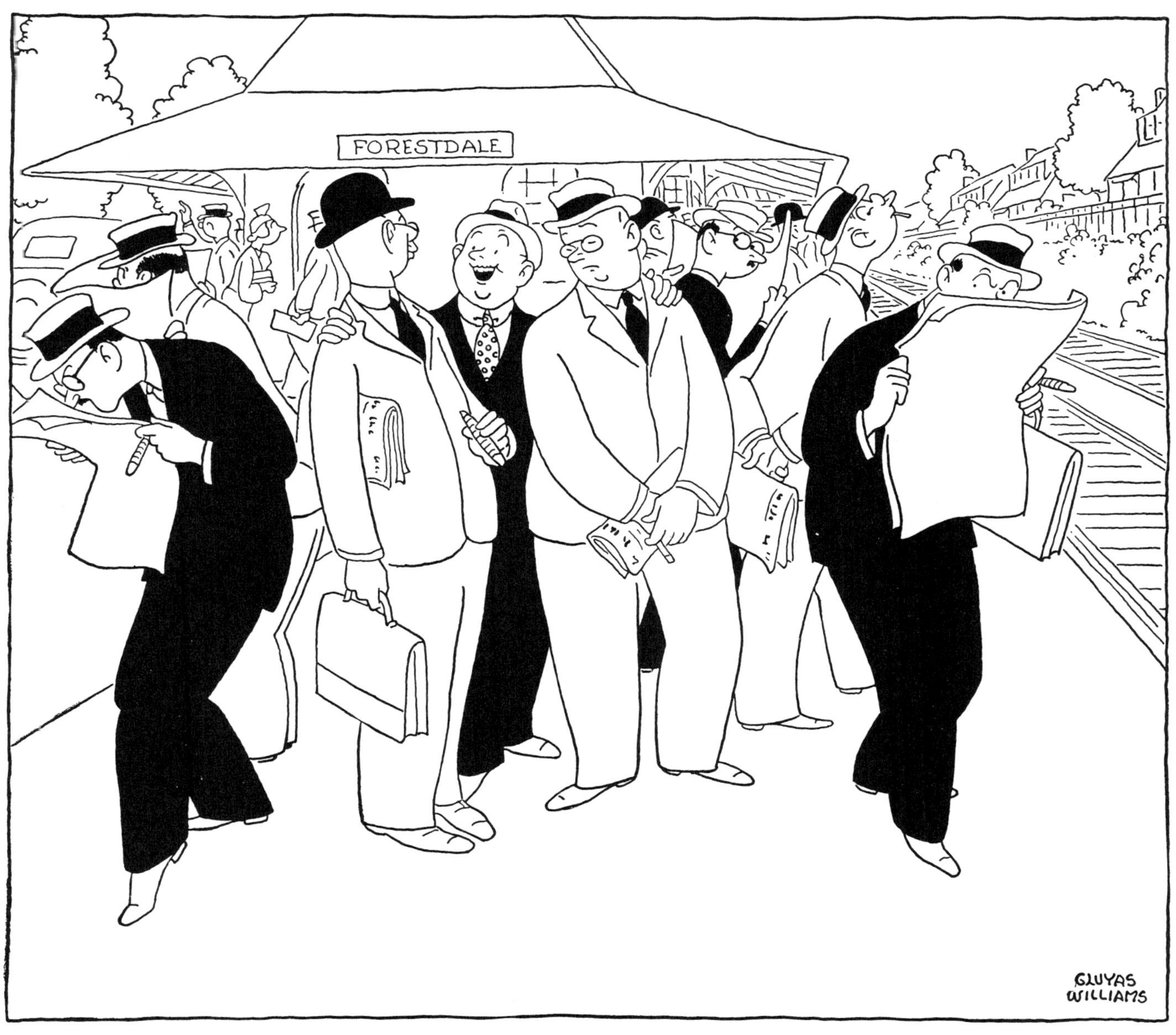

RACONTEURS

"Well, what do you suppose that little tyke of mine said this *morning? We were eating breakfast, and I ought to explain that we've had a new cook at the house for about a week, and the little fellow spoke up and . . ."*

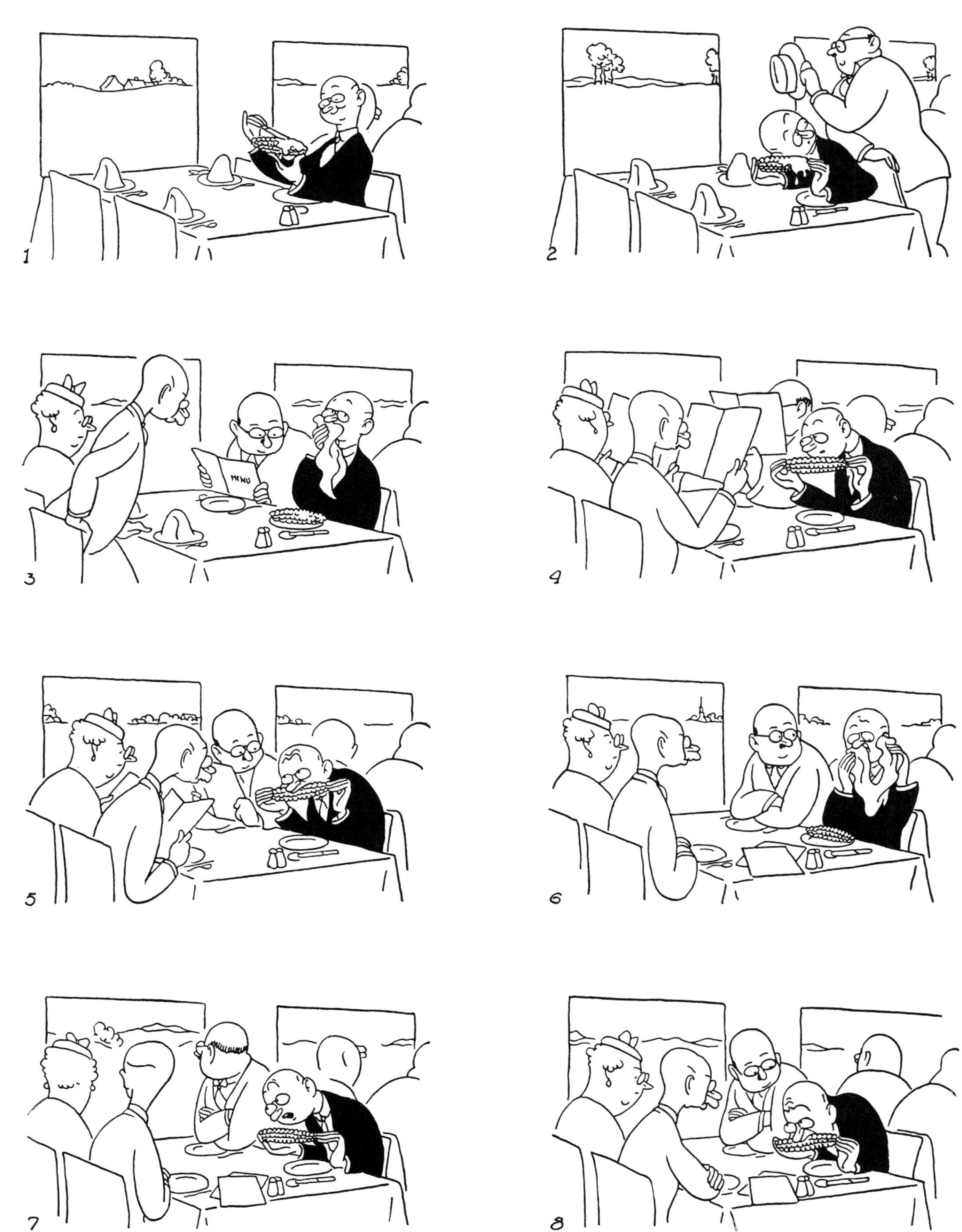

CORN ON THE DINER (I)

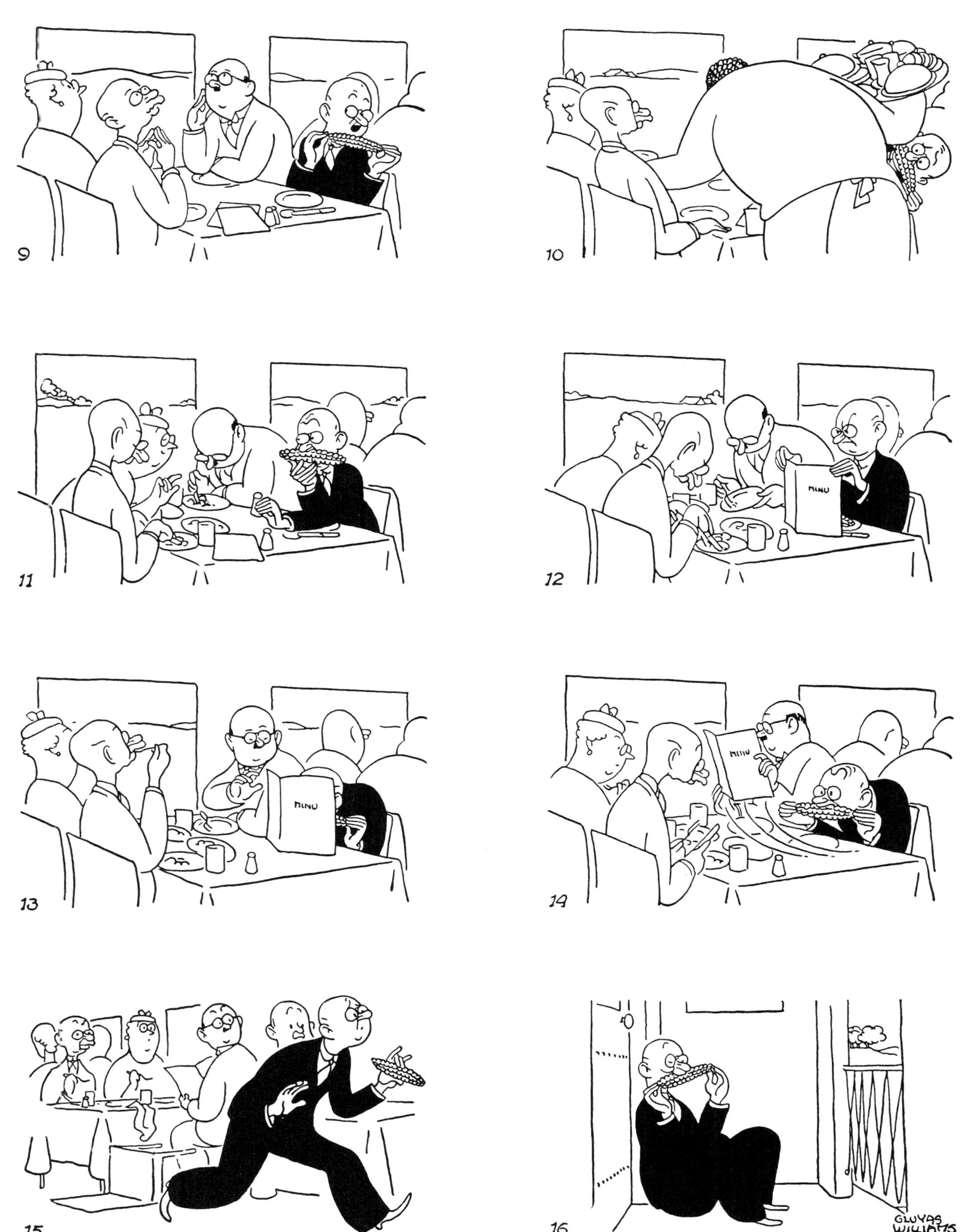

CORN ON THE DINER (II)

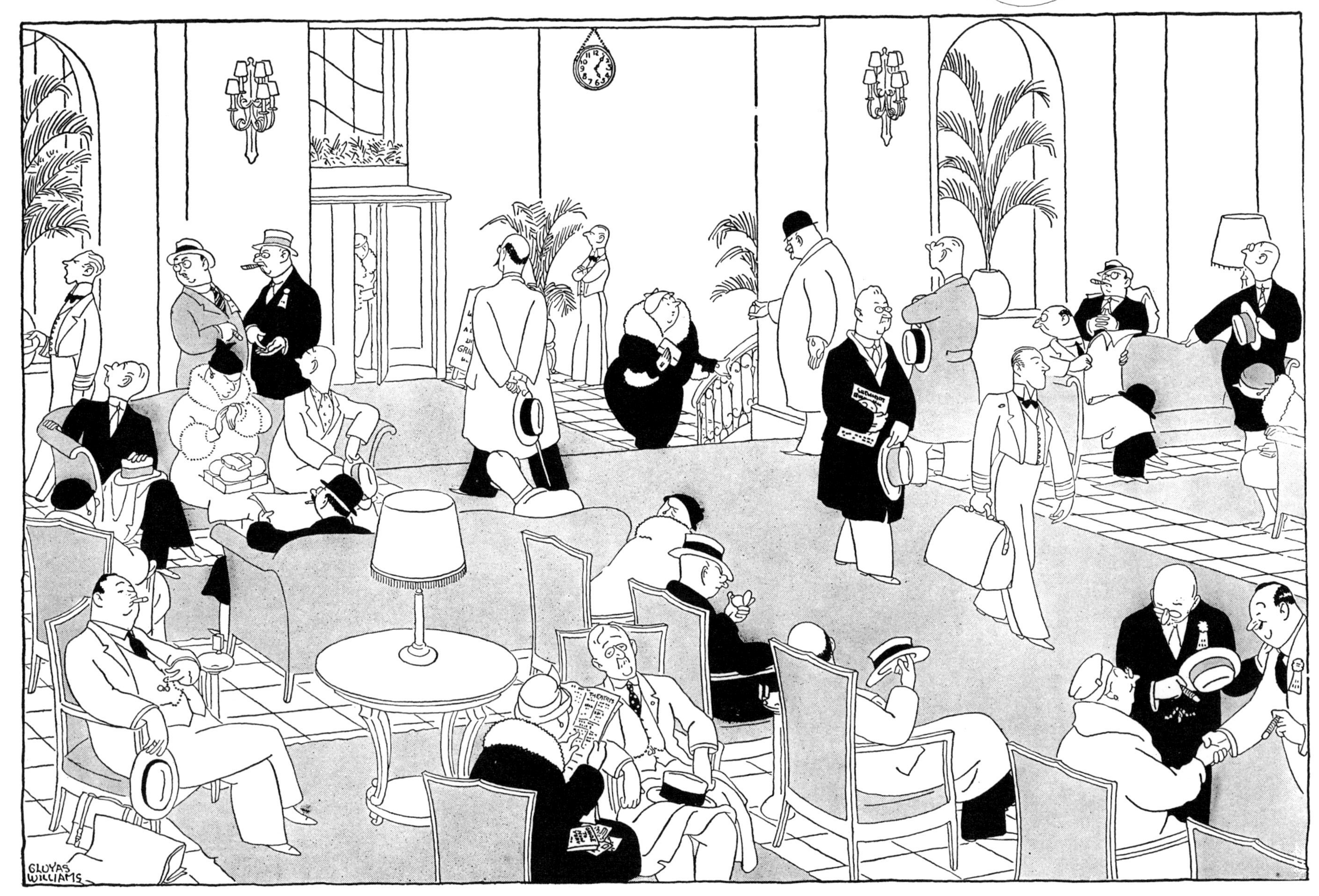

THE HOTEL LOBBY

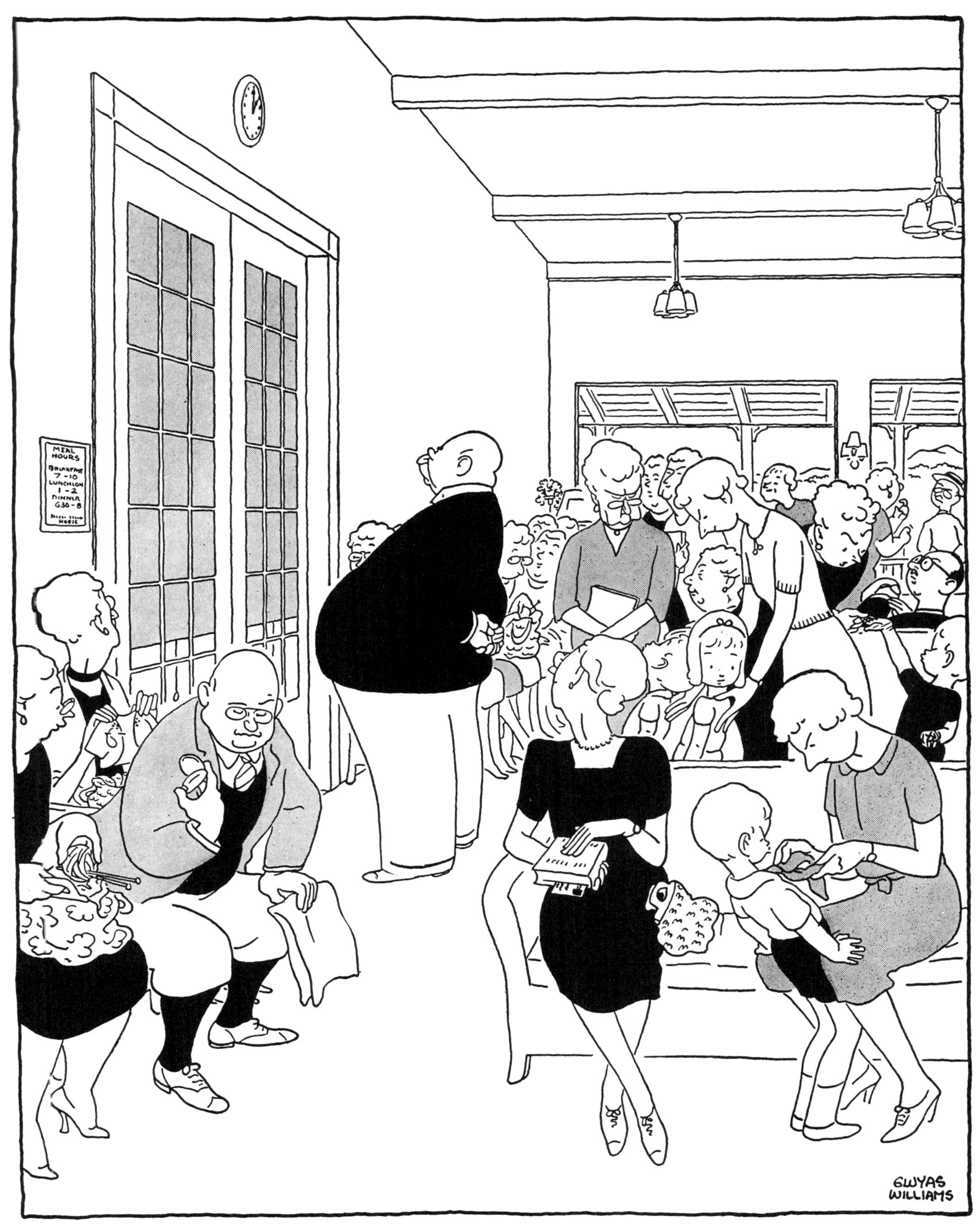

THE INNER MAN LUNCHEON 1–2

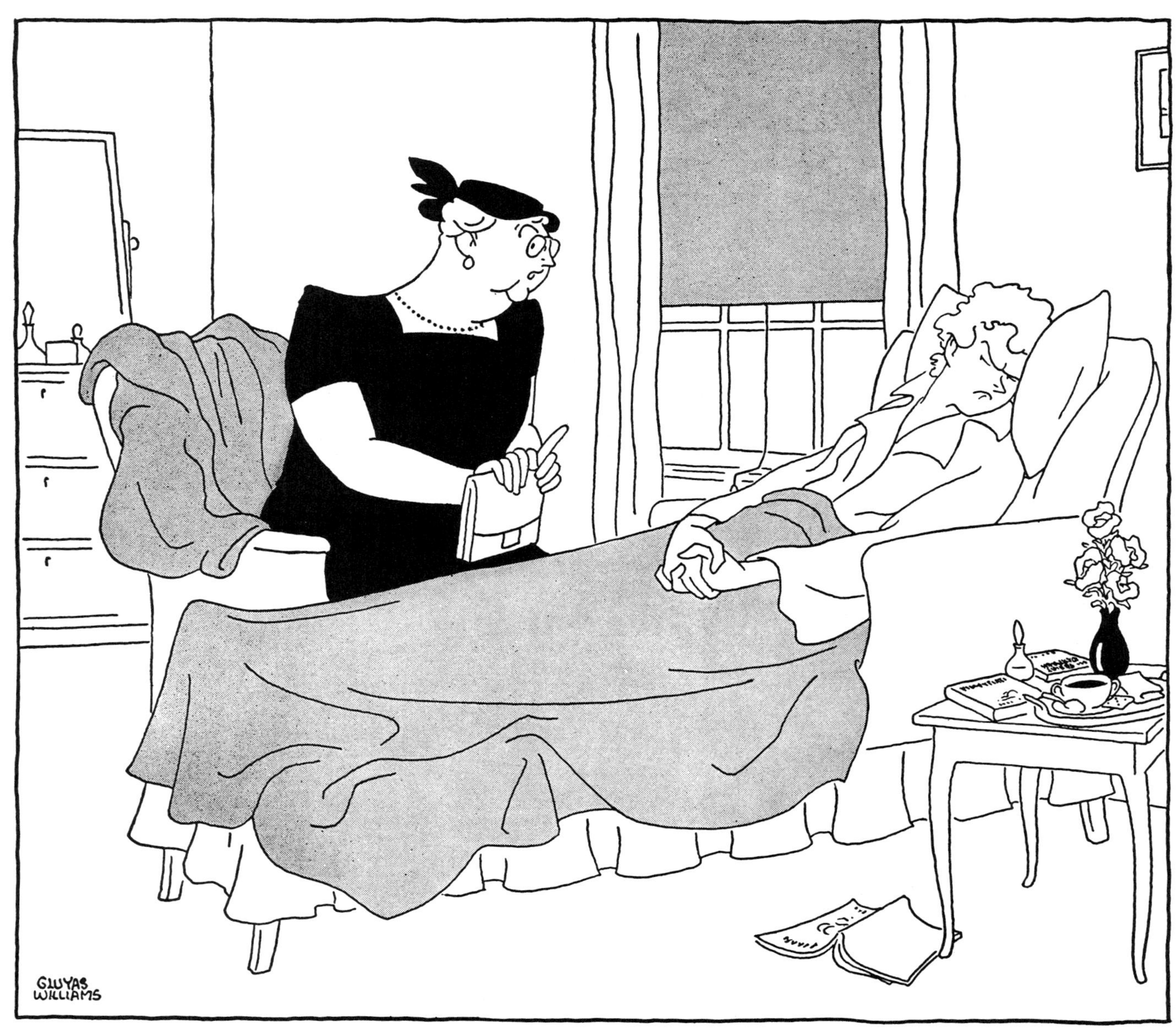

RACONTEURS

"The minute I heard about you I came right over, because I know how lonely you must be. I'm so glad that it's nothing worse than a bad headache, but even so, my dear, I do think you ought to see a doctor right away. Who knows, it may be one of Nature's danger signals. I always remember Mrs. Ramsey—simply the picture of health except for these bad headaches, and the things they found when they got her to the hospital! To begin with . . ."

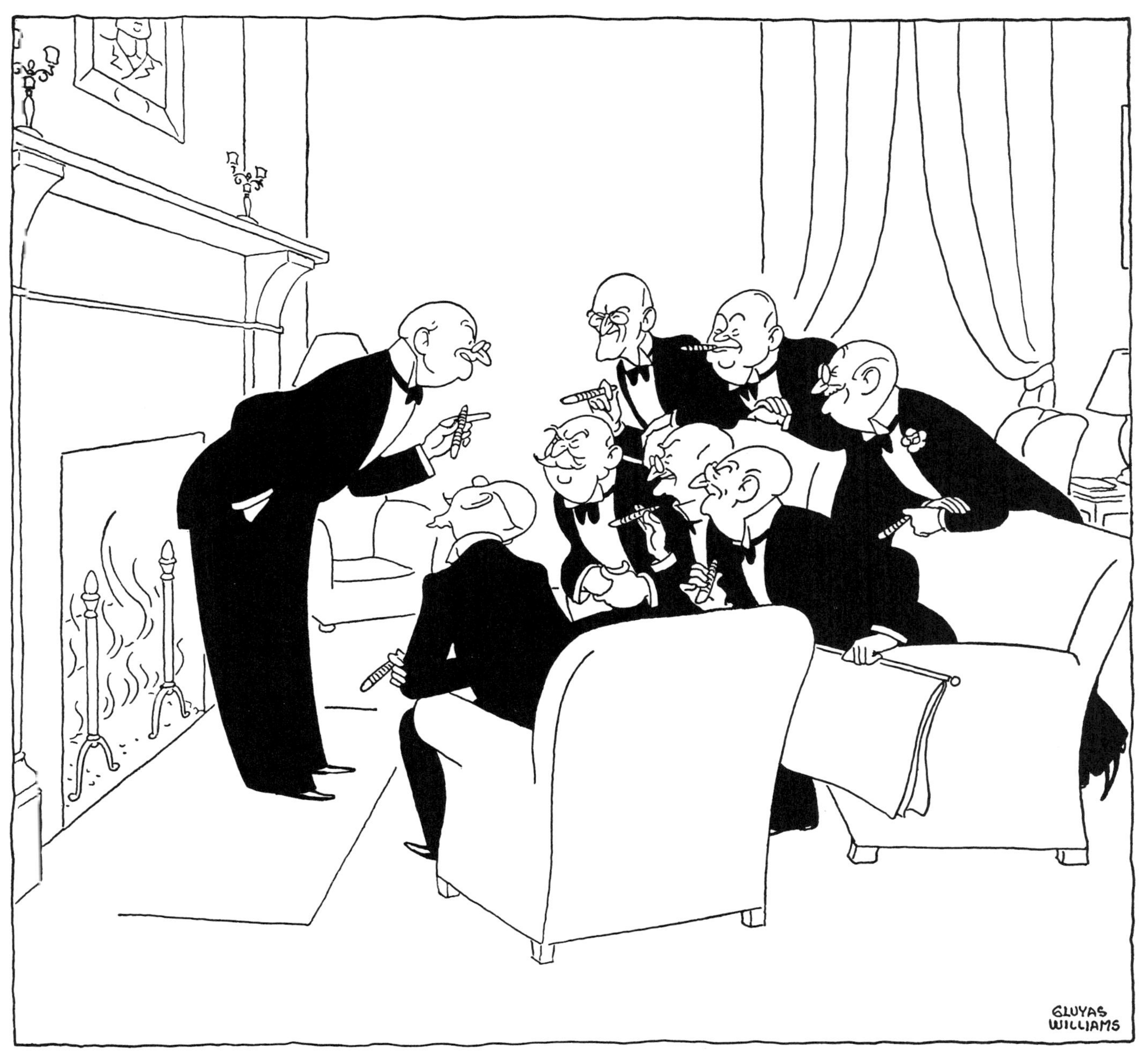

RACONTEURS

"Here's a new one I heard downtown today—F. D. and Eleanor were going shopping, and she said, 'Franklin . . .'"

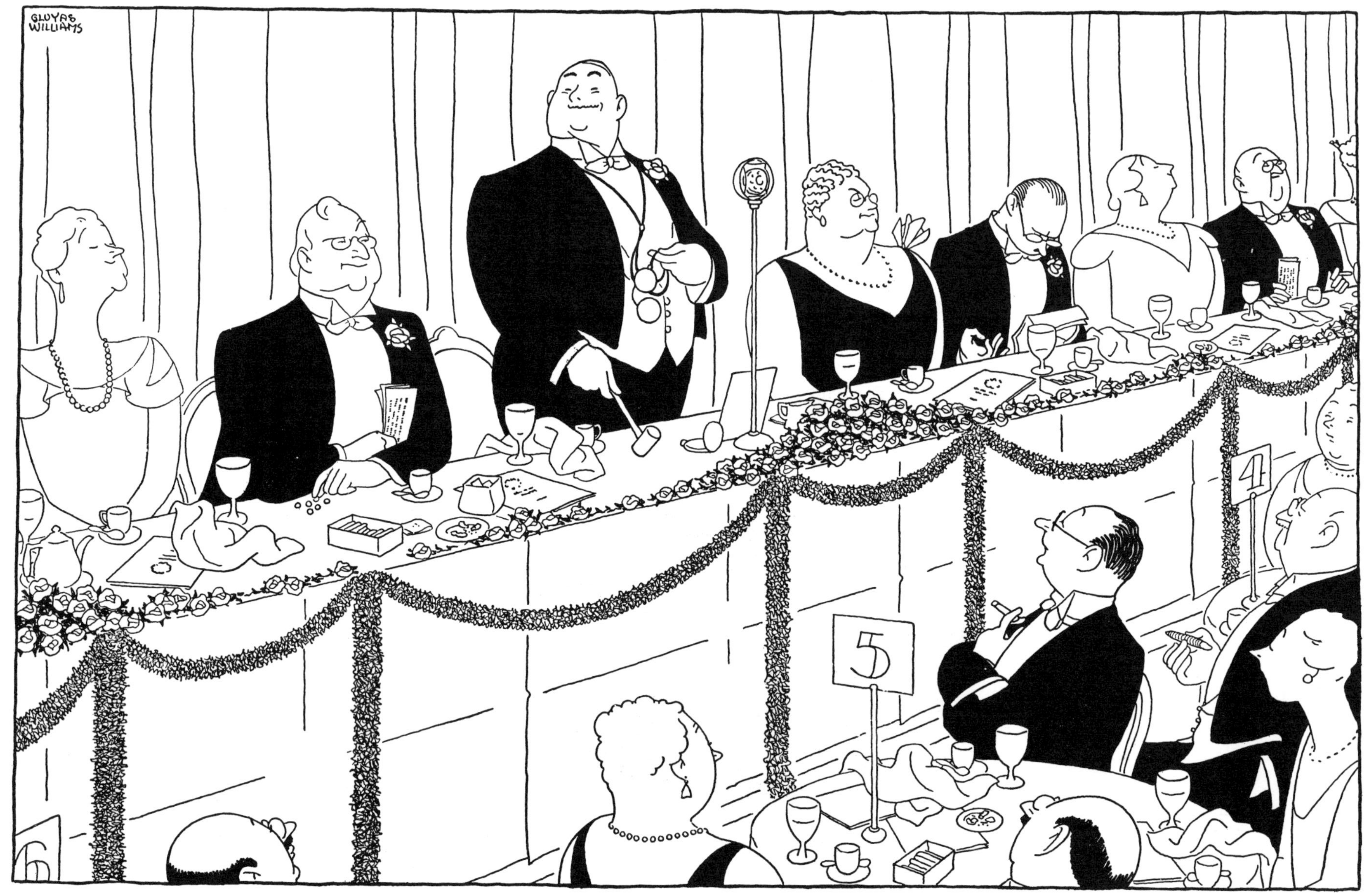

HEAD TABLE

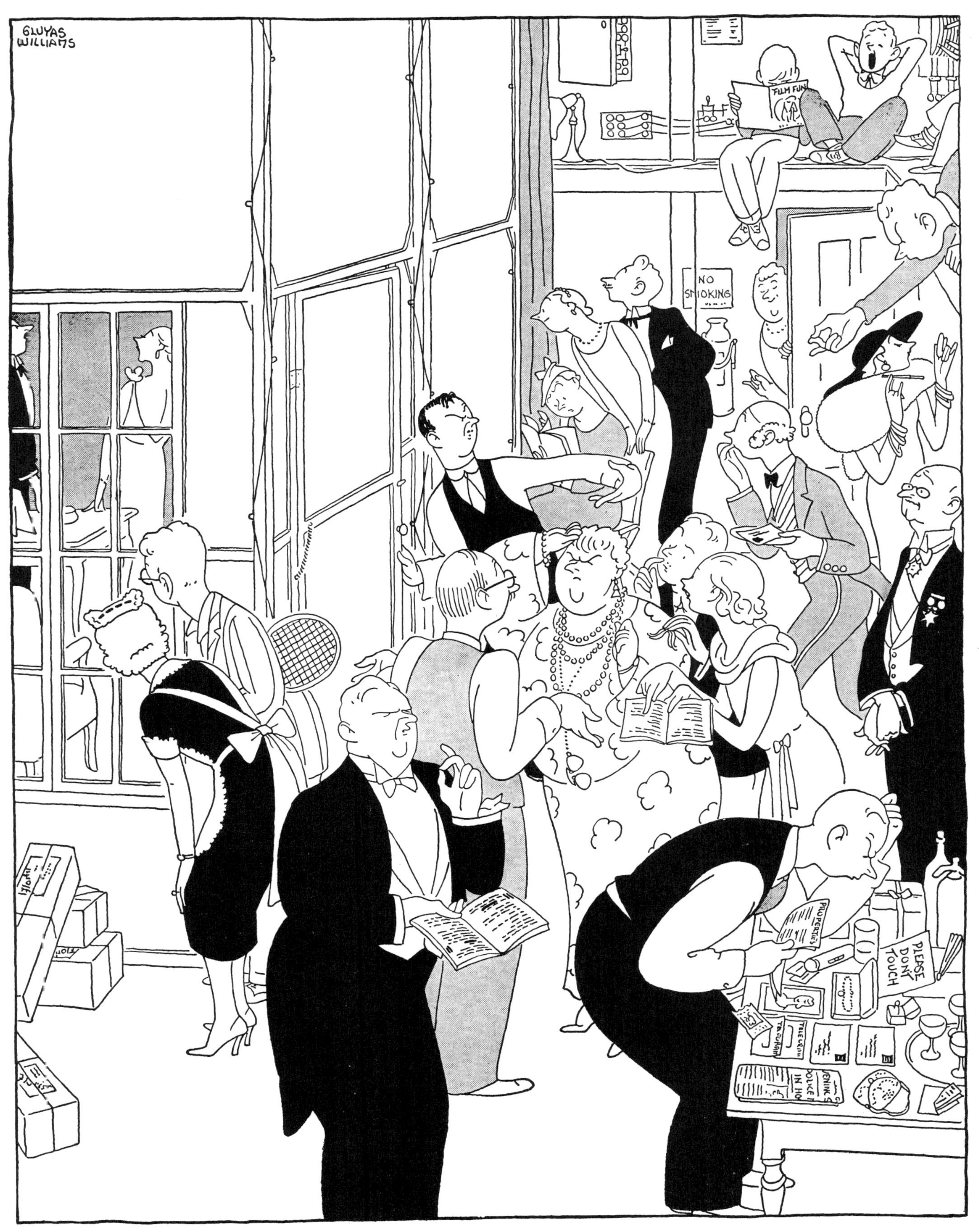

CLUB LIFE IN AMERICA

The Little Stagers Put on a Comedy of Manners

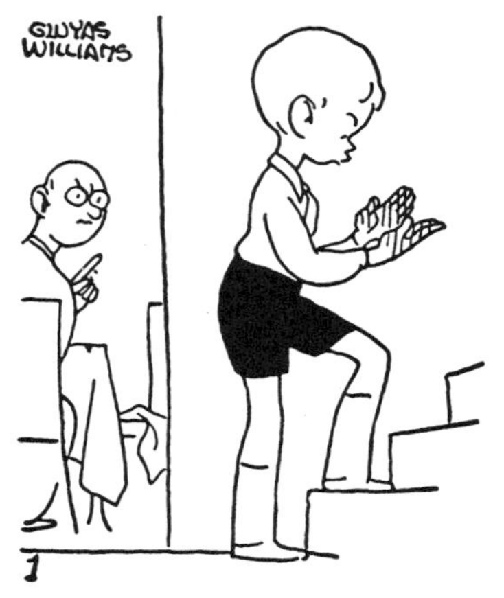

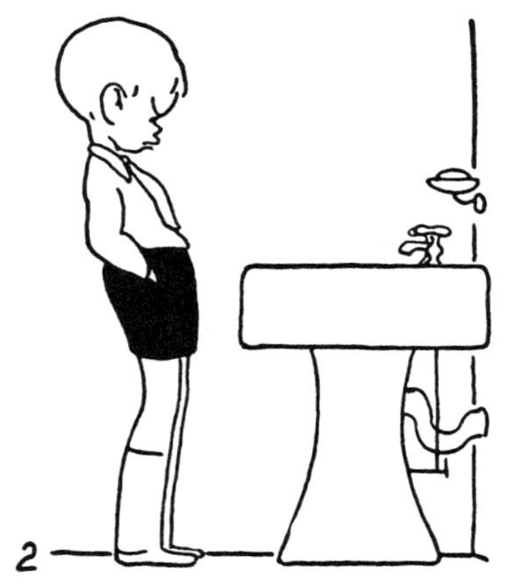

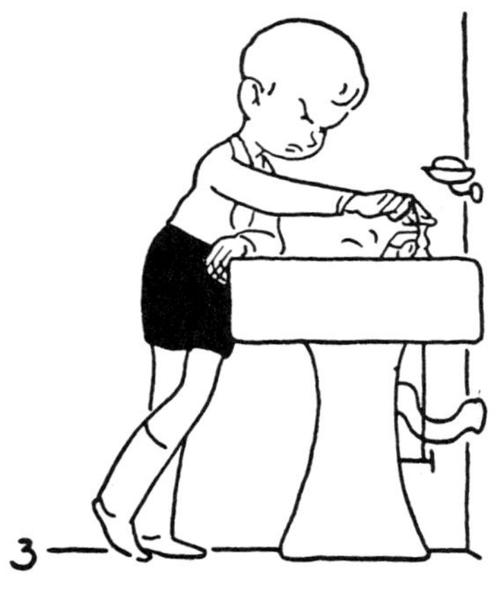

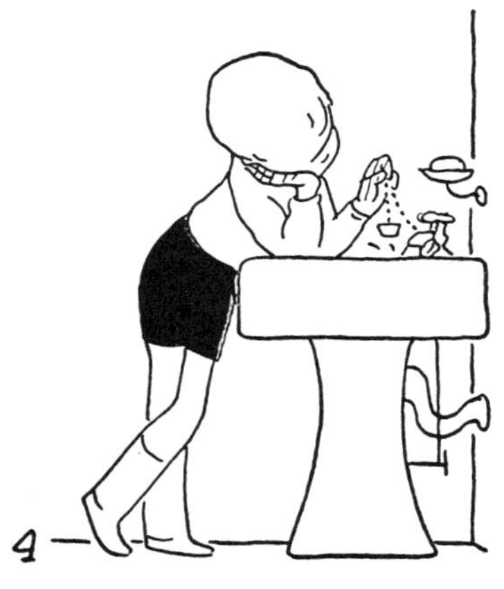

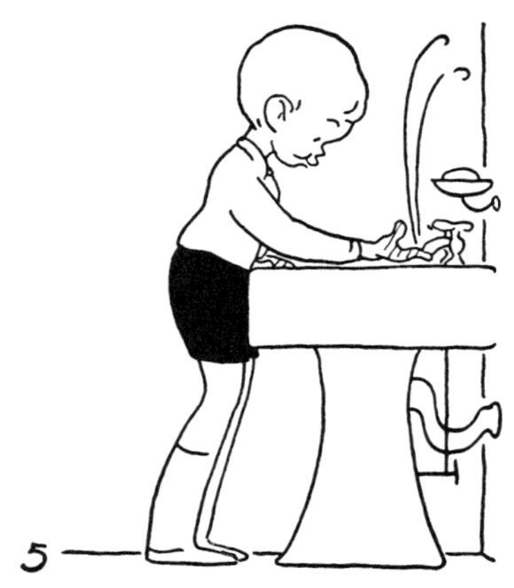

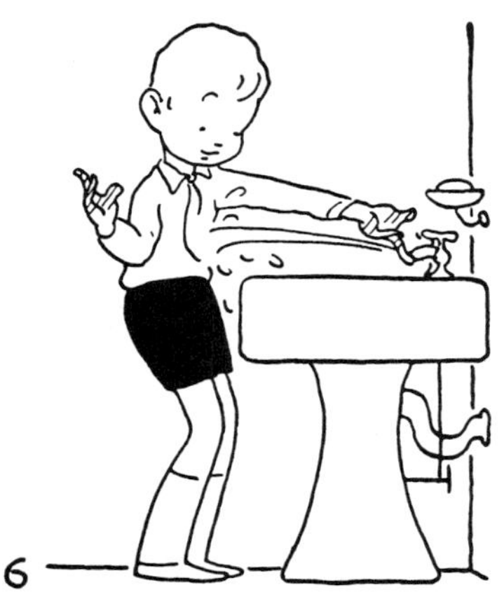

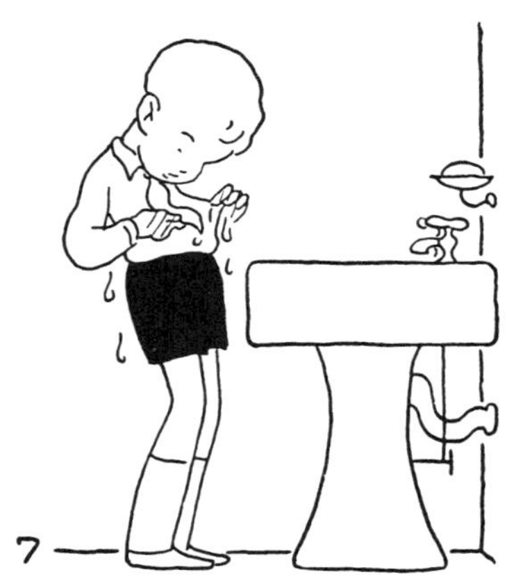

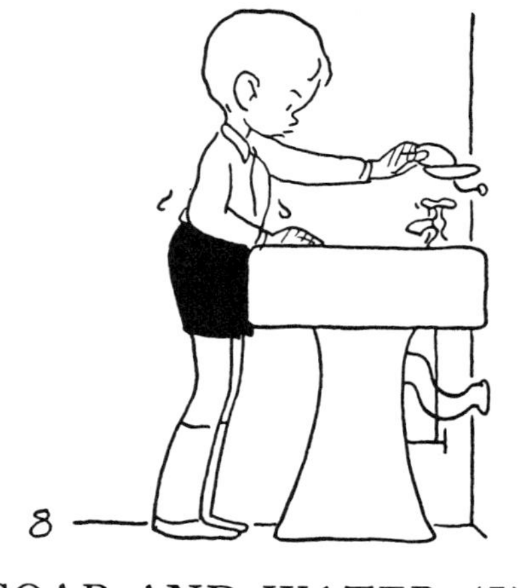

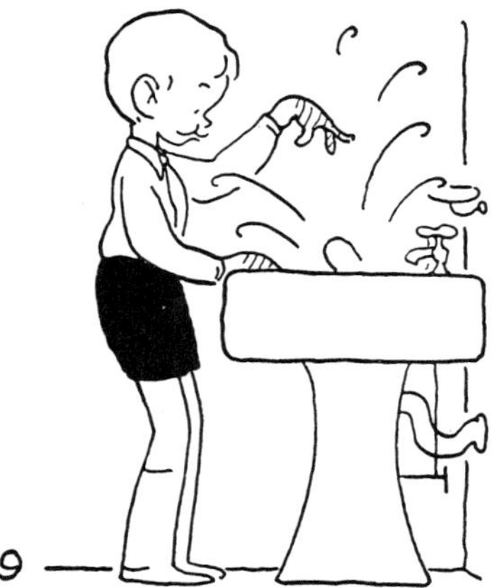

SOAP AND WATER (I)

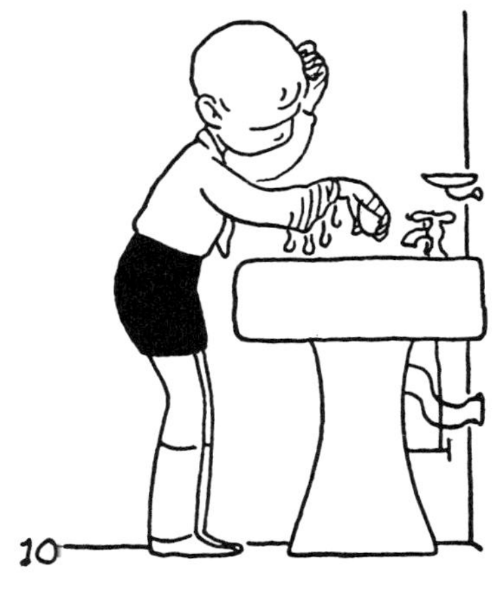

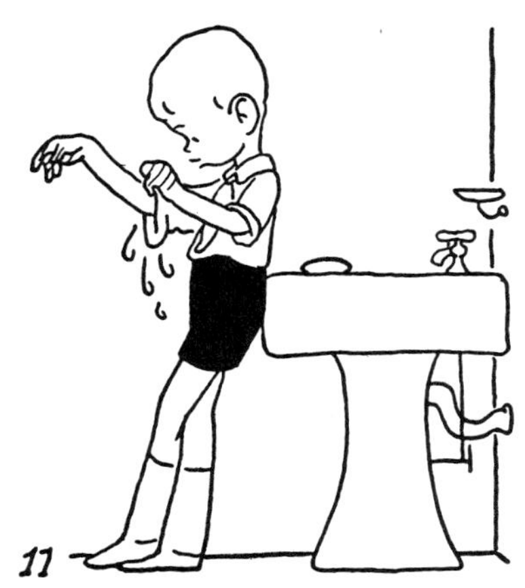

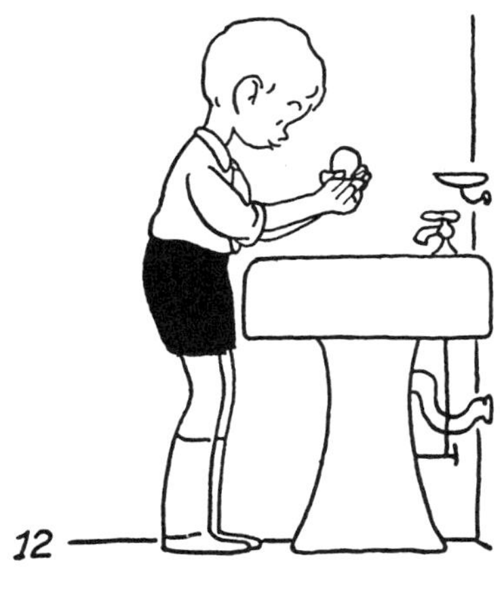

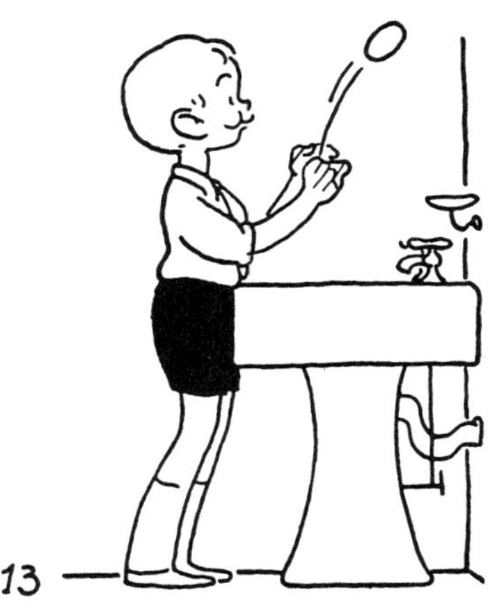

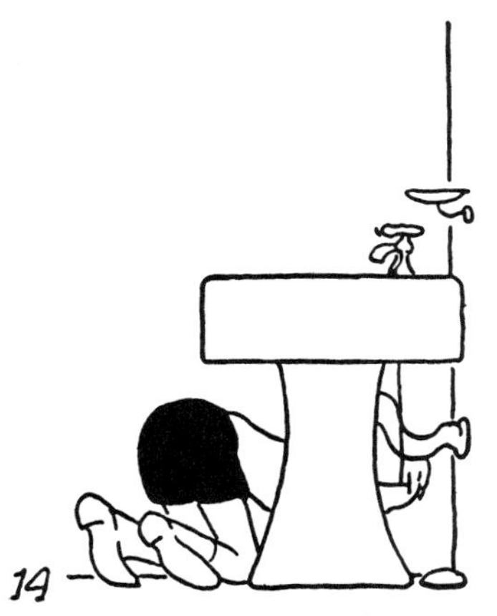

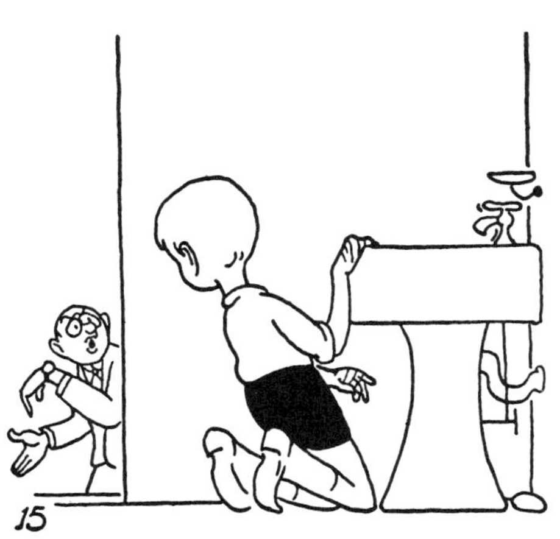

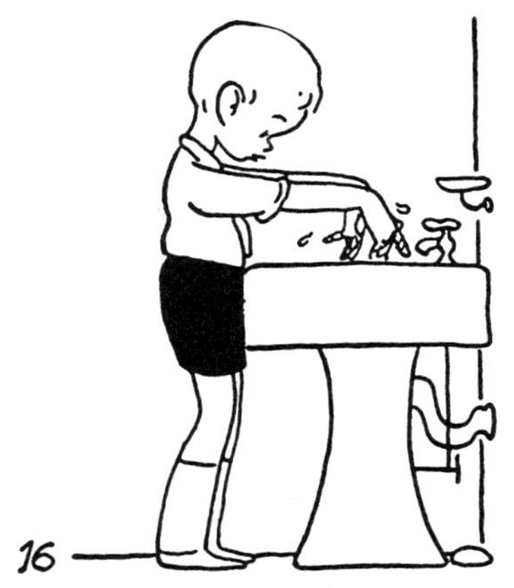

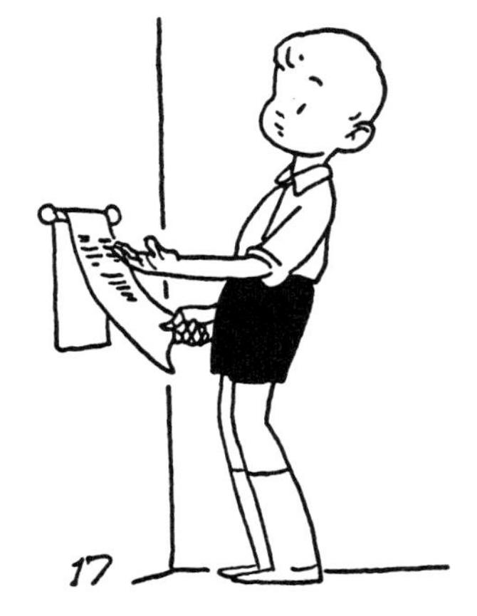

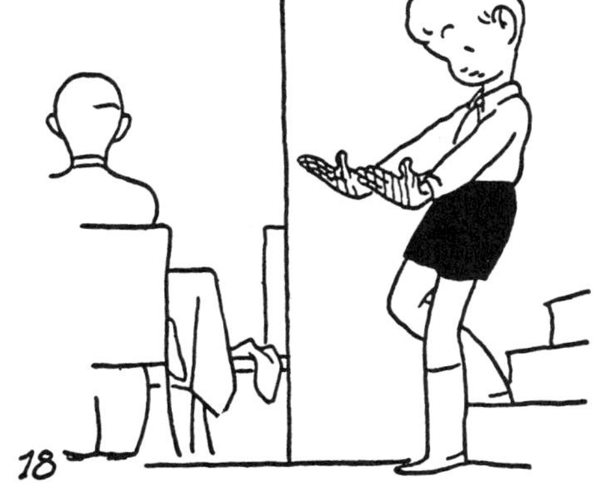

SOAP AND WATER (II)

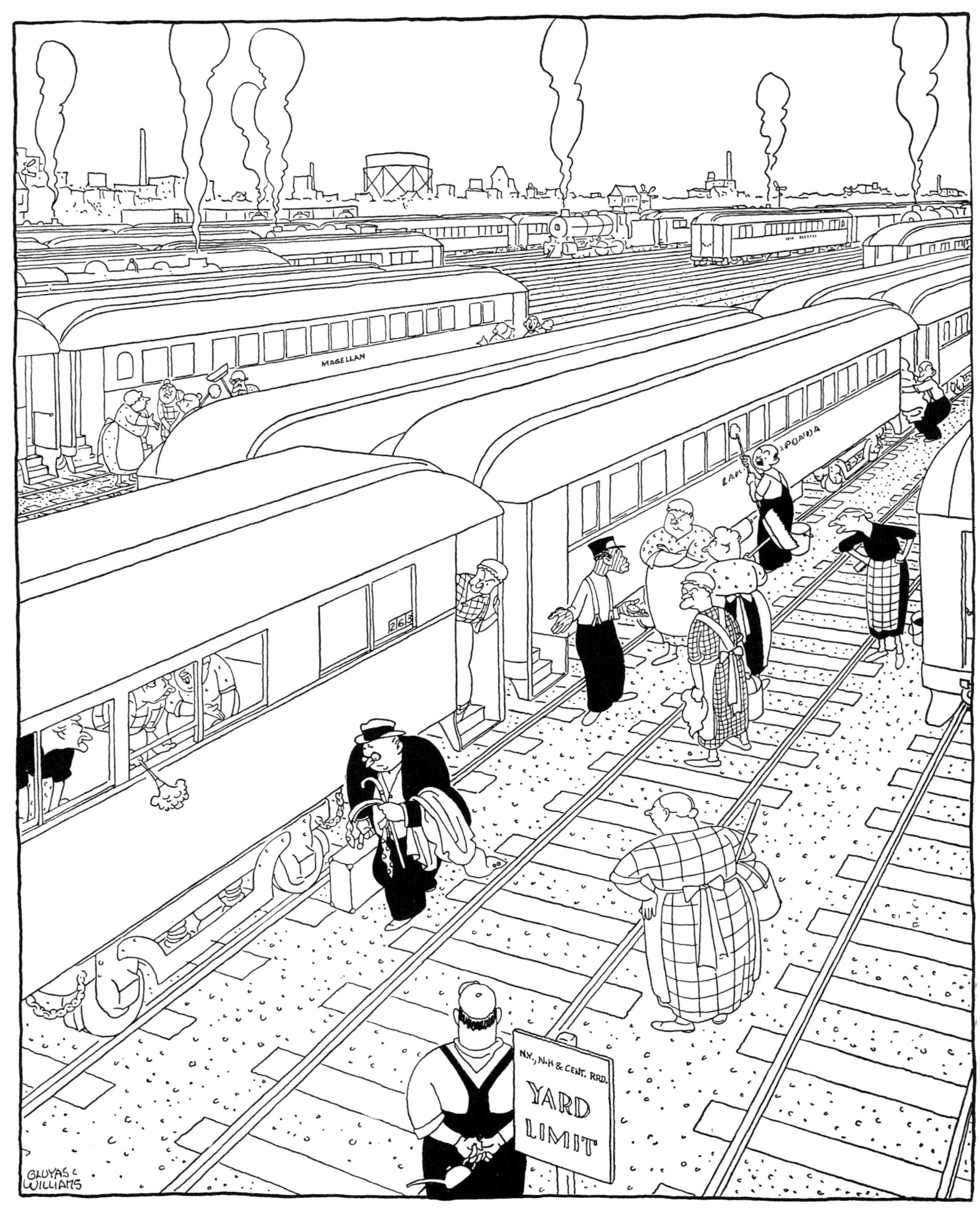

THE MAN WHO OVERSLEPT

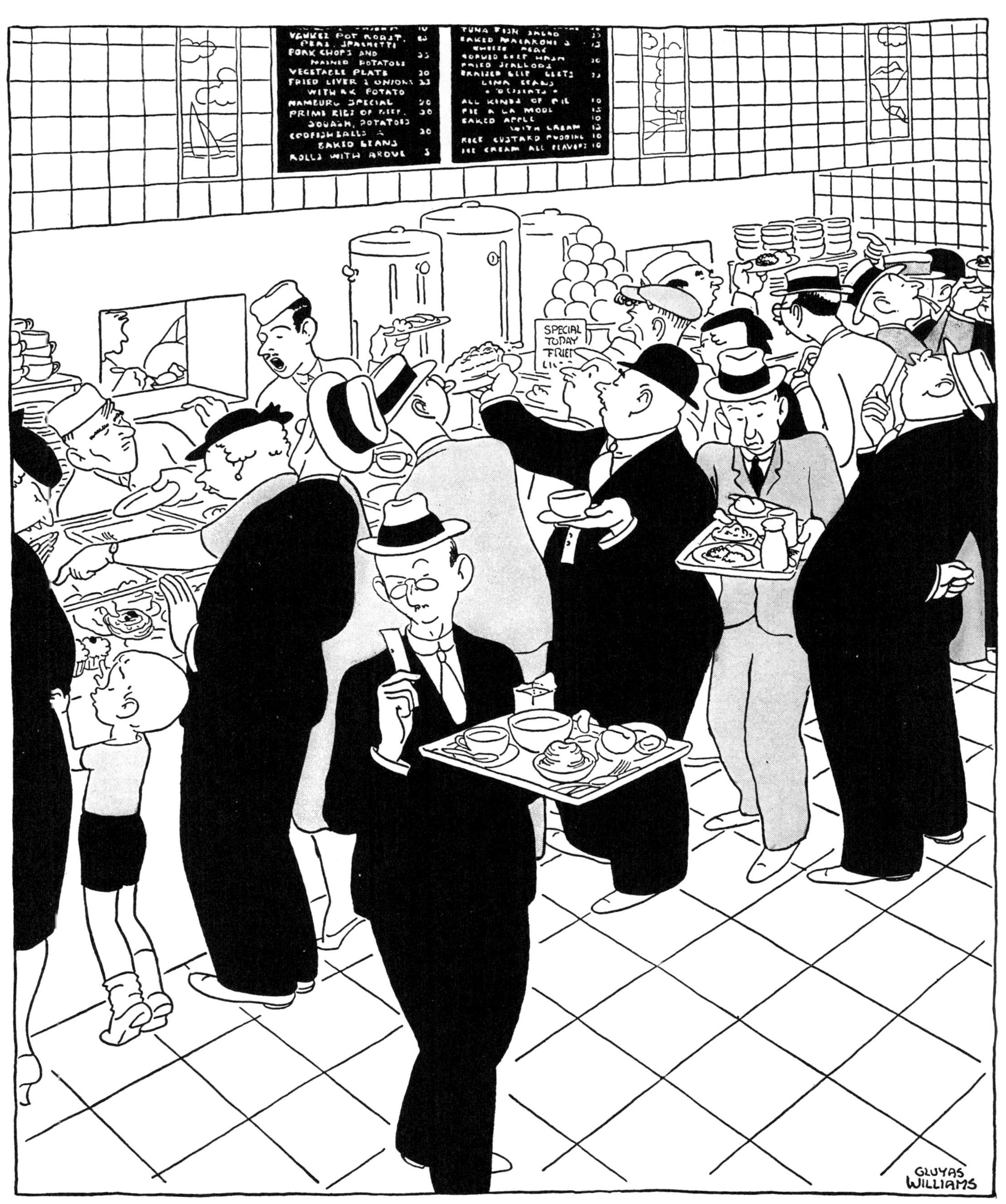

THE INNER MAN

Self-Service

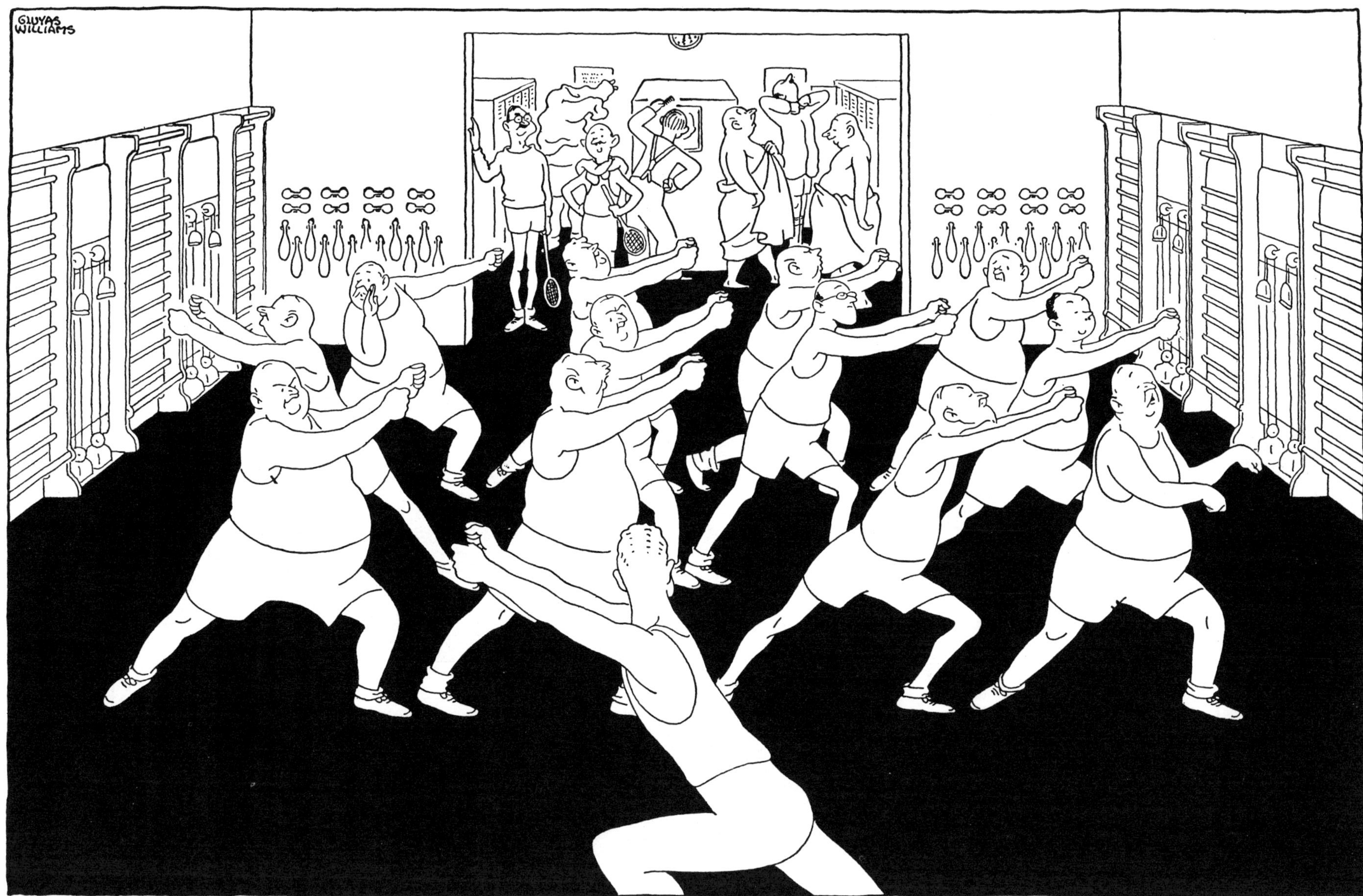

CLUB LIFE IN AMERICA

The Class in Health-Building Meets at the Athletic Club

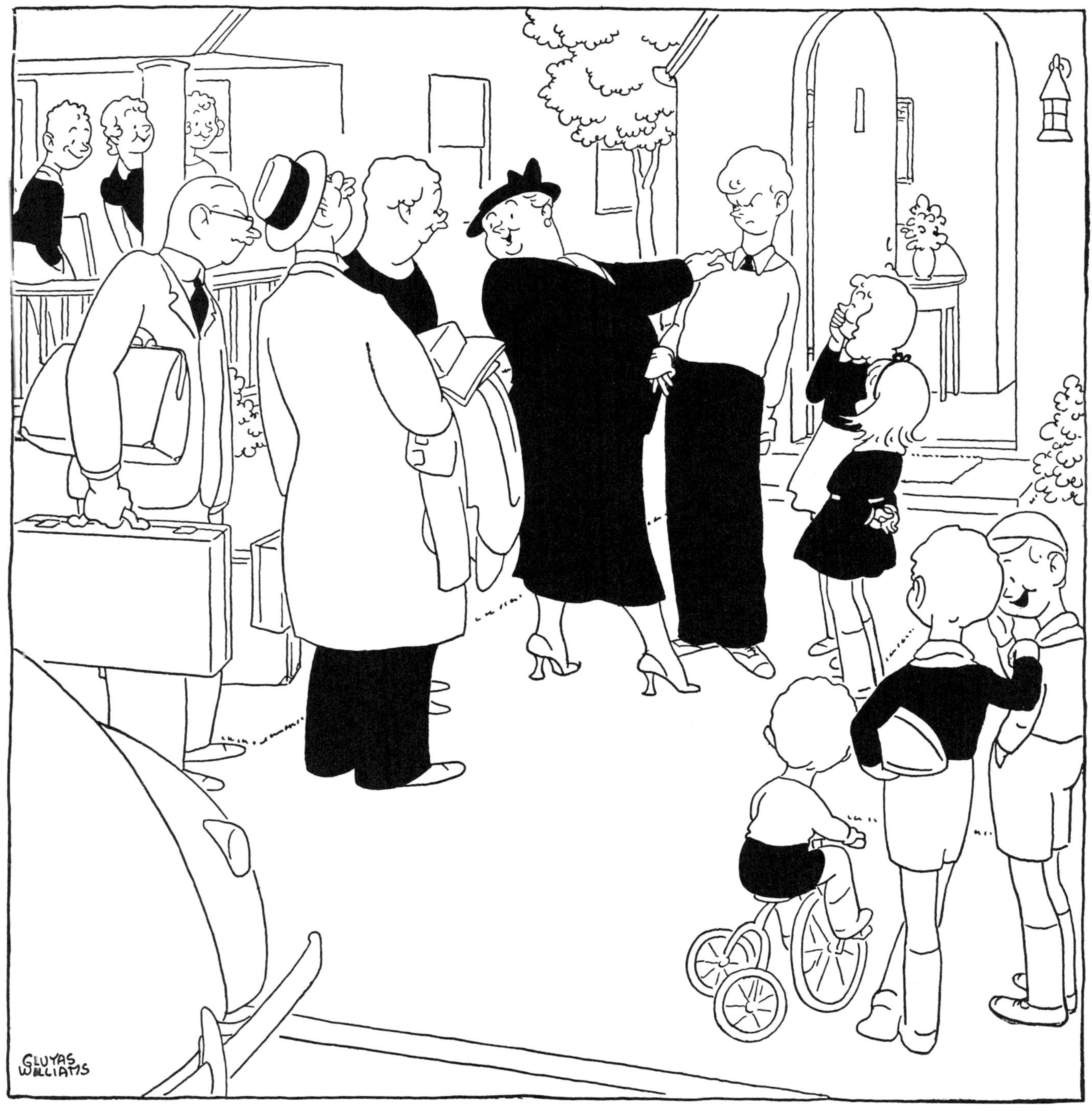

RACONTEURS

"Now don't tell me this young man is Munroe. Well, I can hardly believe it. Seems only yesterday that I'd be giving him his bath and he'd almost wiggle and squirm out of my lap when I tried to dry his stomach. Such a dear little cherub with those fat little legs and golden curls. And do you remember the time when I was visiting you, and he crawled into bed with me and lisped . . ."

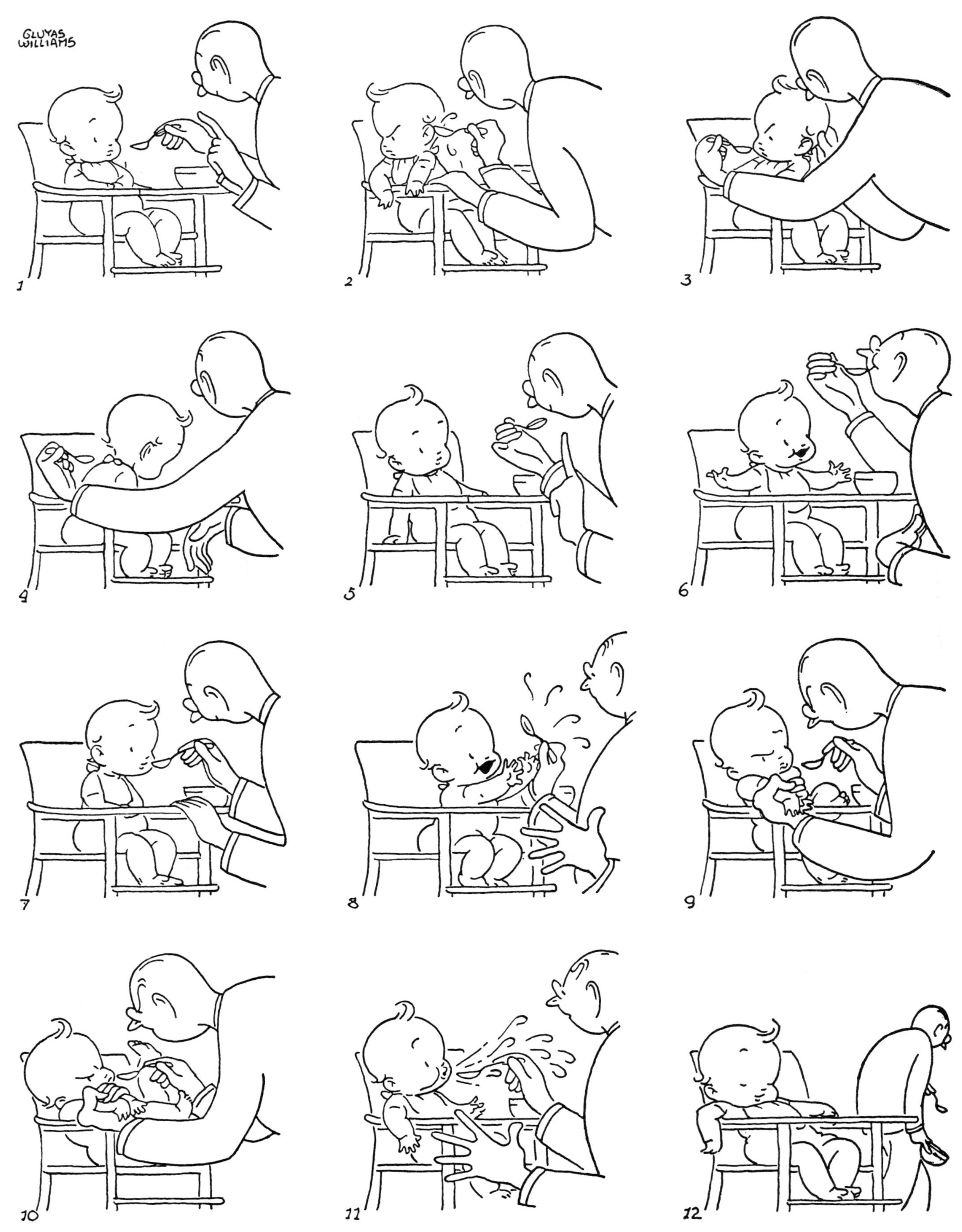

END OF A MEAL

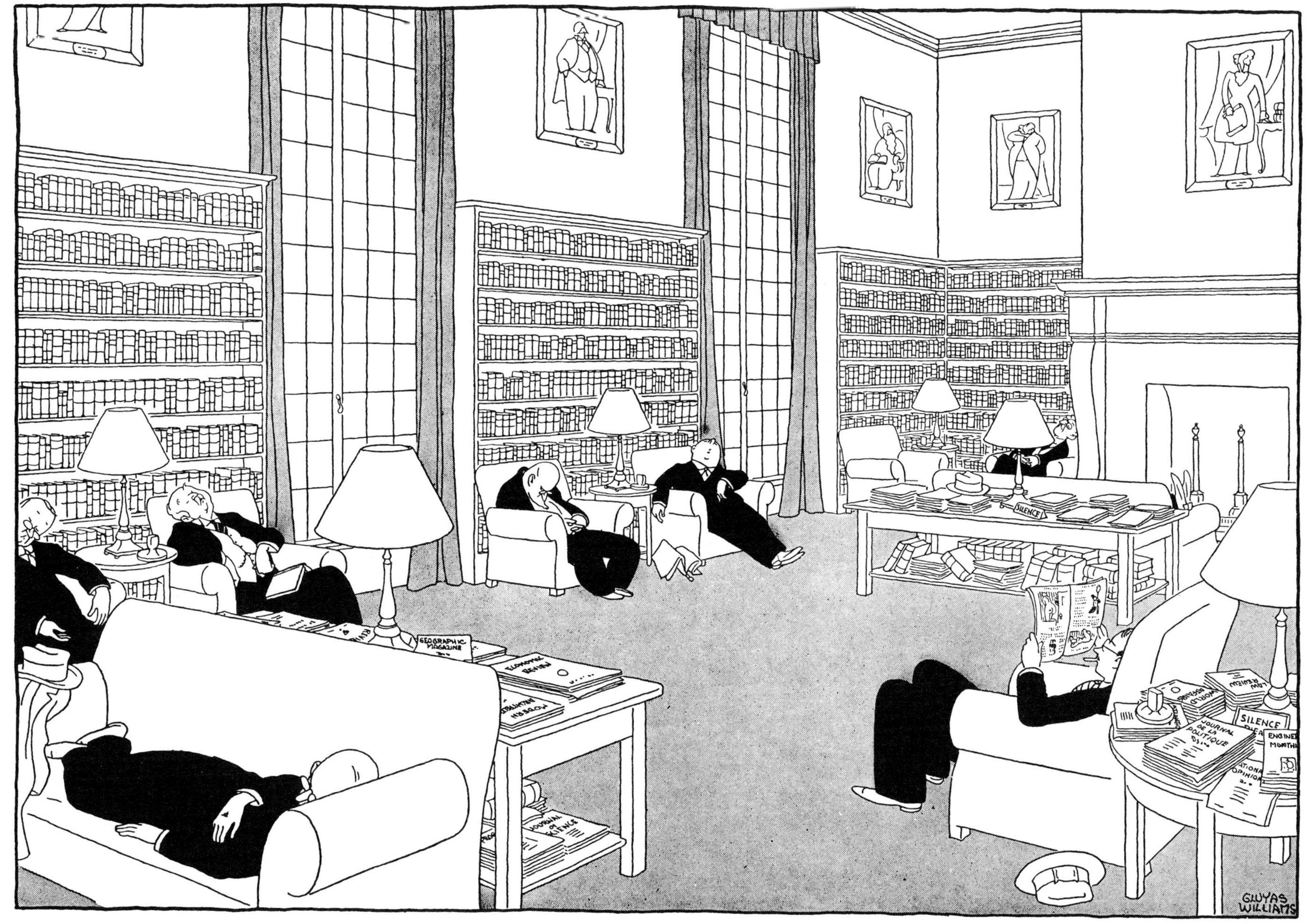

CLUB LIBRARY

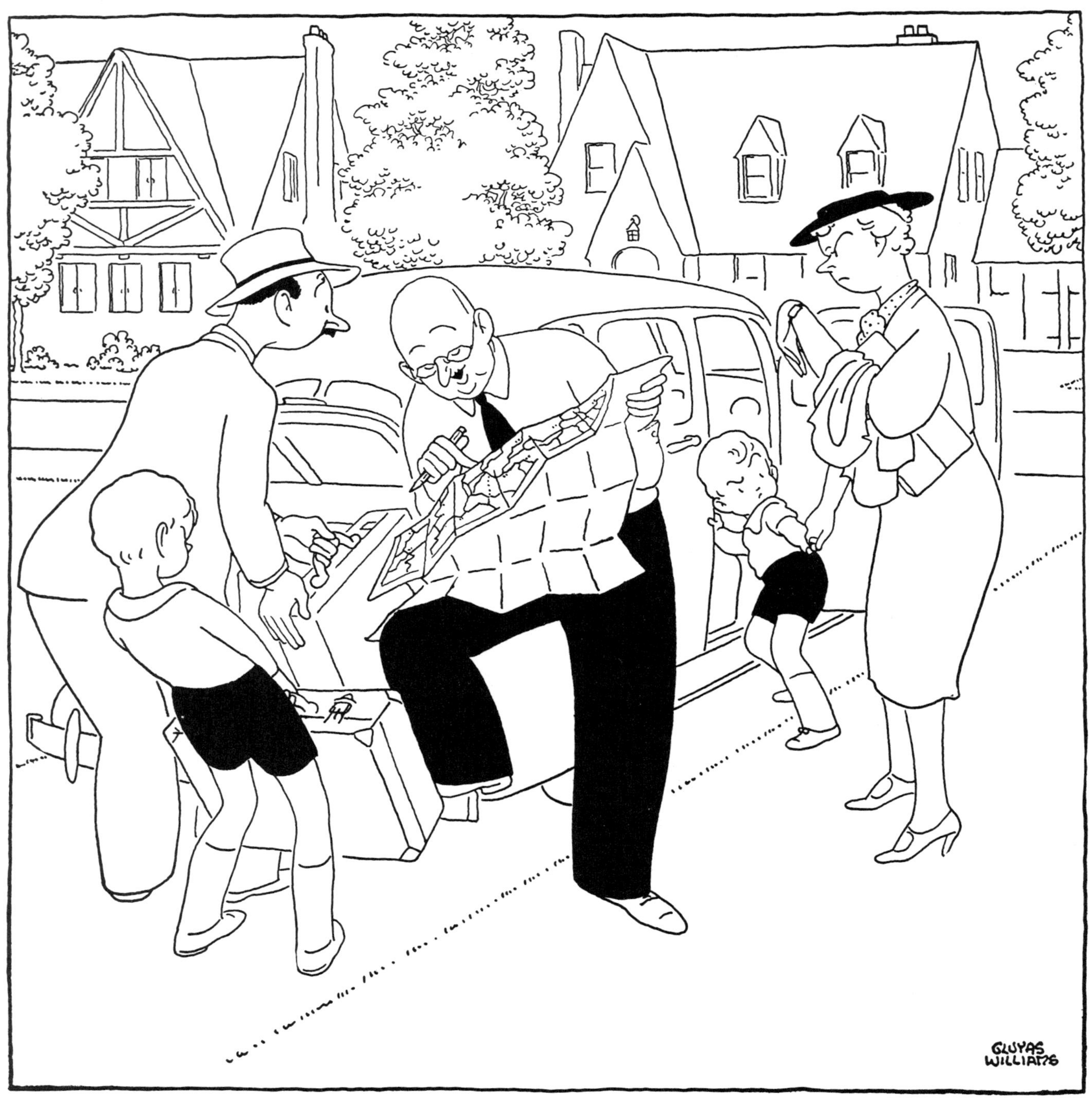

RACONTEURS

"When Eunice told me you were going to the mountains I hurried right over because we know that region like a book. Now don't make the mistake of going the regular way. Take 216 instead, until you come to a church at a four corners. Then take 183, which later becomes 197. Now here's what Eunice and I did last year. We followed 197 until . . ."

THE EIGHT–FIFTEEN

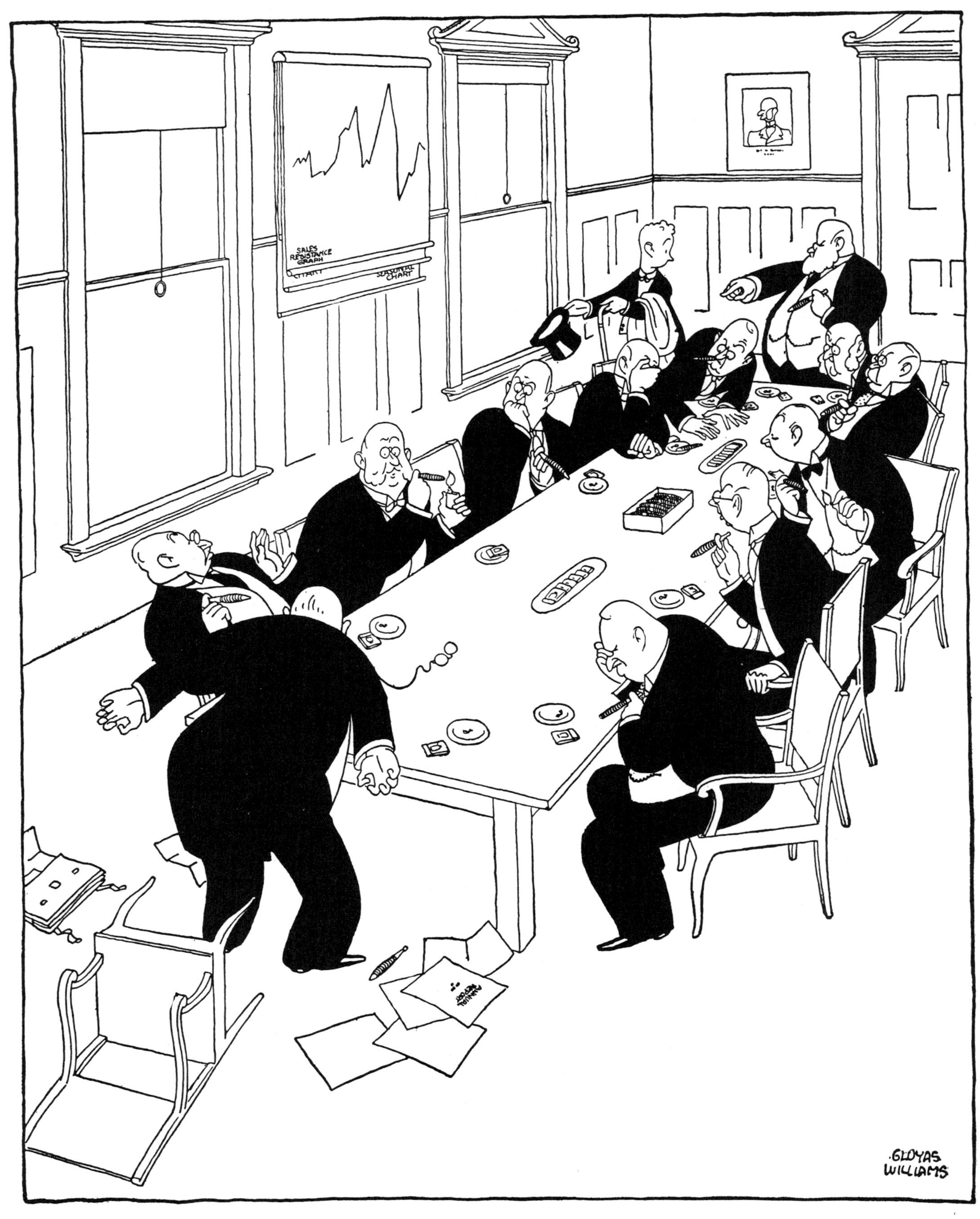

INDUSTRIAL CRISES

A Director of the Diamond Match Company Absent-mindedly Lights His Cigar with an Automatic Lighter

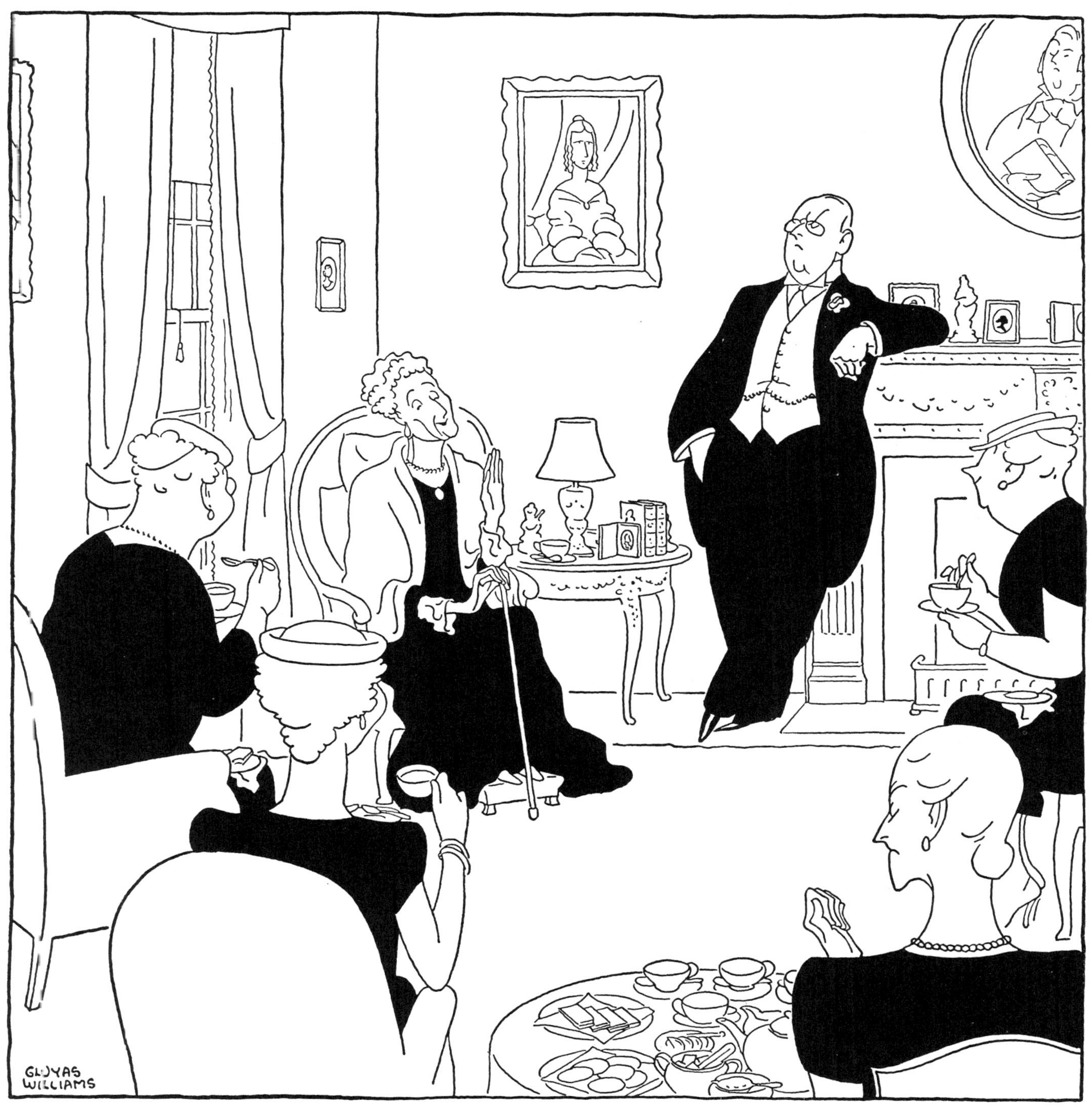

RACONTEURS

"James and Cornelia don't like me to run on about the family, but, goodness me, I can't see any reason for being proud of an ancestor just because he was governor—that was James' great-grandfather, over the mantelpiece there—when you know he was a pompous old windbag who probably cheated the poor. My mother told me of one time when our great-aunt Harriet—who, by the way, was no better than she should be—came to visit and . . ."

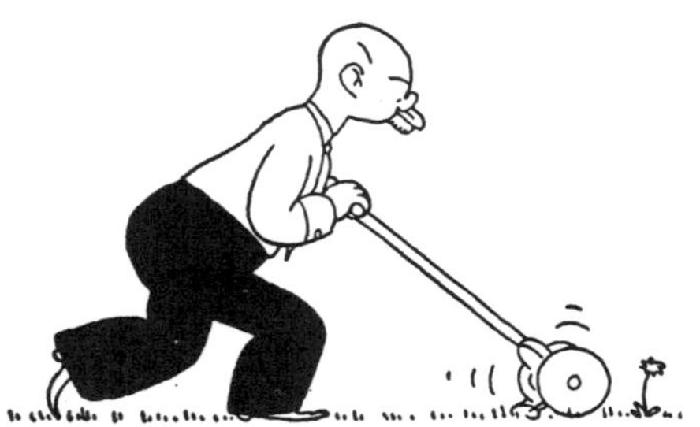
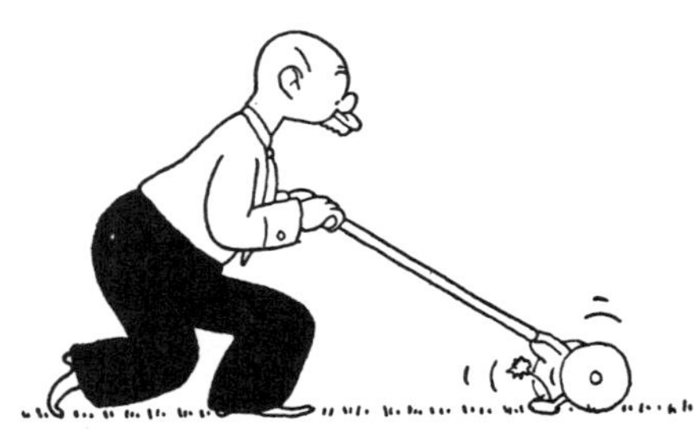
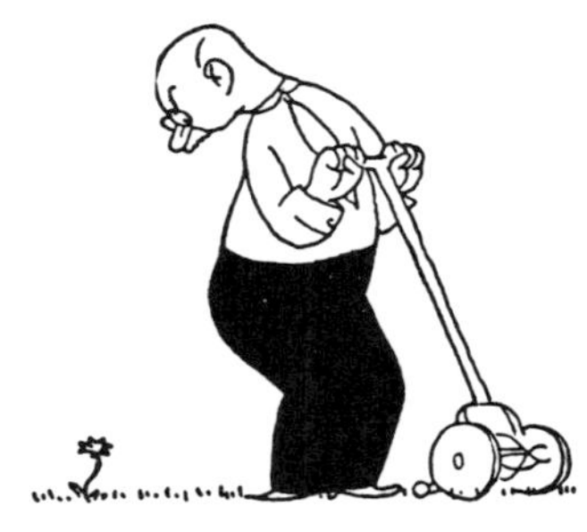
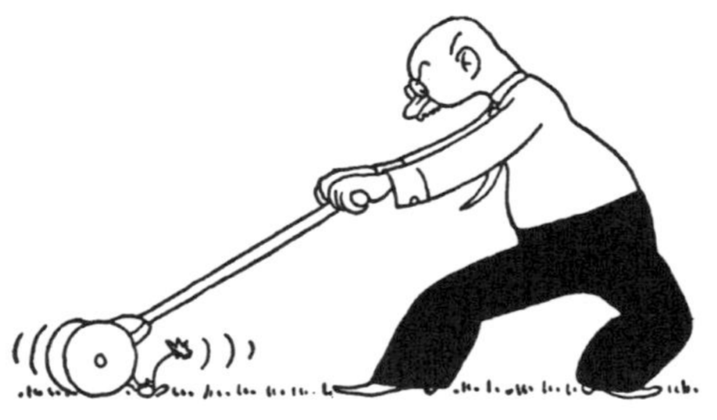
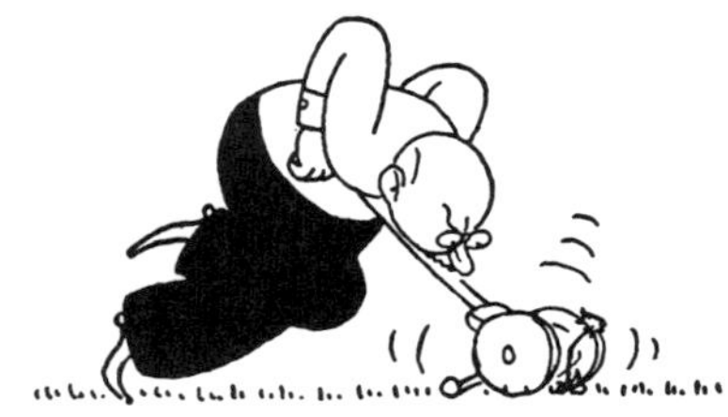
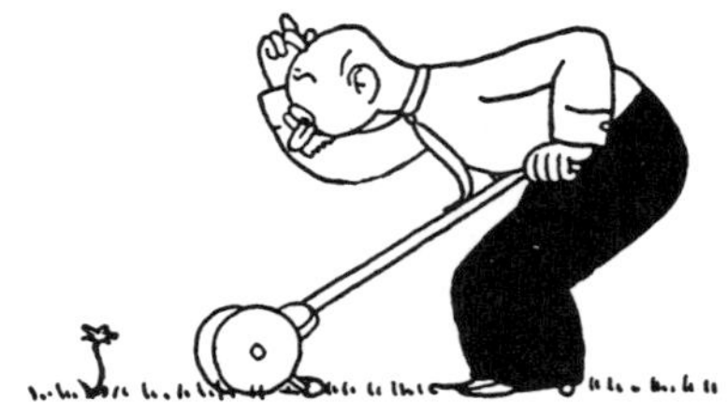
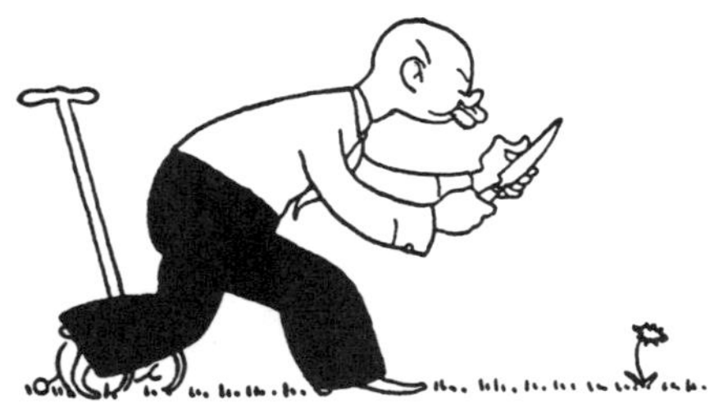
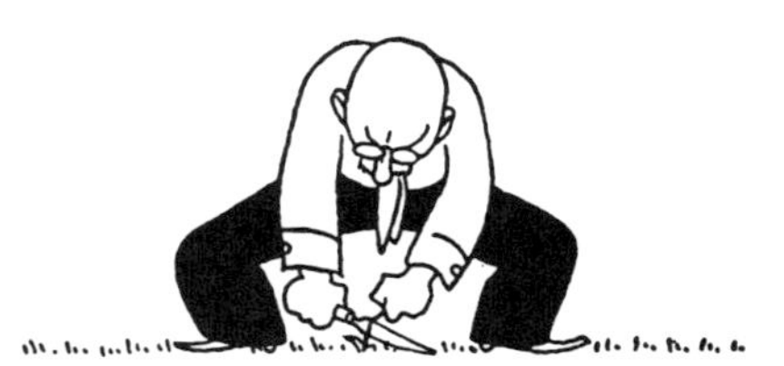
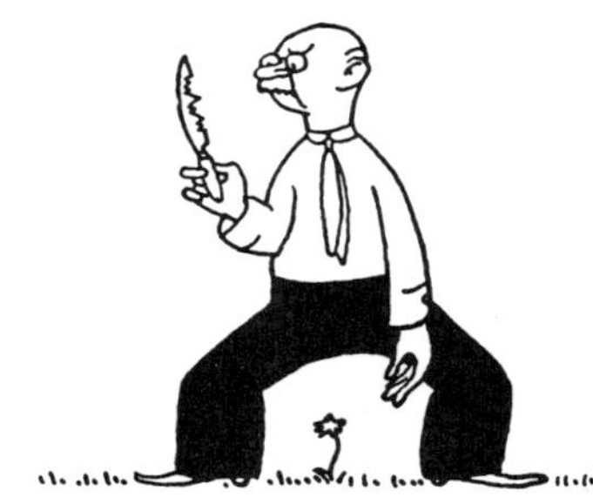
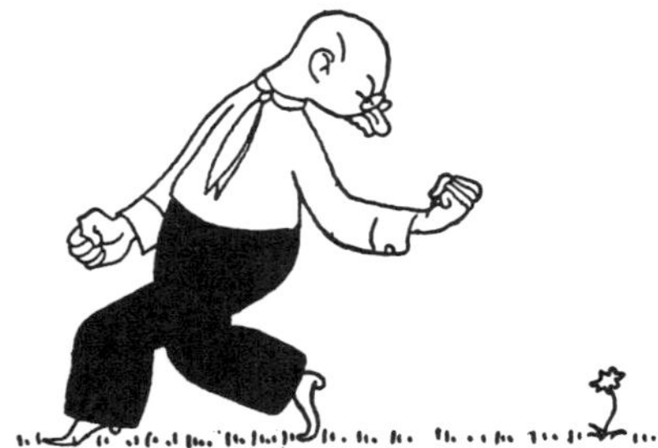
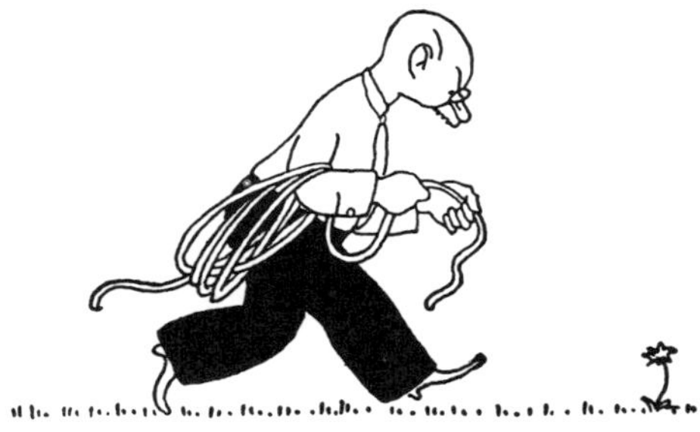

THE DANDELION (I)

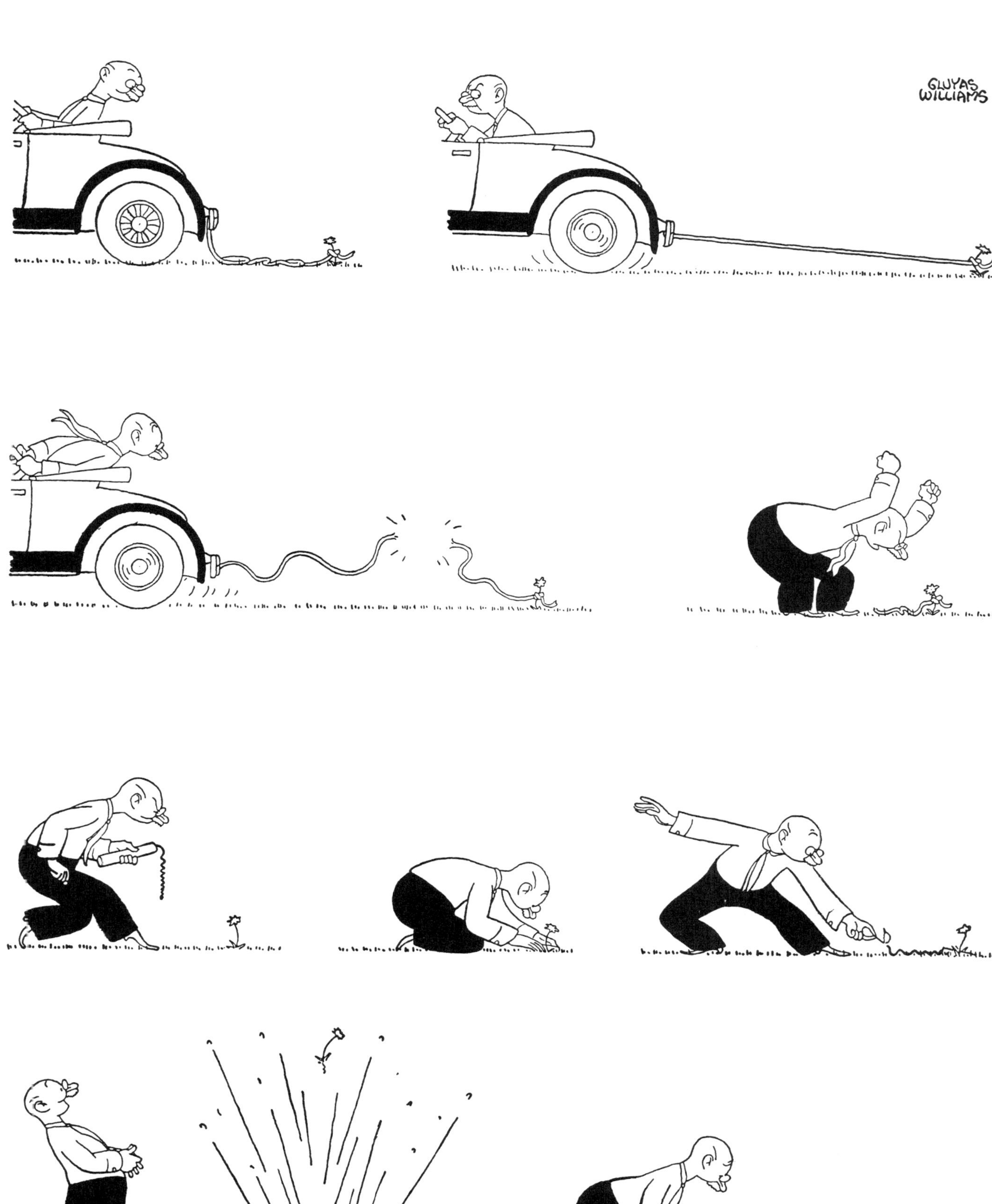

THE DANDELION (II)

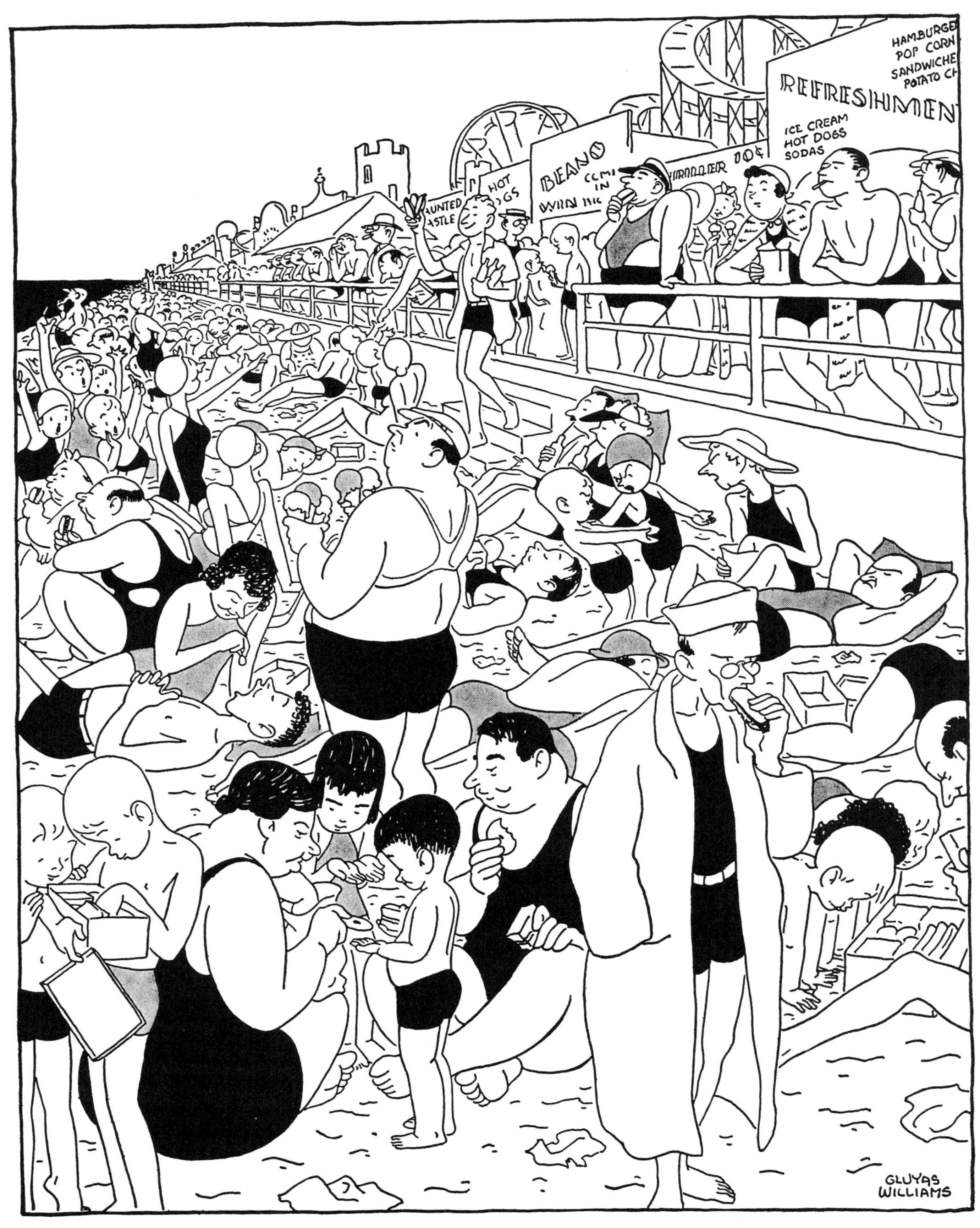

THE INNER MAN

Luncheon on the Beach

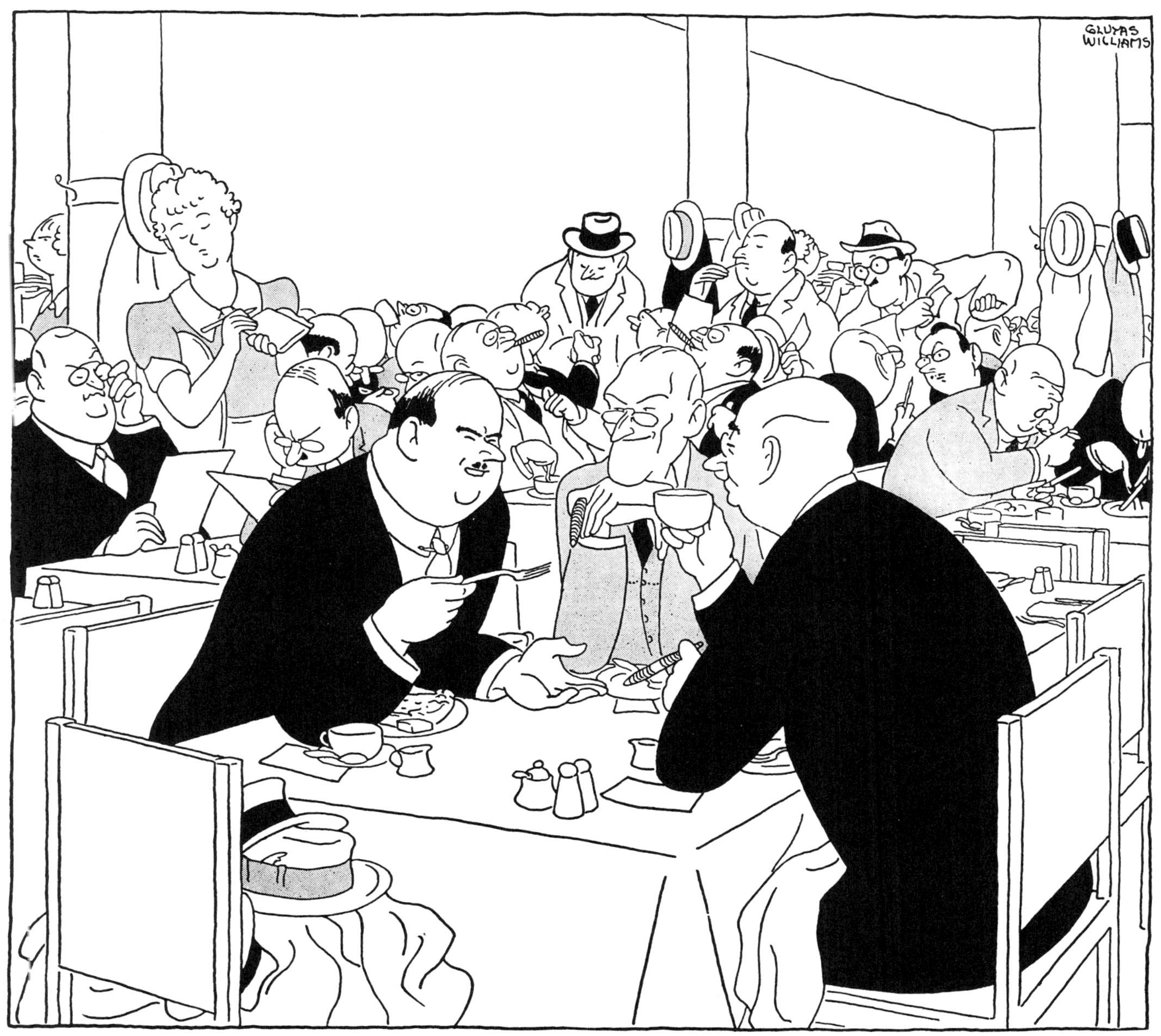

RACONTEURS

"So when he came squawking, I said to him, 'Business is business, Fred, and if you didn't know that clause was in the contract, is it my fault? Sure, I know it's hard on you, Fred,' I said, 'but if we let sentiment get into business, where'd we be? Anyway,' I told him, 'maybe you'd be better off working for someone else than trying to be in business of your own.' You see, with that little clause in there—all perfectly legal, you understand—I was sitting pretty, because . . ."

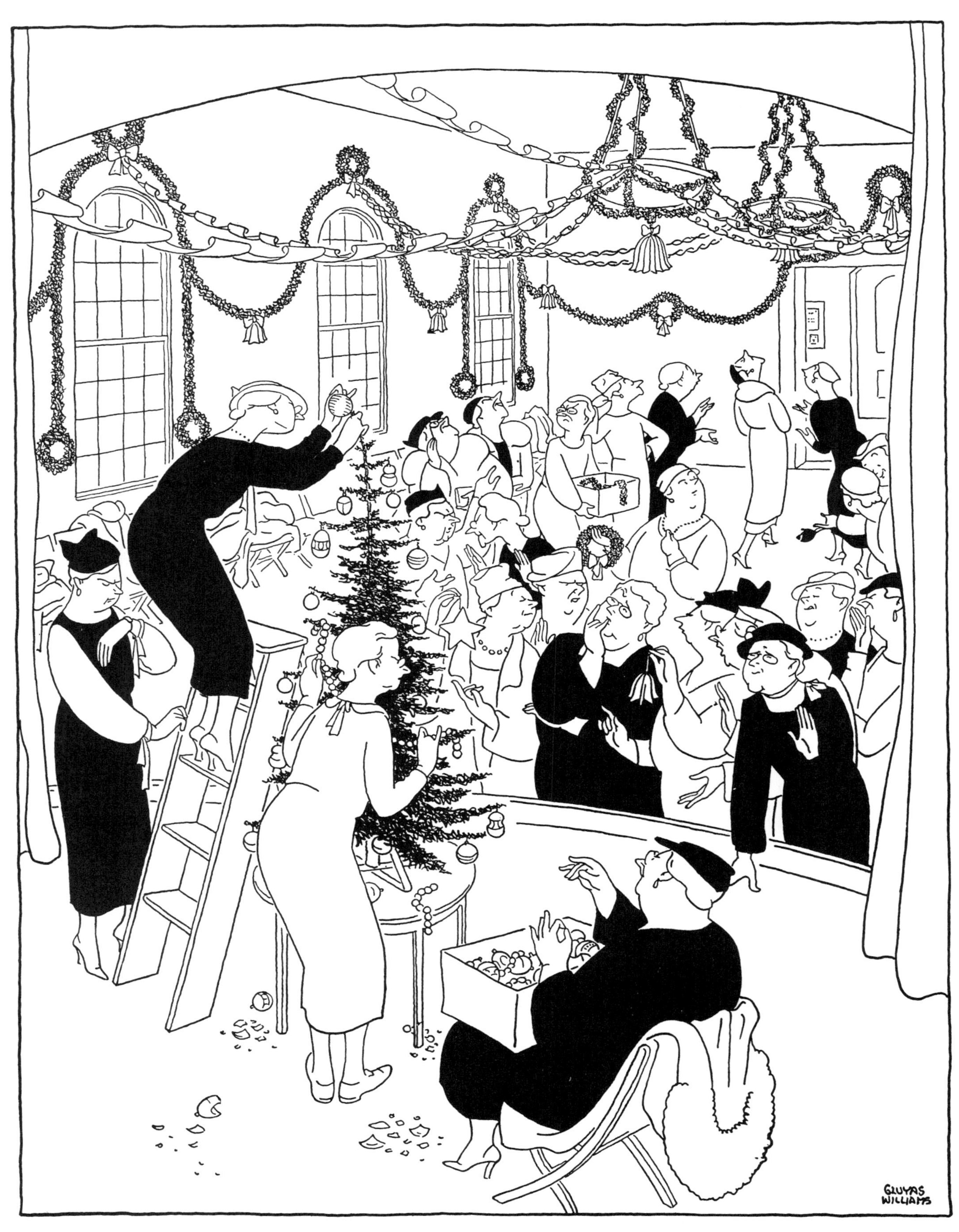

CLUB LIFE IN AMERICA

The Community Service Ladies Bring Peace and Good Will to the Town Hall

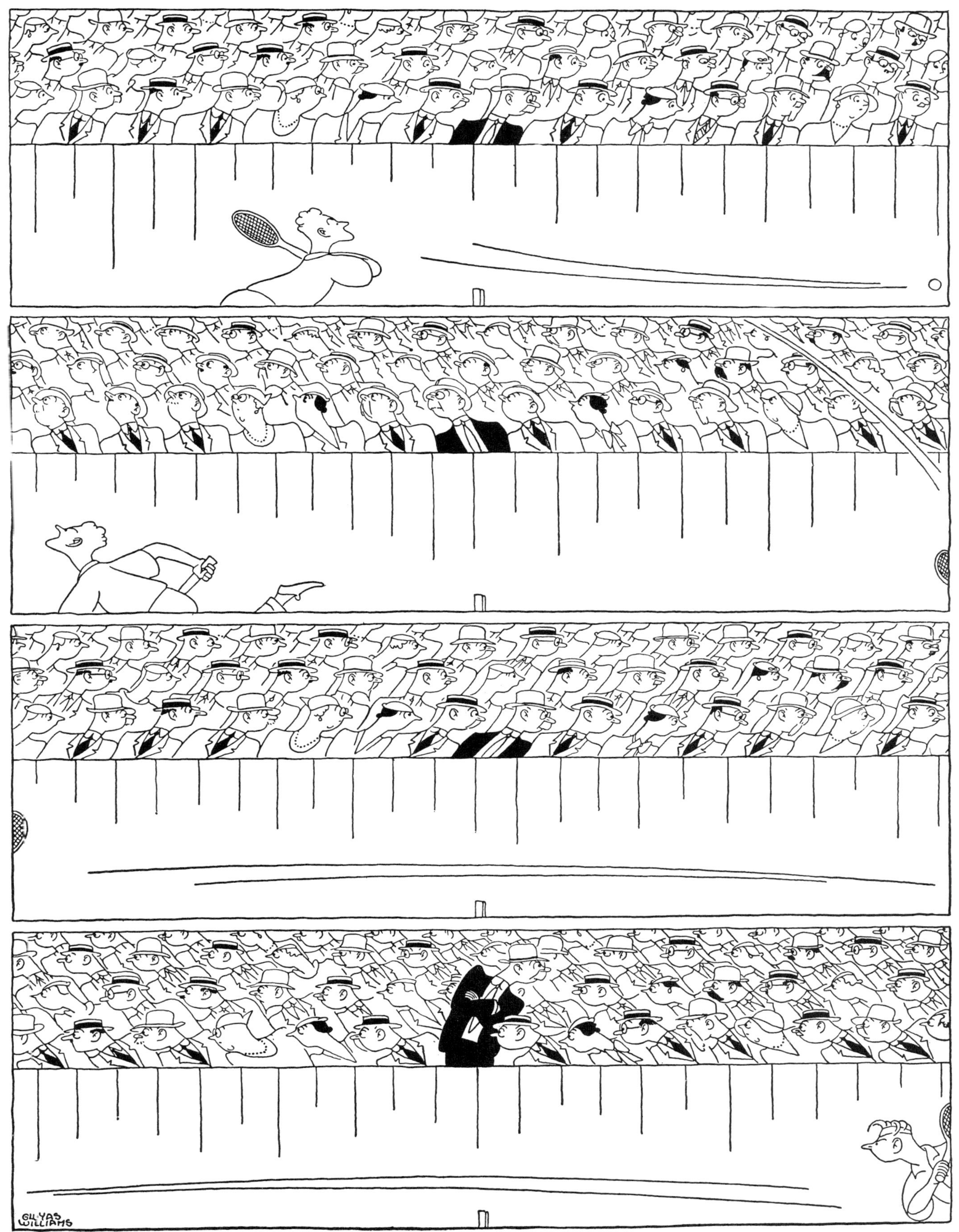

THE REBEL

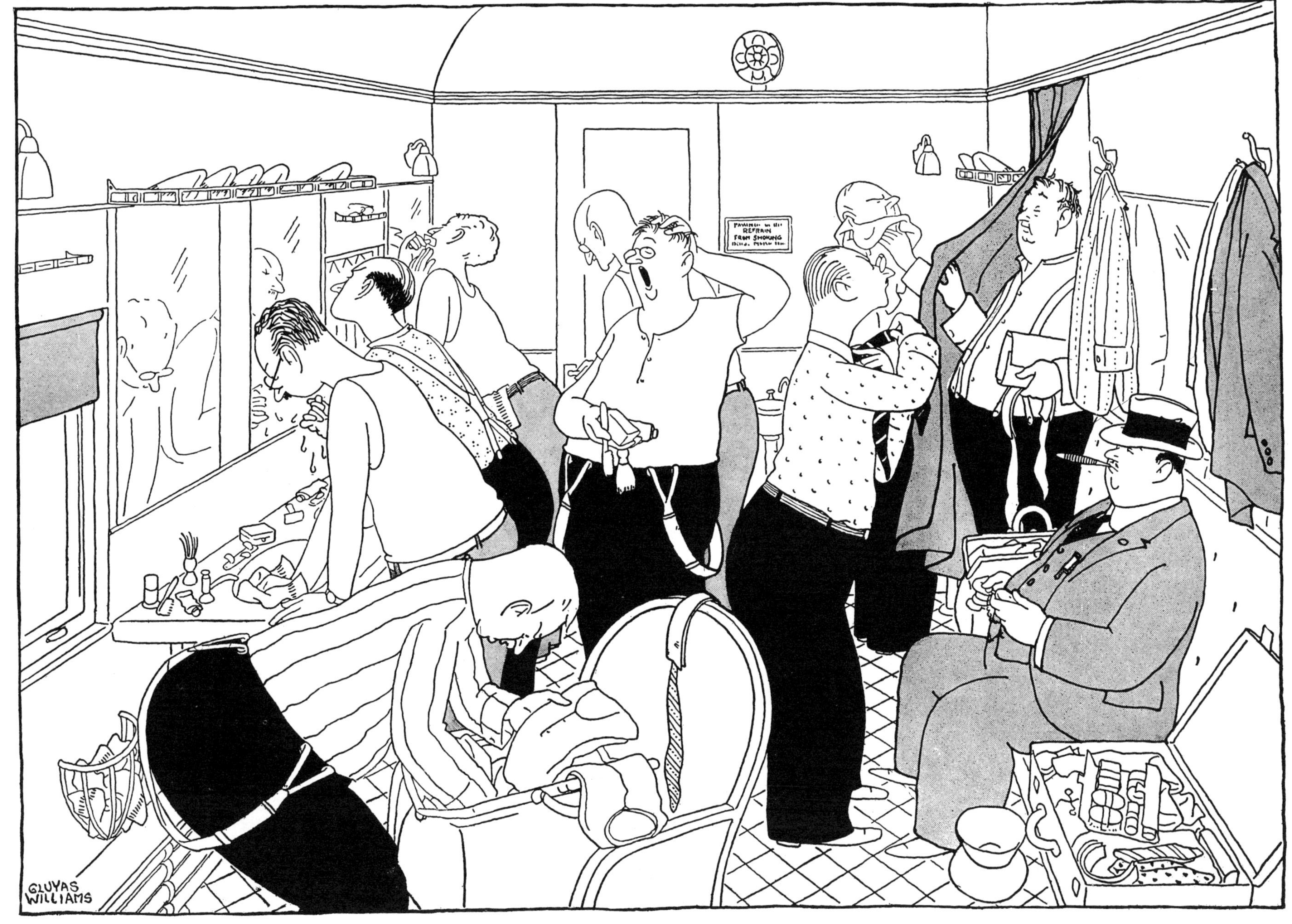

MORNING ON THE MIDNIGHT

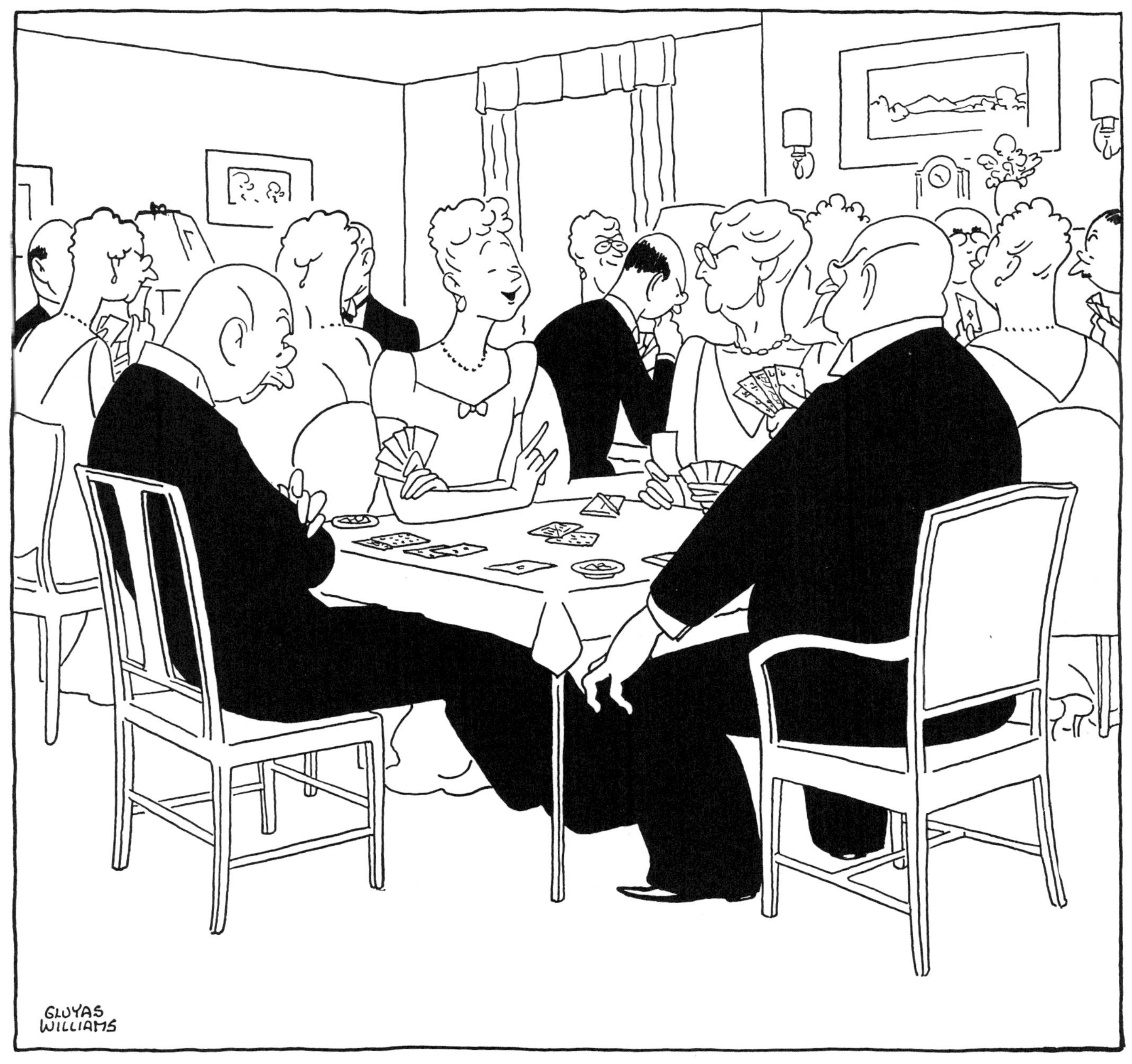

RACONTEURS

"It's really the very best picture I've seen in years—all about international spies and jewel thieves and things—and you mustn't miss it. I do wish I could remember its name, but it all begins on a transatlantic liner, and the duchess—that was Edna May Oliver, and perfectly screaming, although she turns out later to be a swindler—misses her necklace. Well, after that . . ."

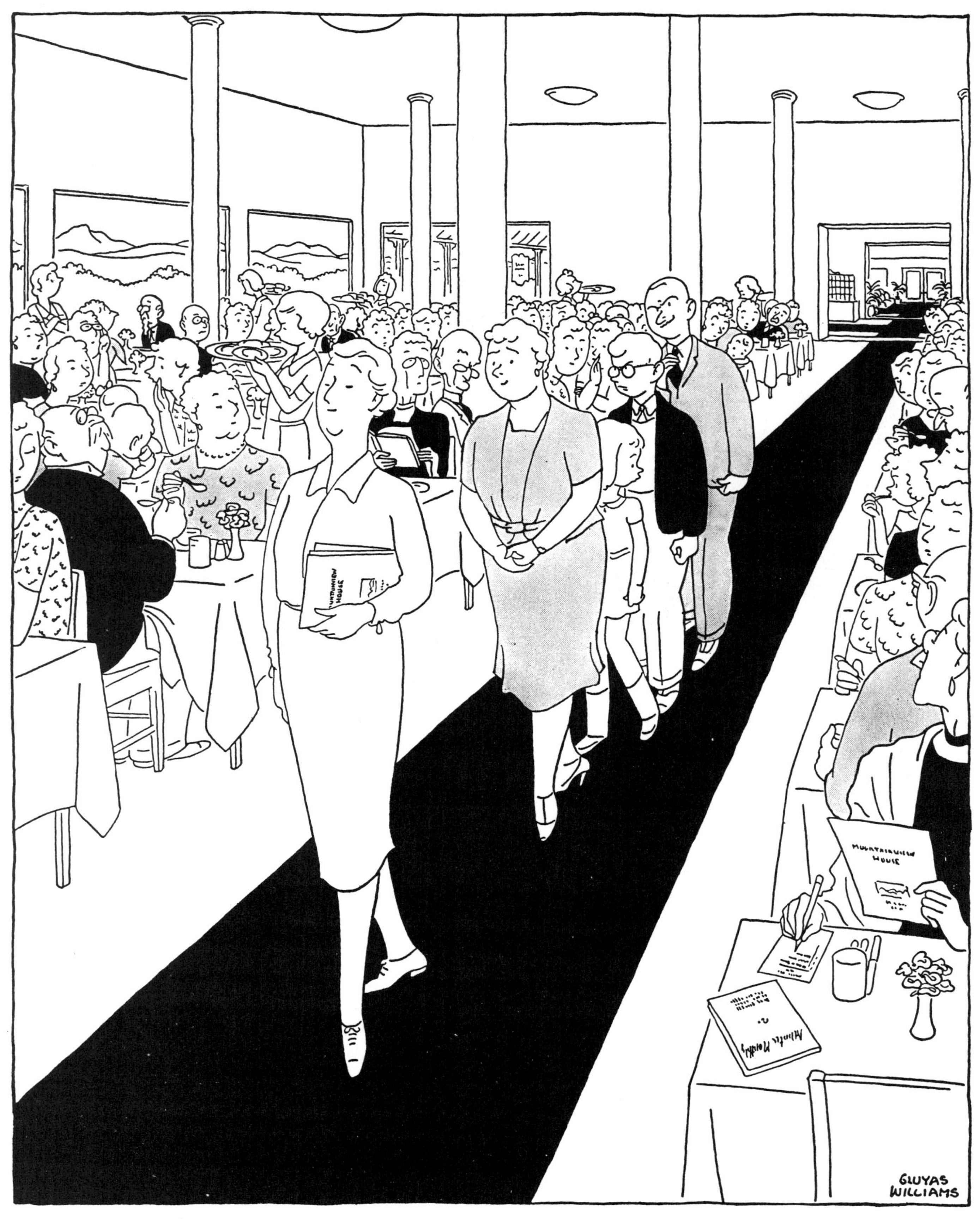

THE INNER MAN

New Arrivals

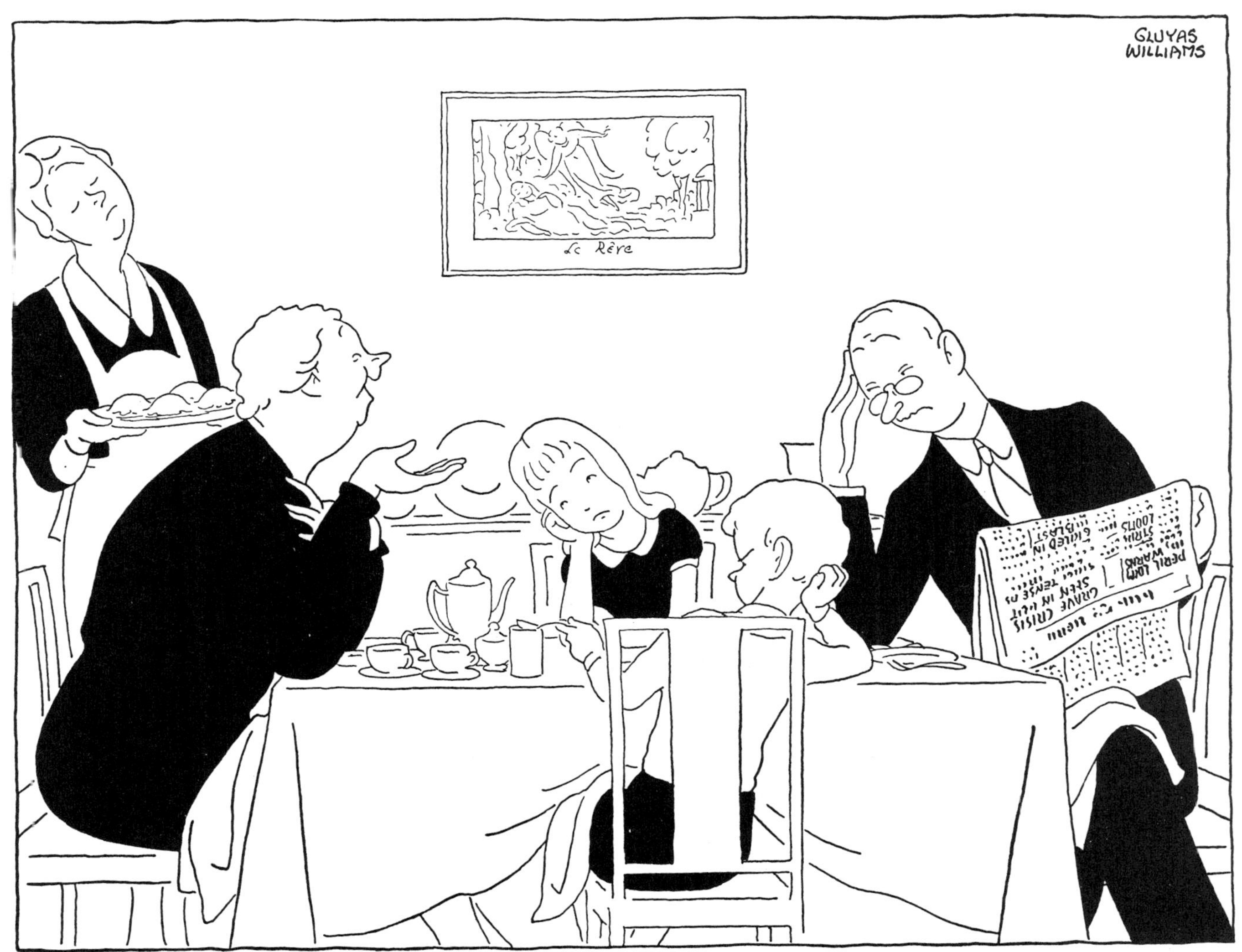

RACONTEURS

"I had the funniest dream last night. We were house guests of the Windsors, only I seemed to be the Duchess and yet me too—you know how it is in dreams. Well, we were having dinner, only now it seemed to be on a ship, and the captain kept biting people. Really, it was screaming. Well, it kept getting more and more mixed up, because I remember Wendell Willkie got into it somehow, and then . . ."

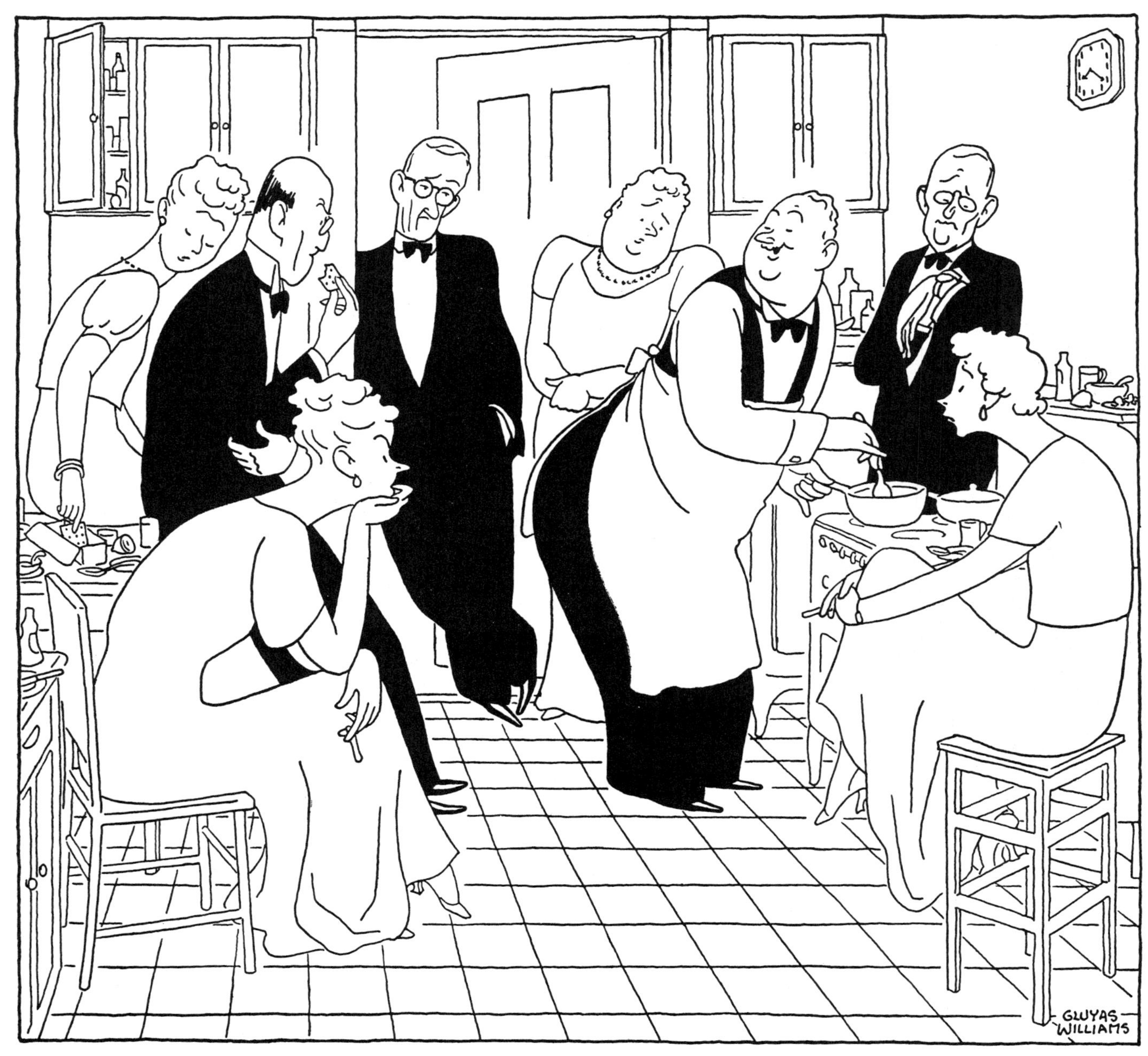

RACONTEURS

"I let my Jap have the evening off because I wanted you folks to see how bouillabaisse should really be prepared. The steward on that Mediterranean cruise told me how to make it, though I do think I've added a few touches of my own. I hope you're not getting too hungry waiting, but I didn't want to begin until you all got here, and we can't hurry with bouillabaisse. Now then, first we cook carrots, onions, garlic and leeks in olive oil until golden brown. Then we . . ."

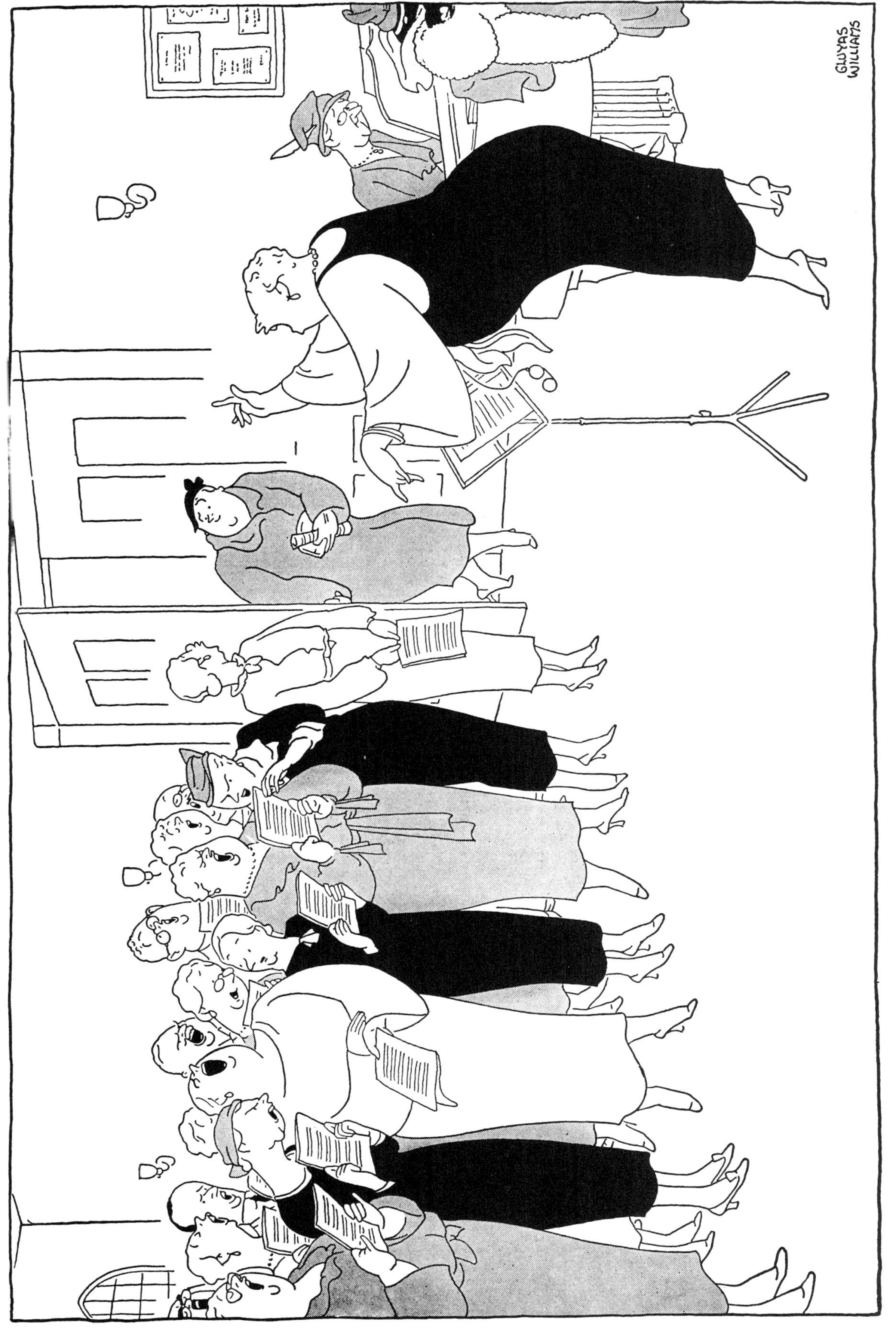

CLUB LIFE IN AMERICA

The Choral Society Polishes Up for the Spring Recital

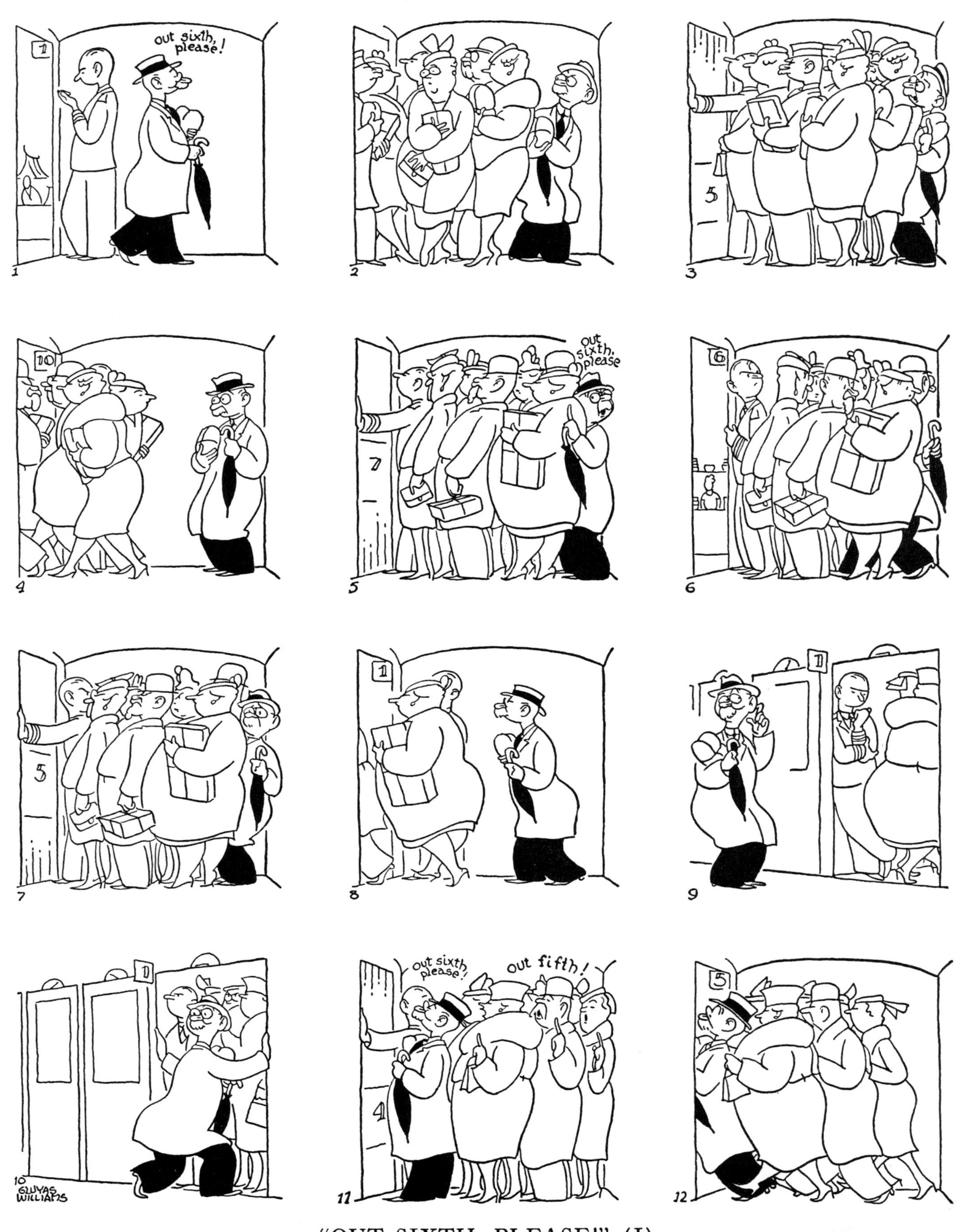

"OUT SIXTH, PLEASE!" (I)

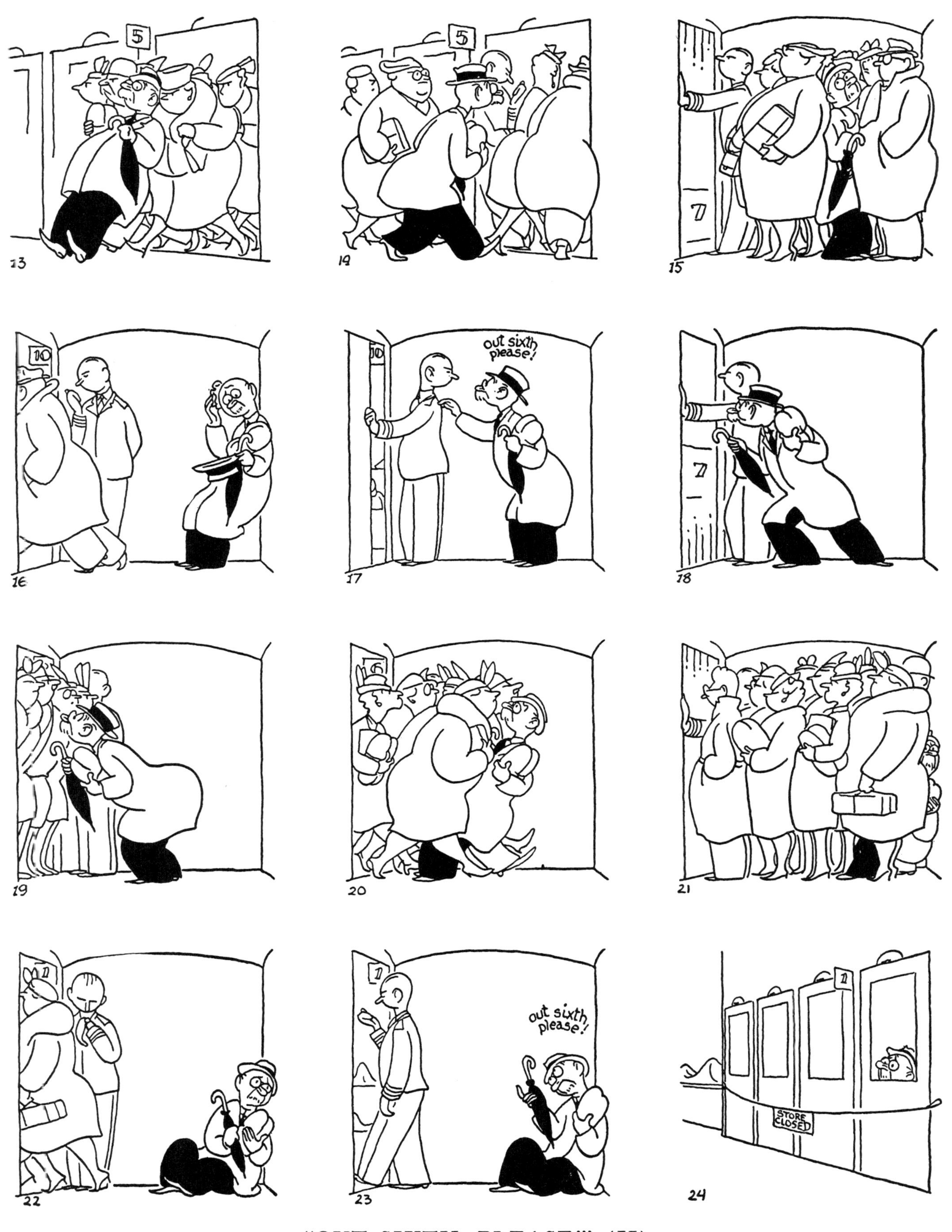

"OUT SIXTH, PLEASE!" (II)

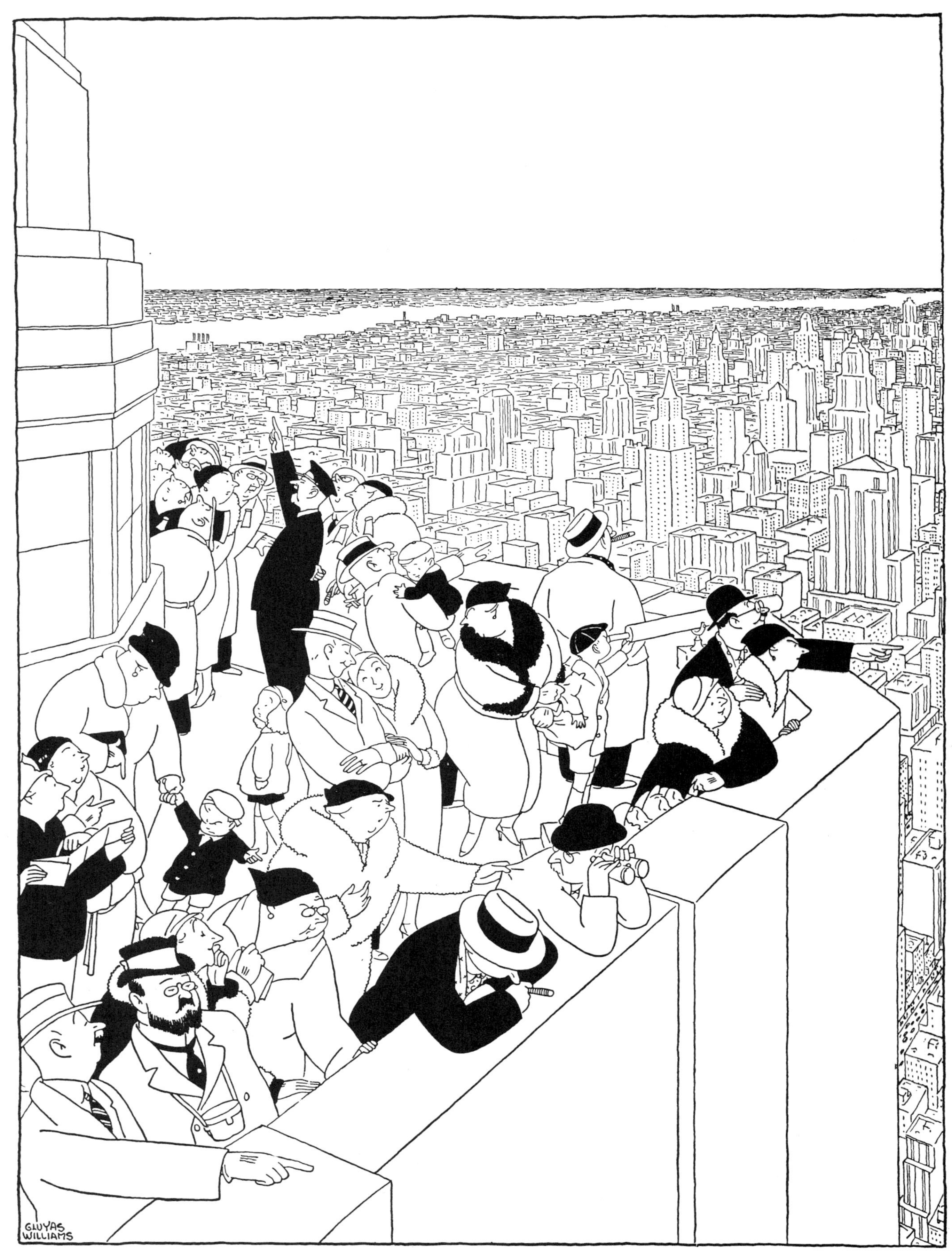

OBSERVATION PLATFORM

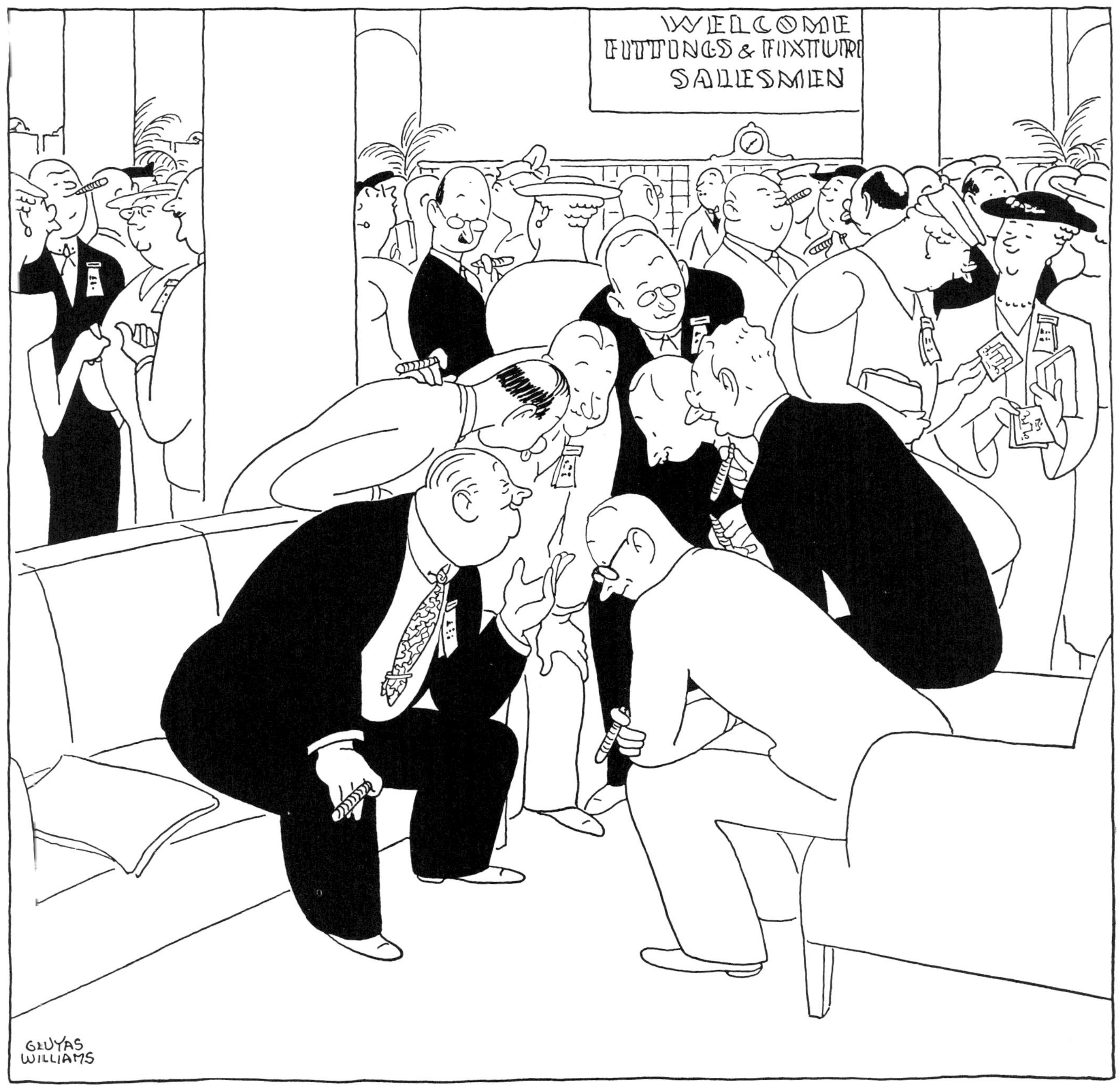

RACONTEURS

"Have you boys heard this one? I don't go in much for this kind of story myself, you understand, but a fellow told me this one out in Detroit last week and it struck me as really funny. Come a little closer. Well, it seems a couple of newlyweds drove up to this country hotel and the old geezer at the hotel winked at the fellow and said . . ."

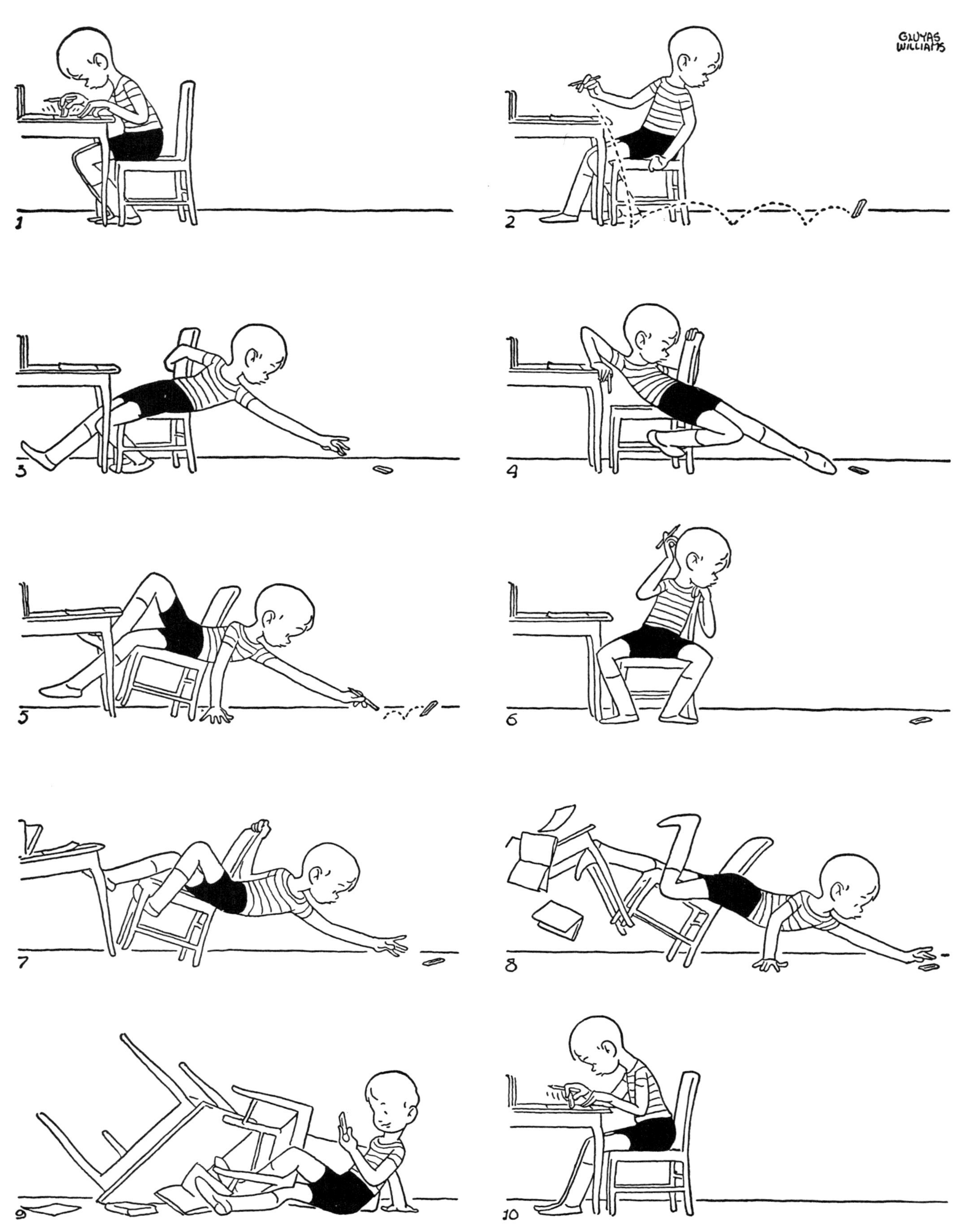

PICKUP

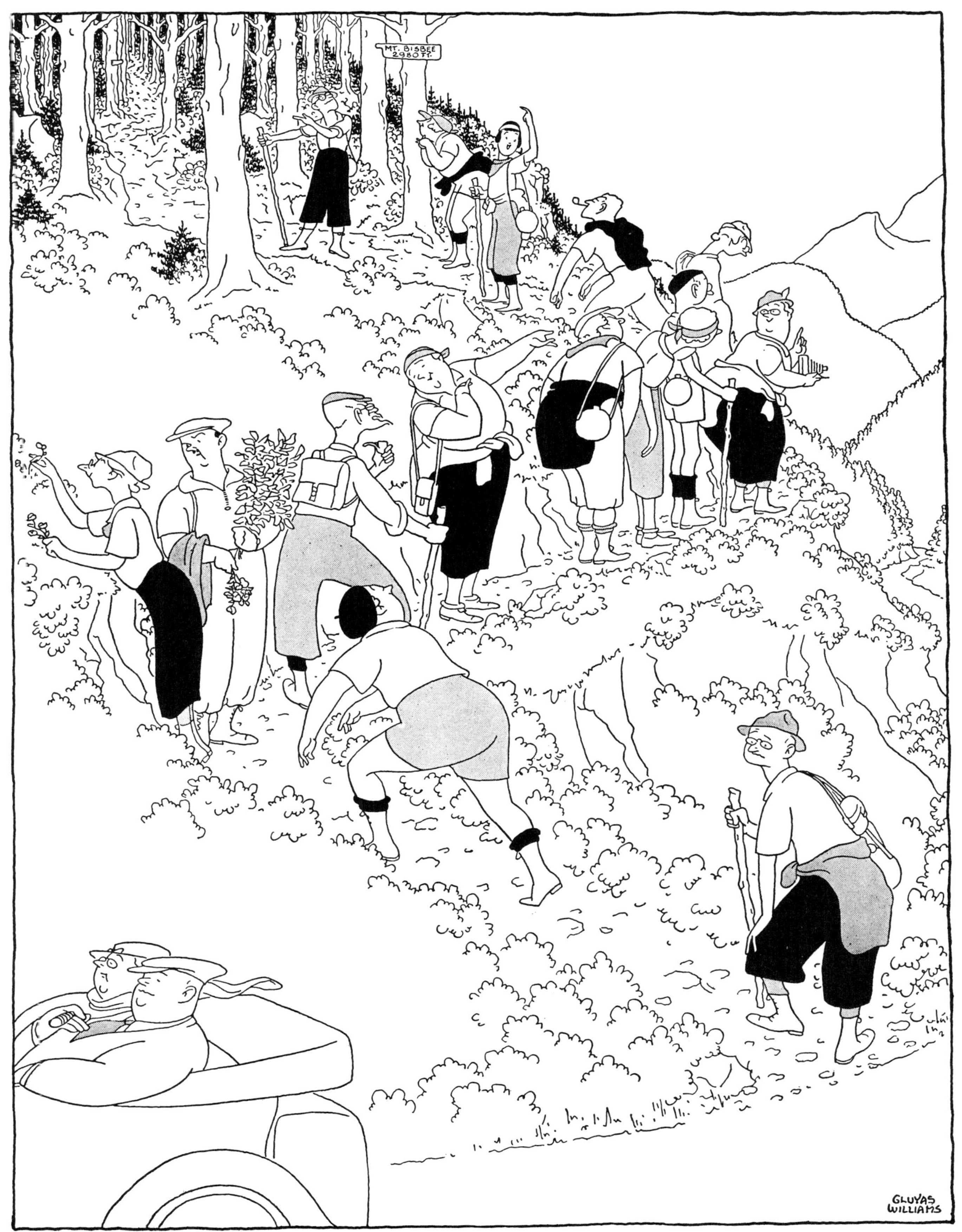

CLUB LIFE IN AMERICA

The Alpine Wanderbirds Hit the High Spots

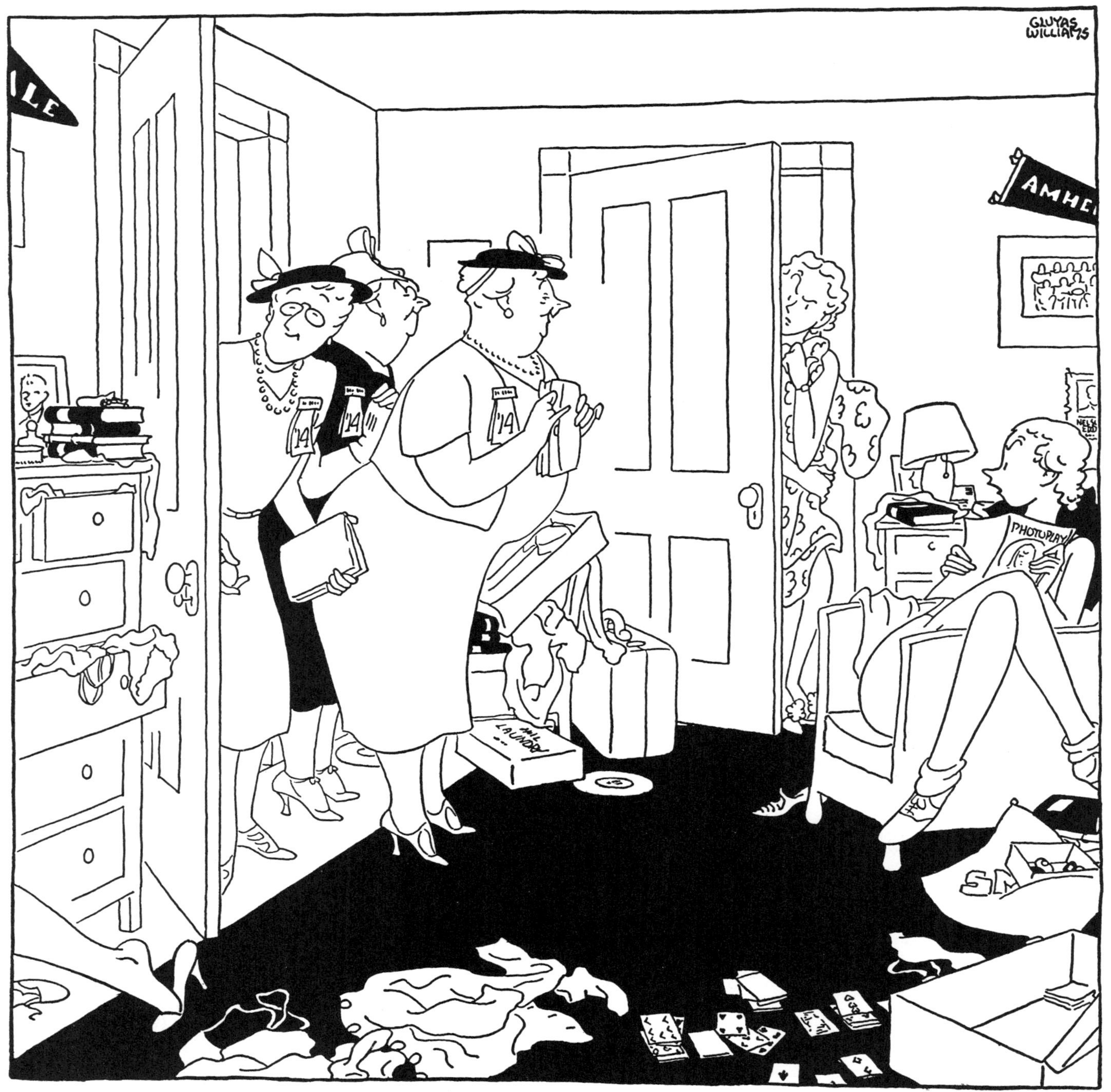

RACONTEURS

"I hope you won't mind if the girls and I peek in. It's almost like a pilgrimage to us to come back to the rooms where we spent those four golden years. Oh, it does bring it all back so! The Three Musketeers, we called ourselves, and the high jinks that these four walls could tell of! Oh, girls, do you remember the time that . . ."

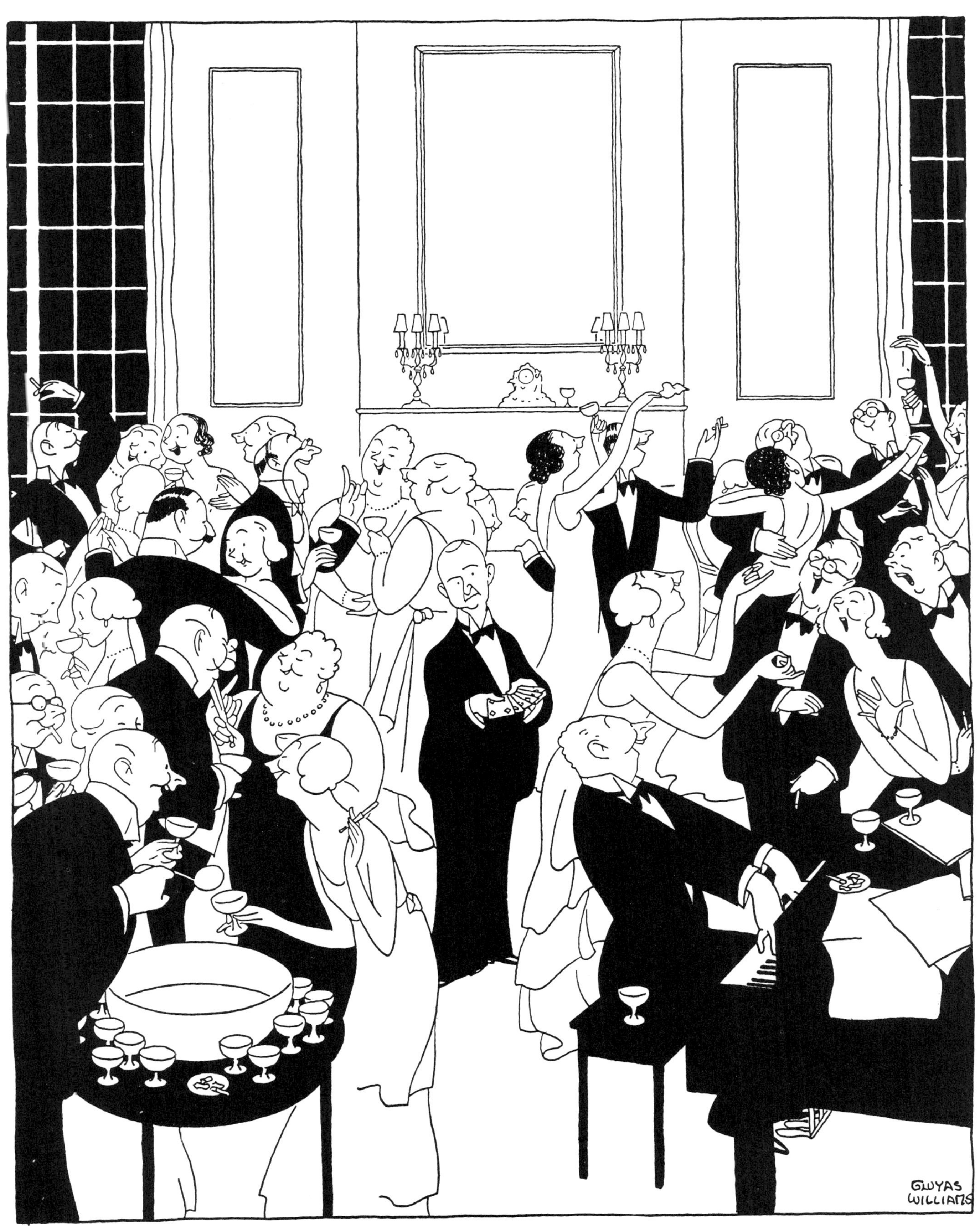

"WILL SOMEBODY PICK A CARD, ANY CARD?"

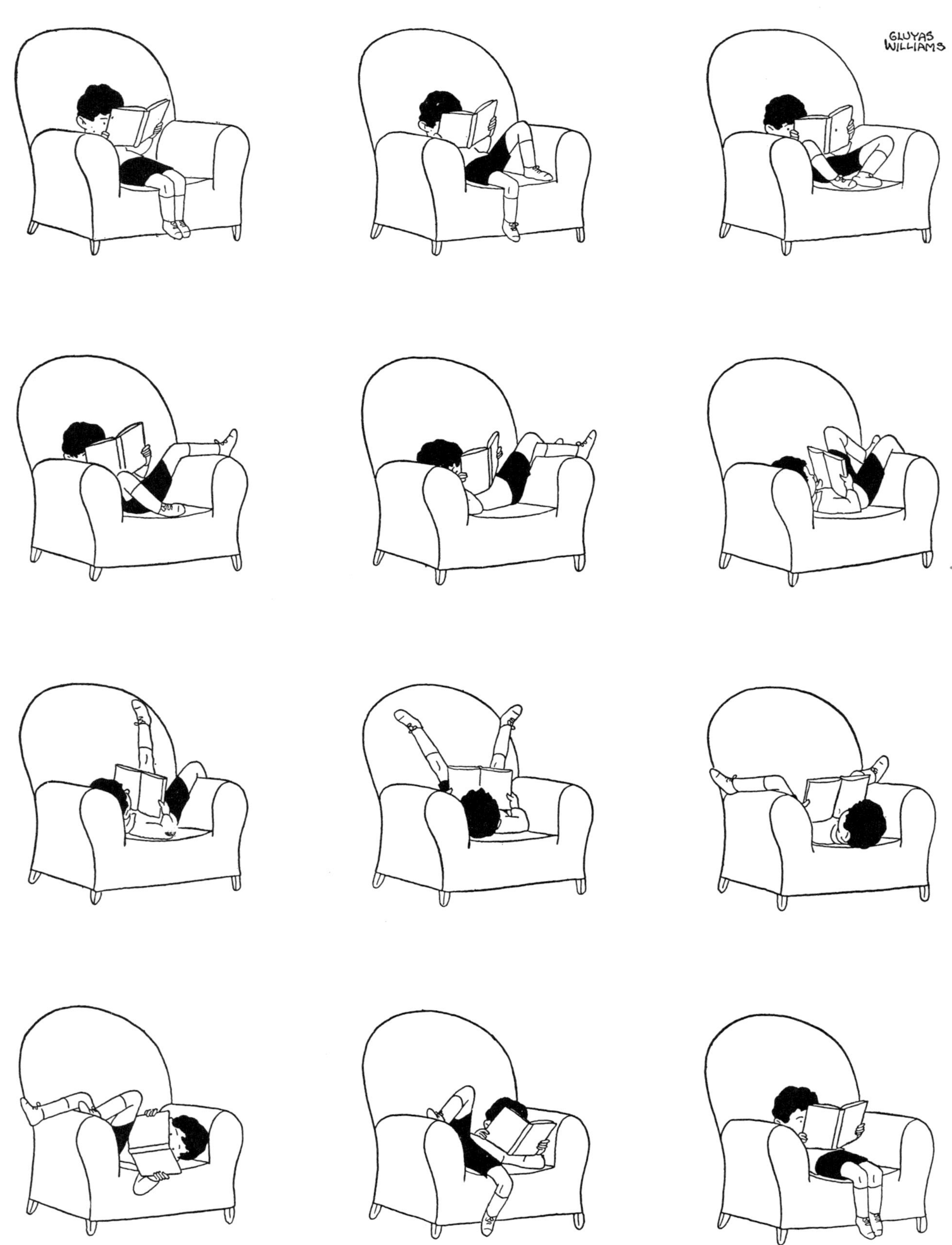

PORTRAIT OF A SMALL BOY READING

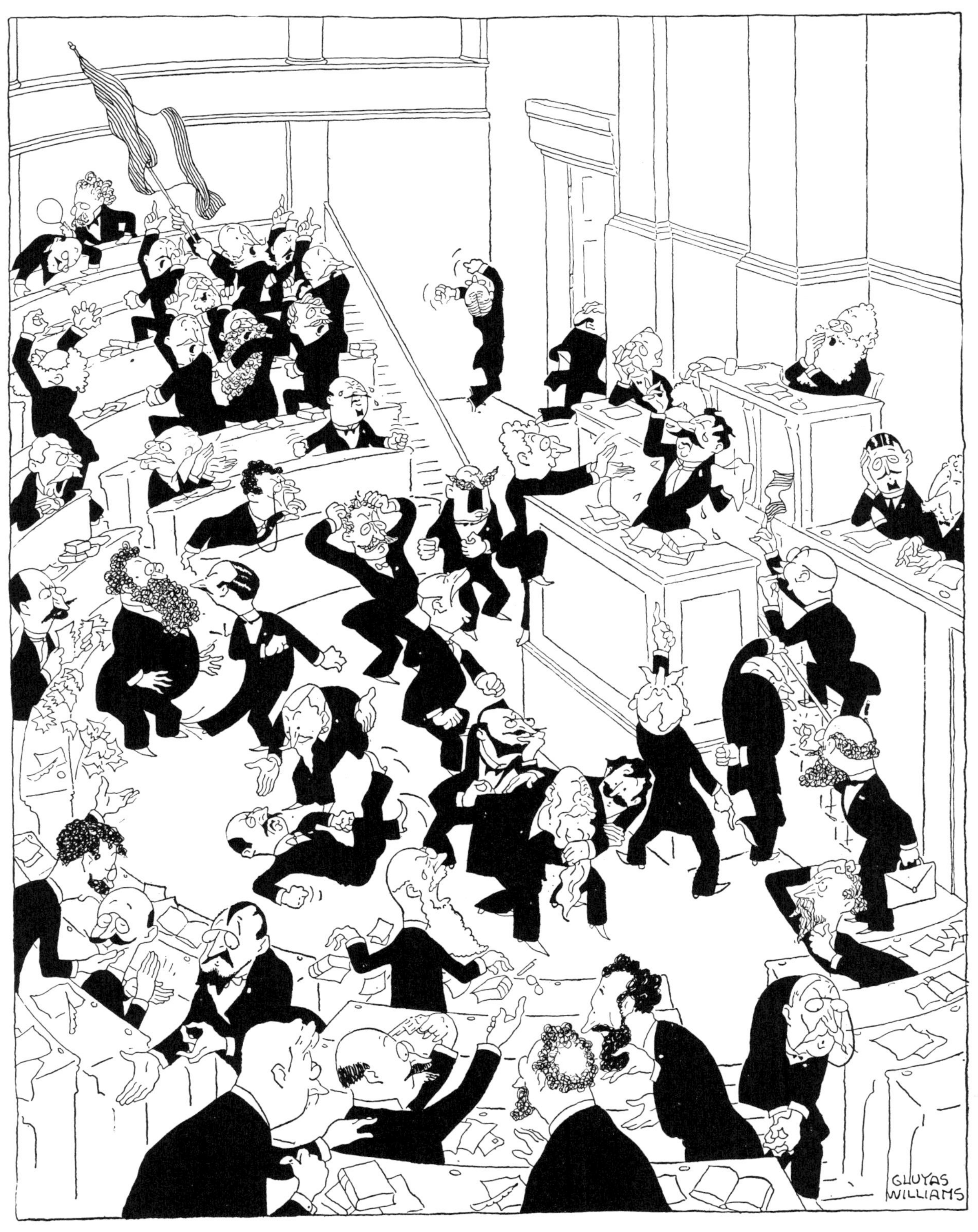

THE FRENCH CHAMBER OF DEPUTIES DEBATES A MINOR APPROPRIATION BILL

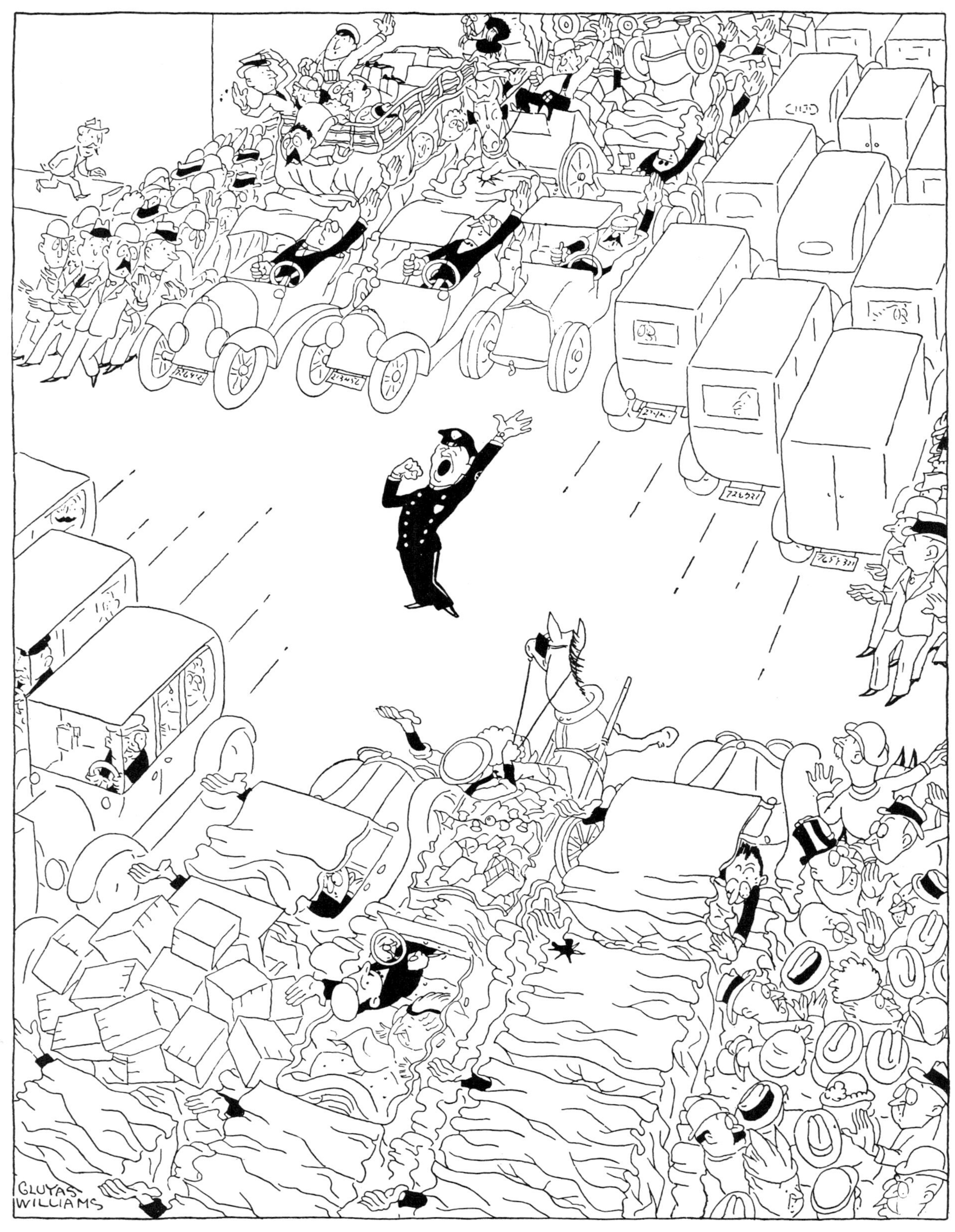

WHEN THE TRAFFIC COP YAWNED

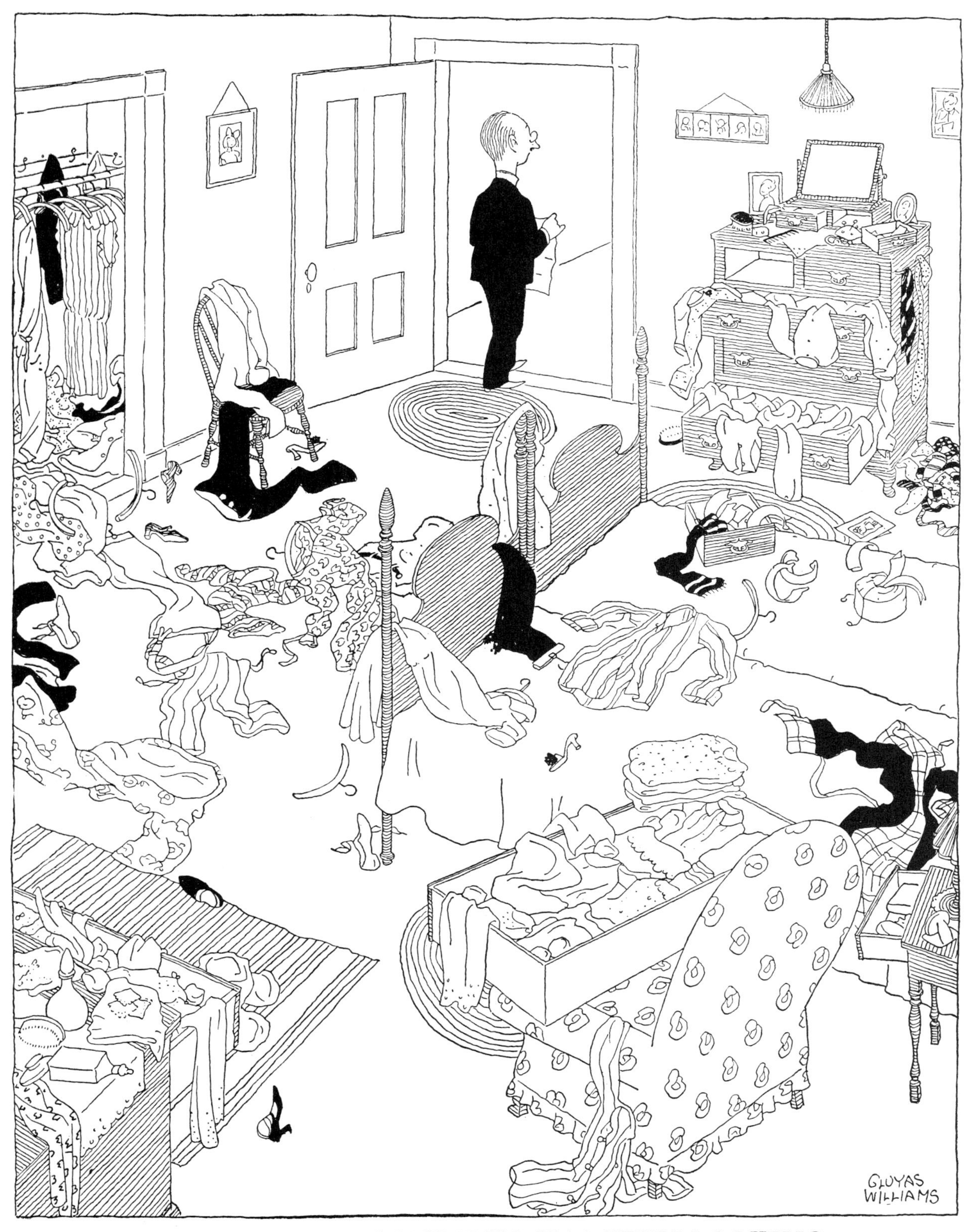

PORTRAIT OF A MAN WHO HAS BEEN LOOKING FOR A HANDKERCHIEF

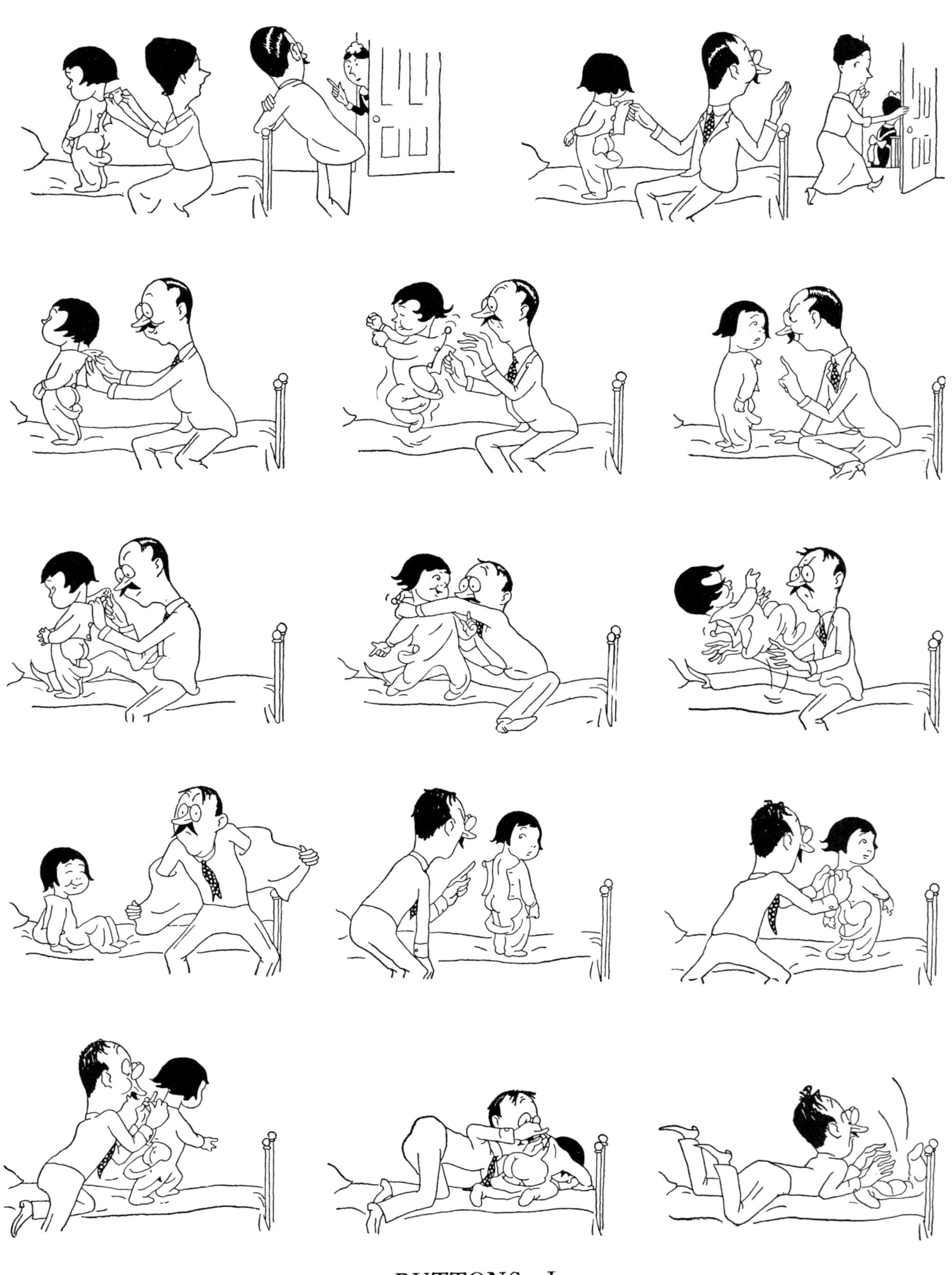

BUTTONS—I

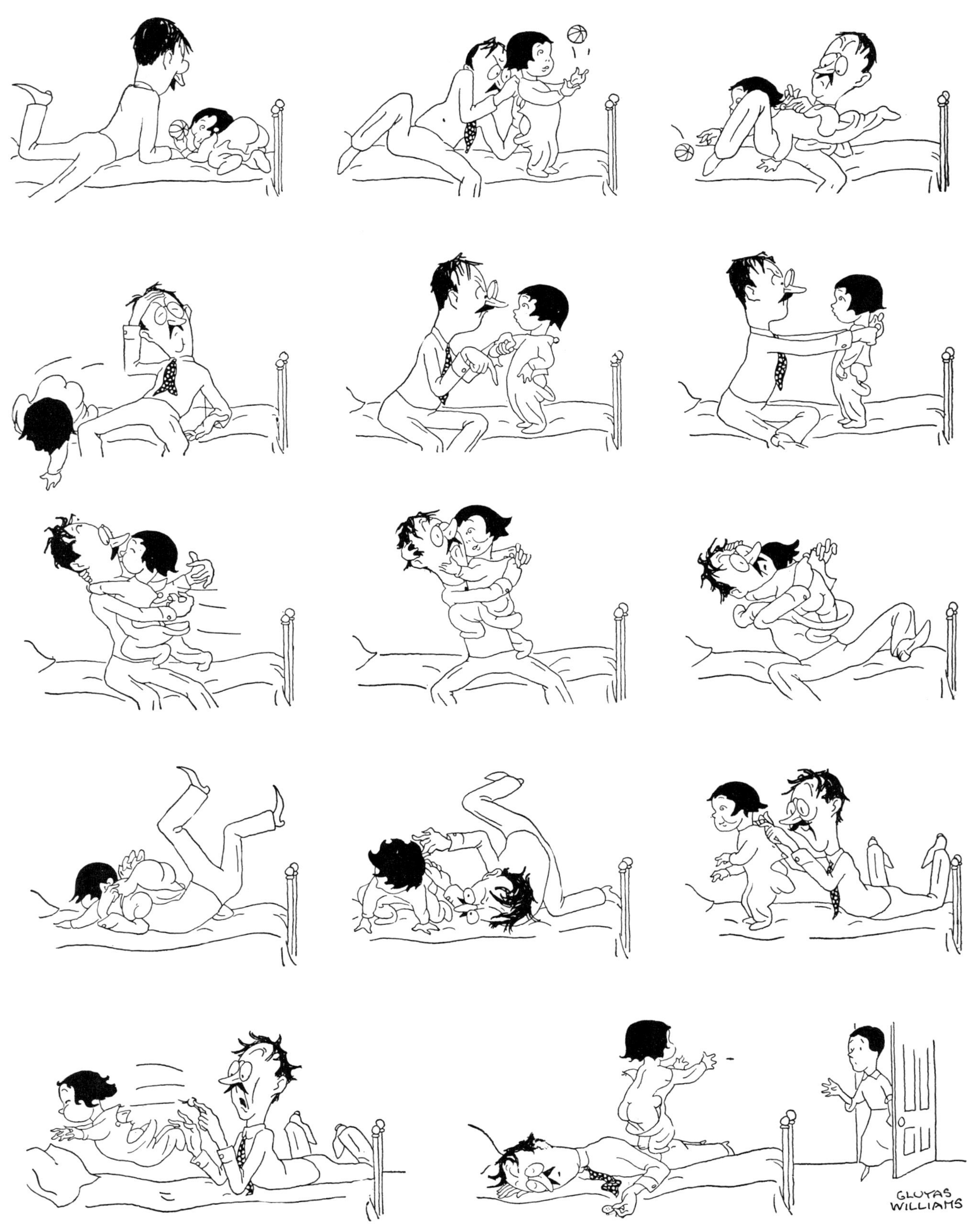

BUTTONS—II

"GOD REST YE MERRY GENTLEMEN"

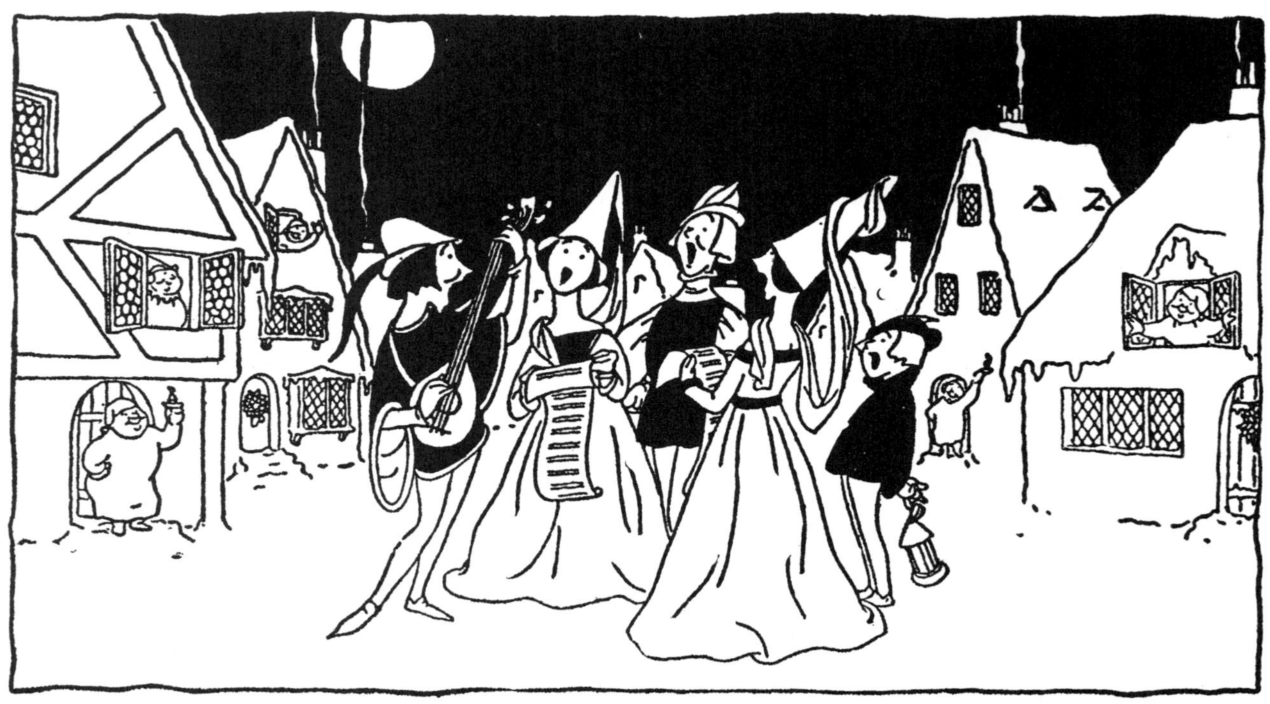

The custom of singing carols always looks so attractive on the Christmas cards but—

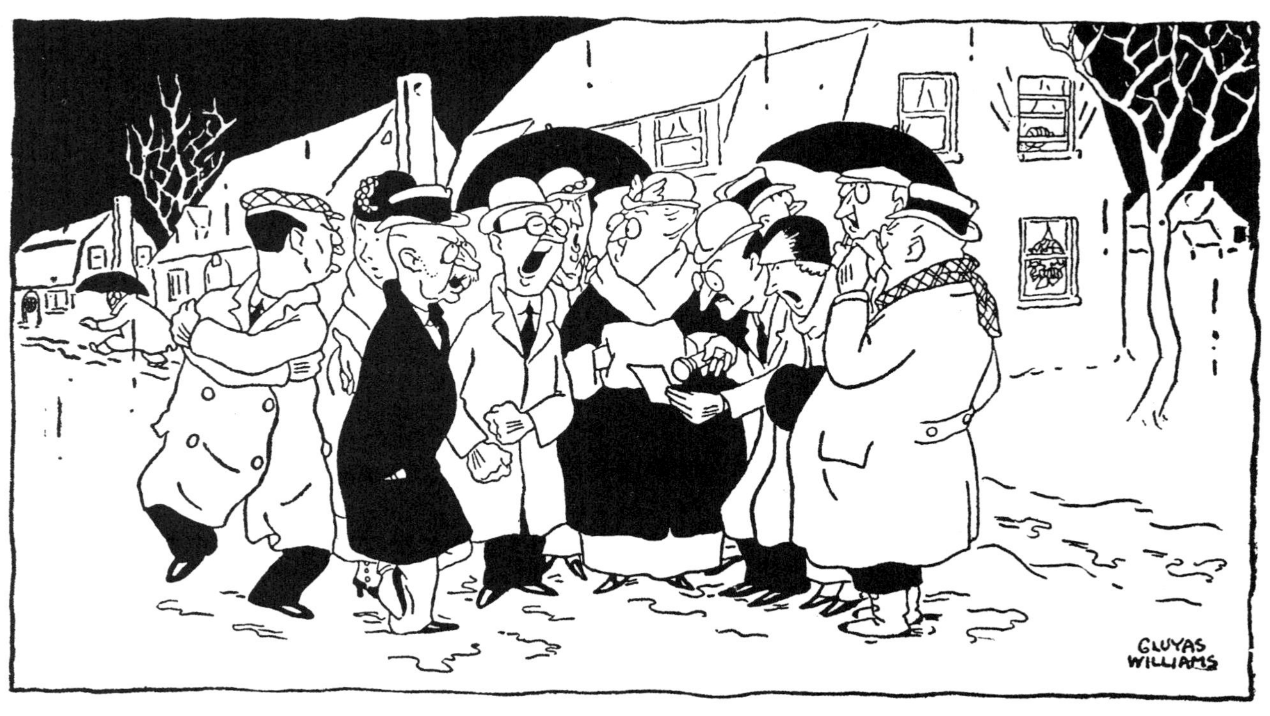

in our suburb it doesn't seem to work out so well

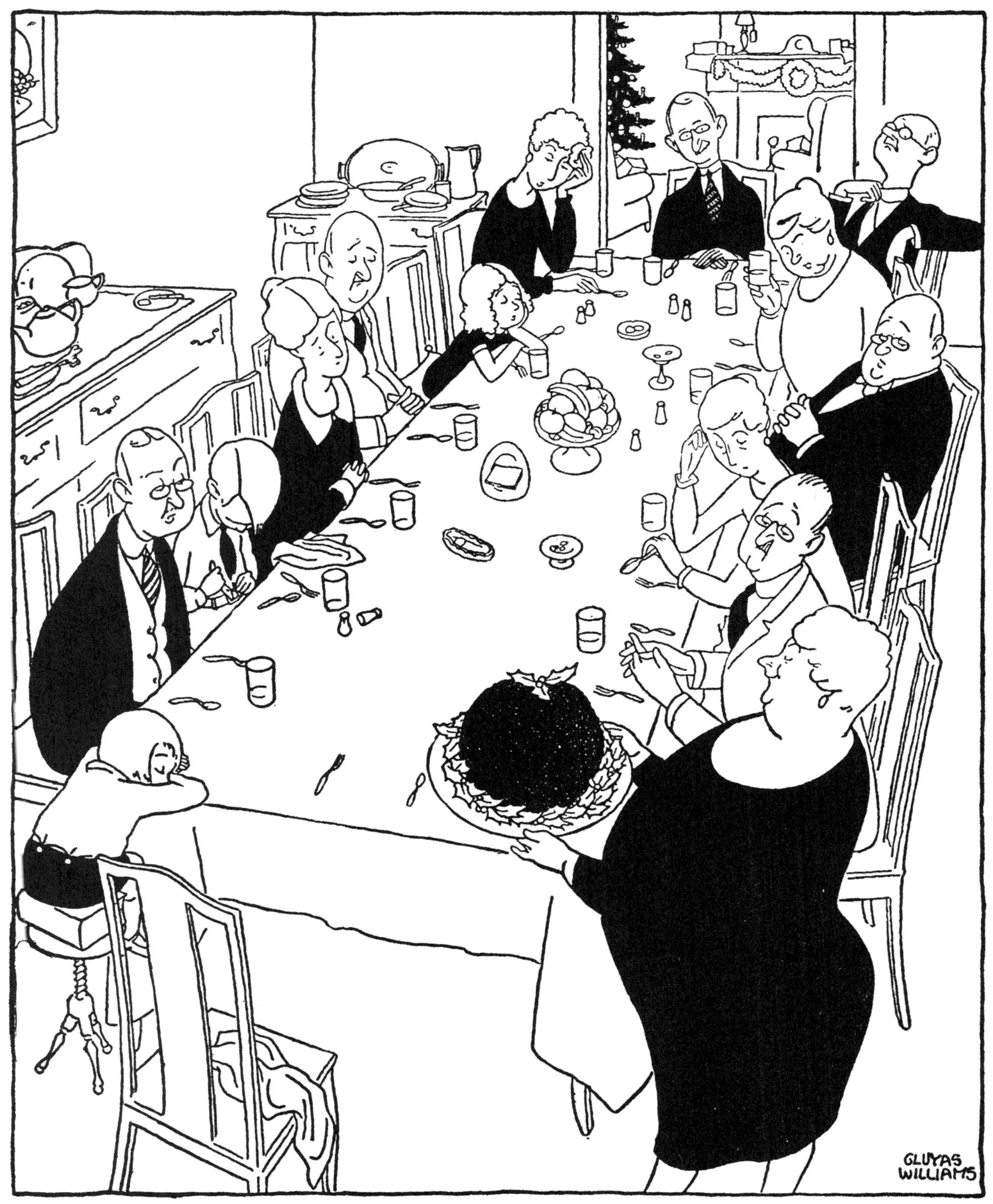

THE CHRISTMAS PLUM PUDDING

Which comes in looking a little soggy after everyone has eaten too much, and which no one can refuse or feelings are hurt

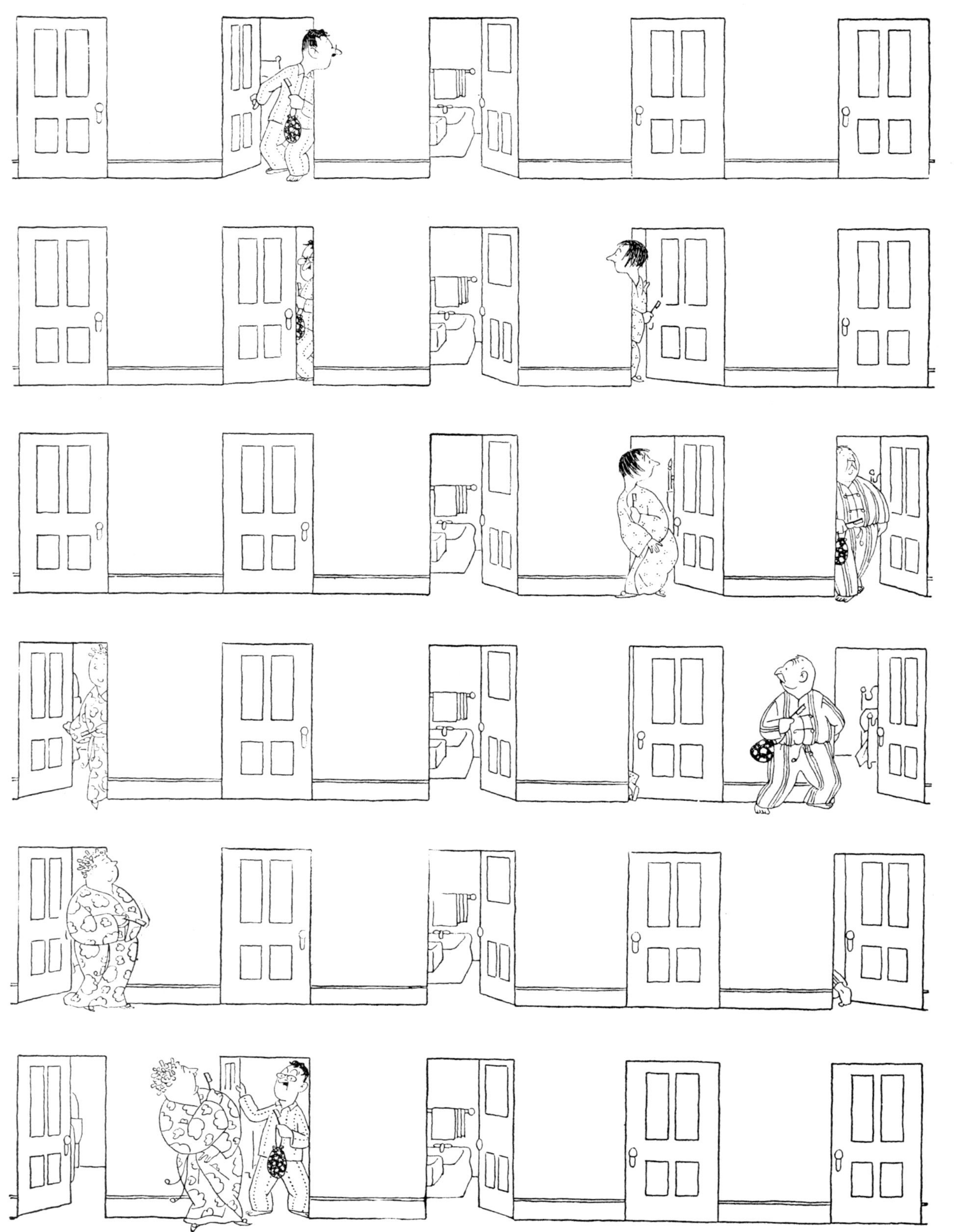

THE WEEK-ENI

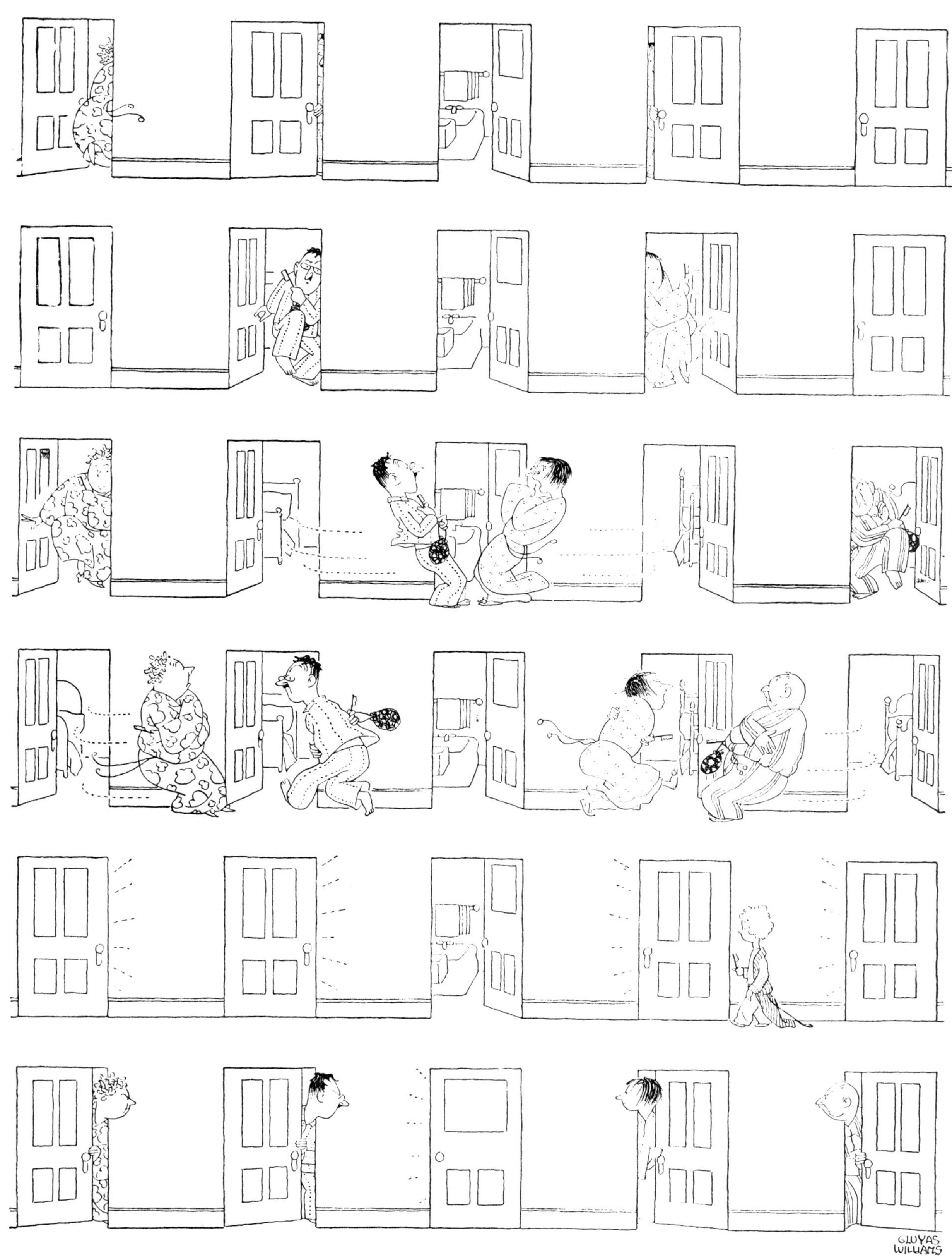

BATH ROOM

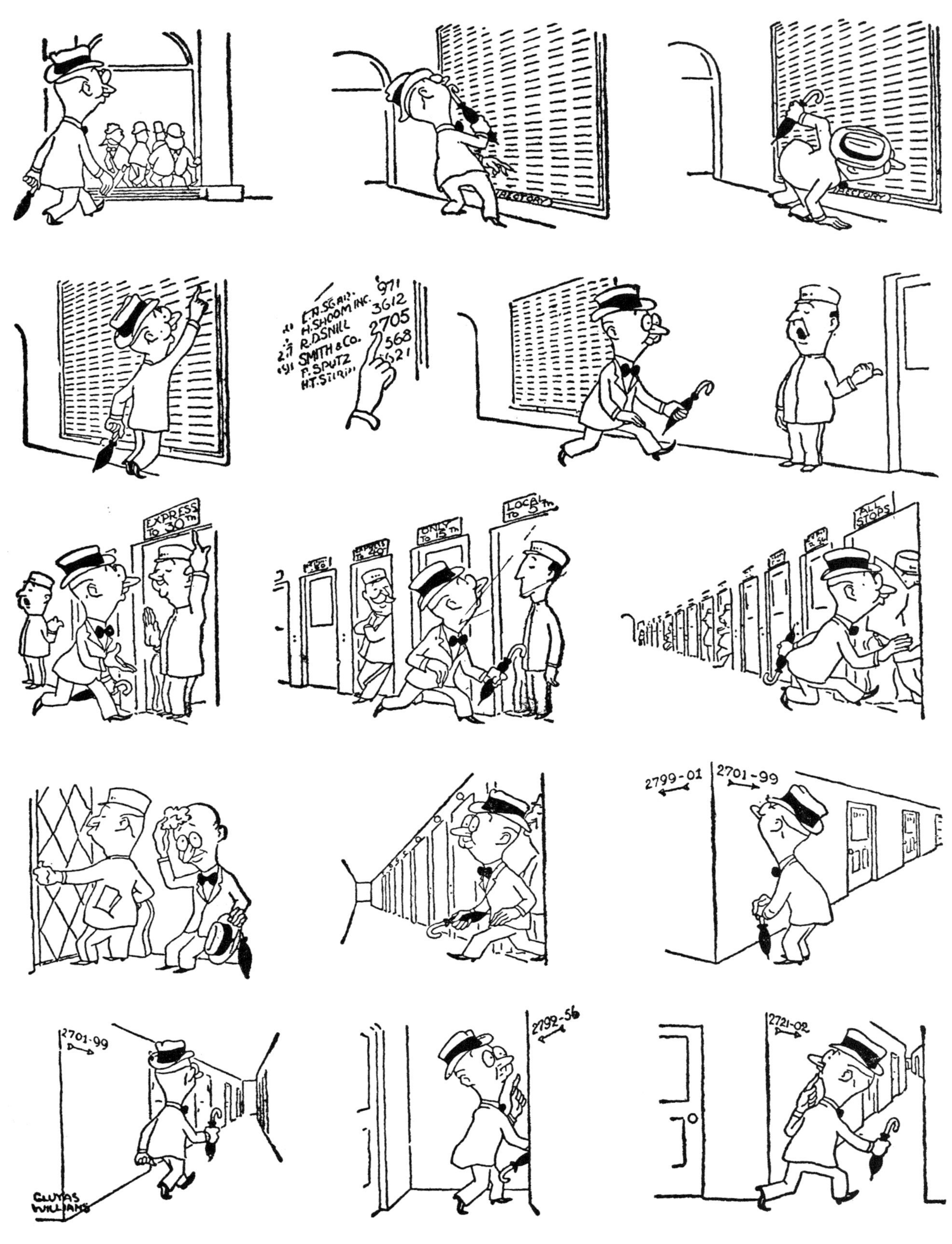

THE MODERN OFFICE BUILDING—I

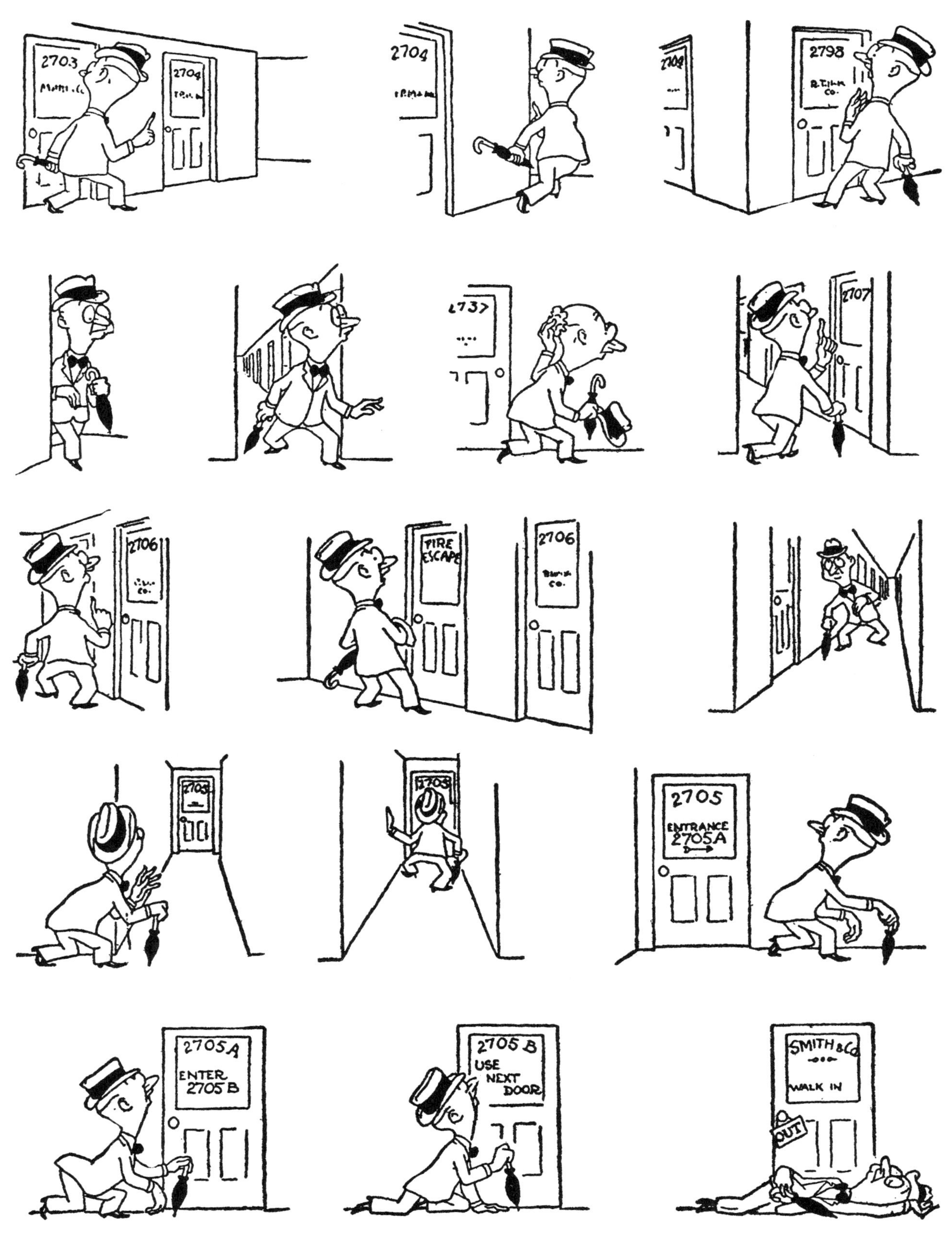

THE MODERN OFFICE BUILDING—II

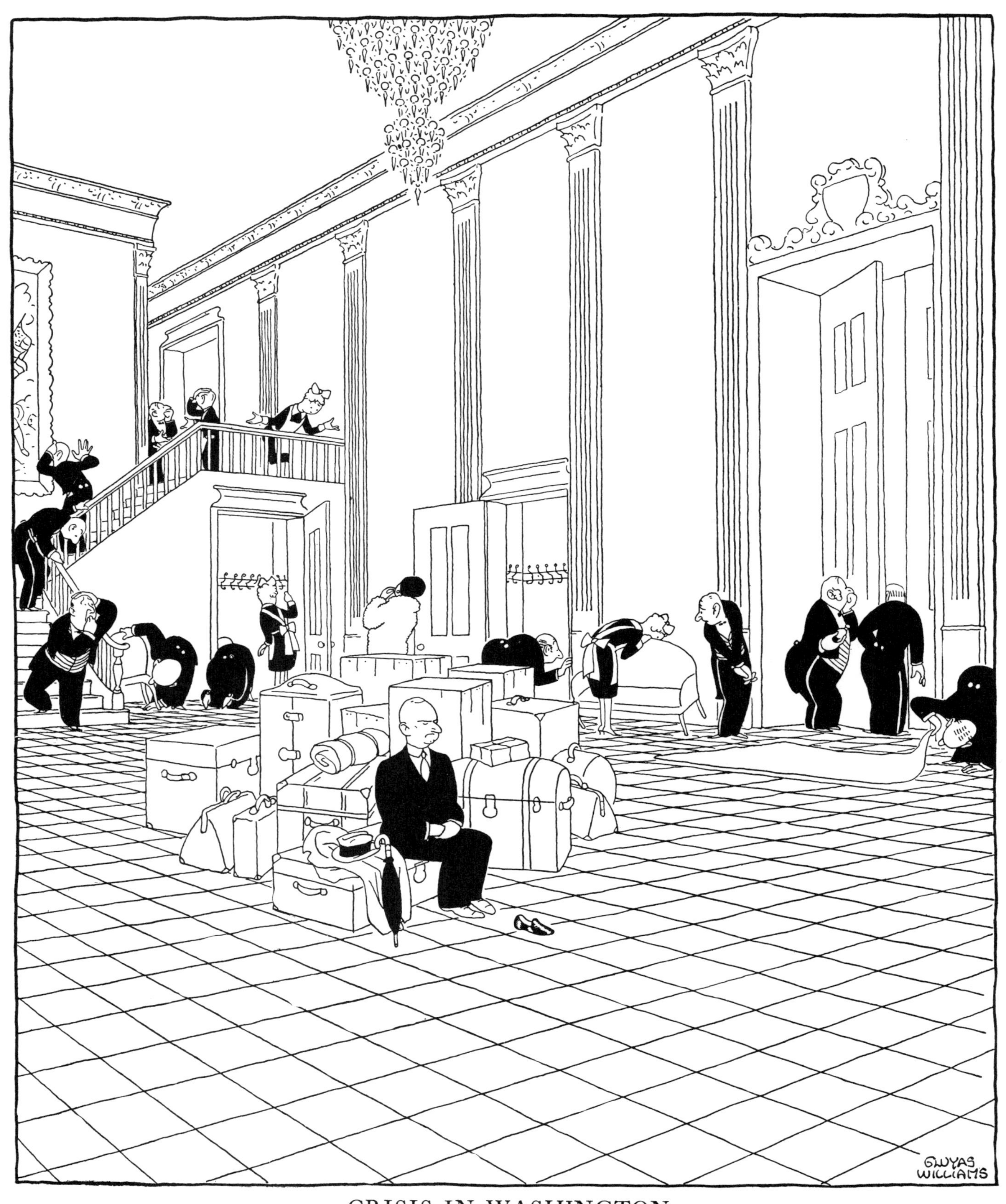

CRISIS IN WASHINGTON

Mr. Coolidge refuses point blank to vacate the White House until his other rubber is found

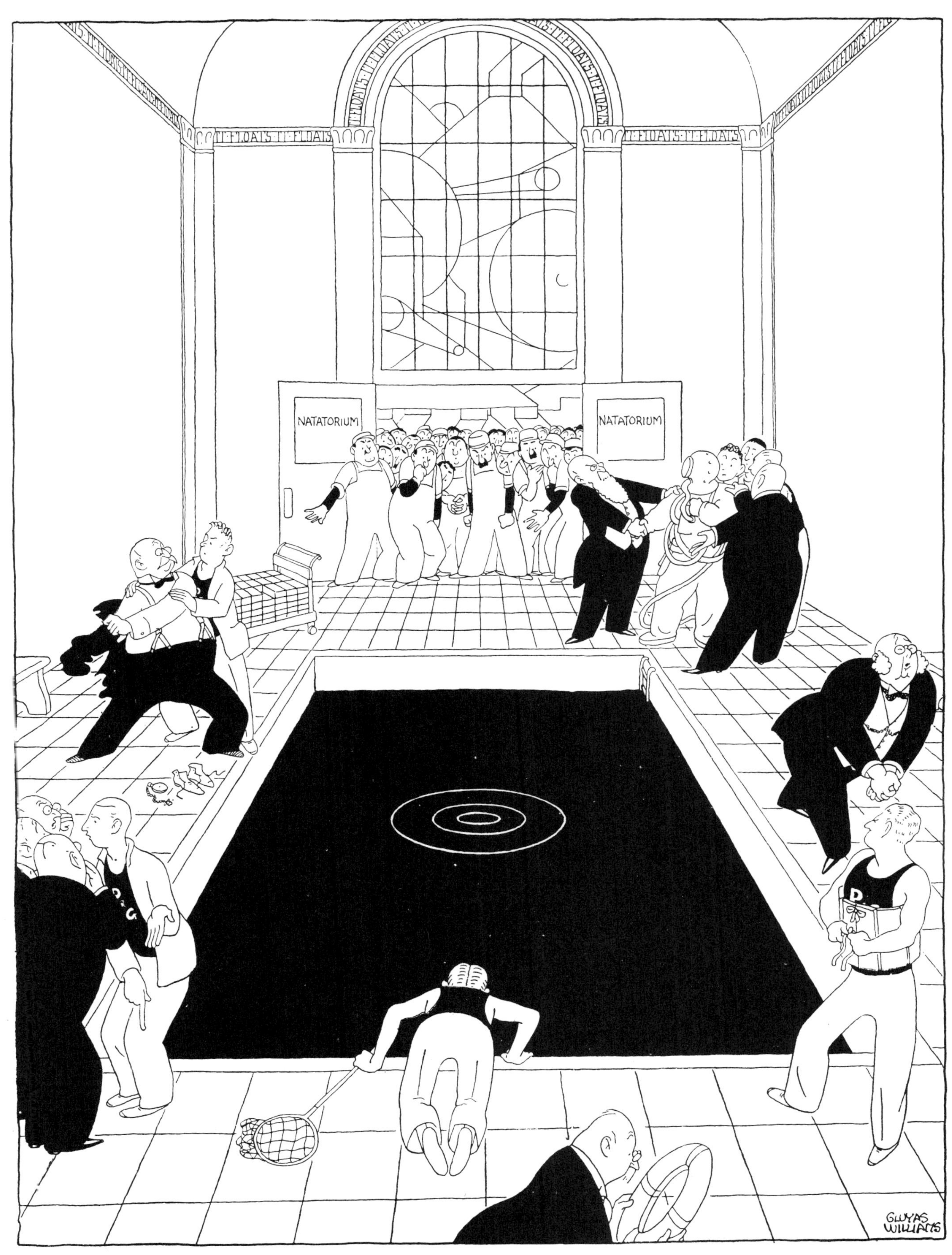

INDUSTRIAL CRISIS

The day a cake of Ivory sank at Proctor & Gamble's

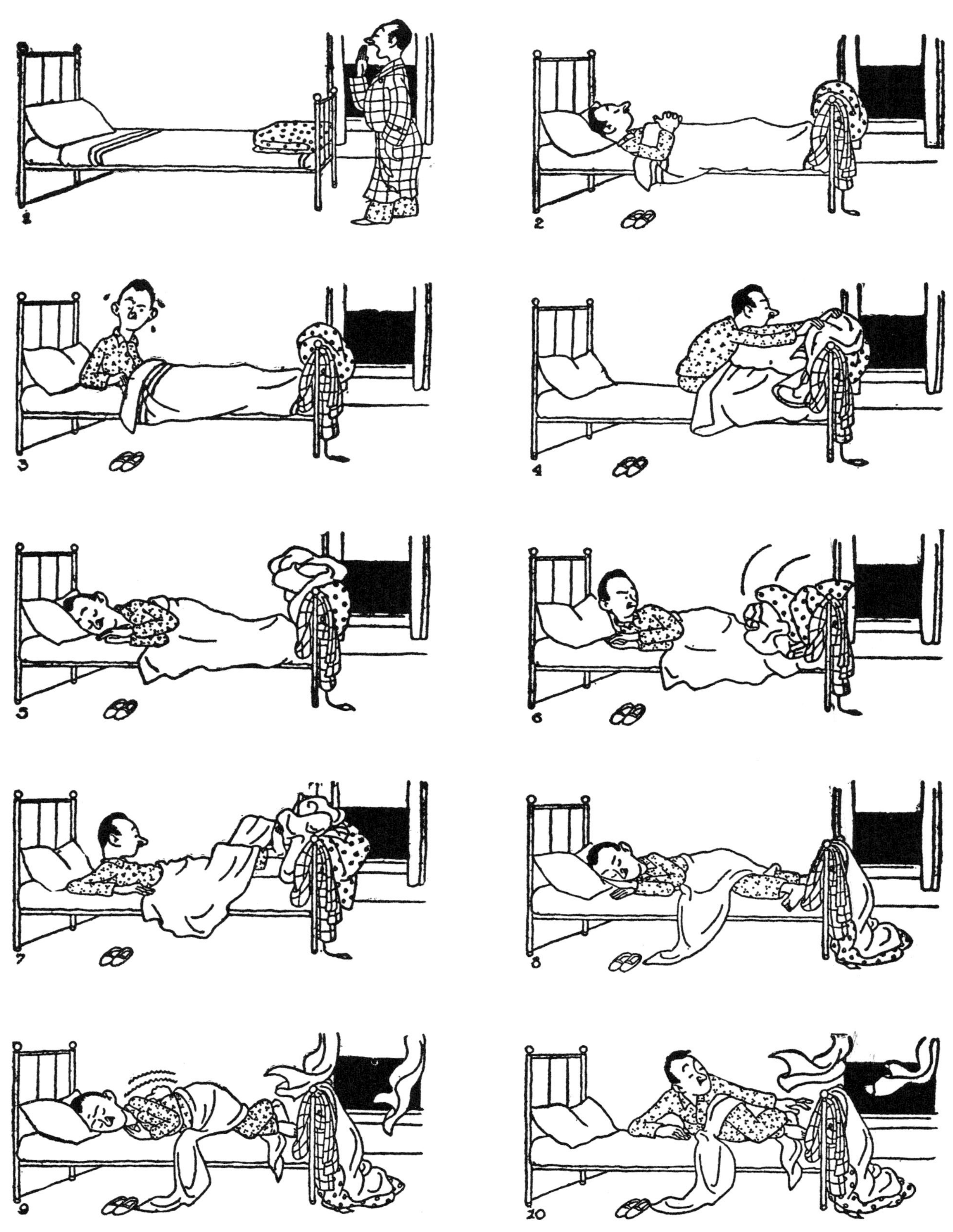

SUMMER BEDCLOTHES—I

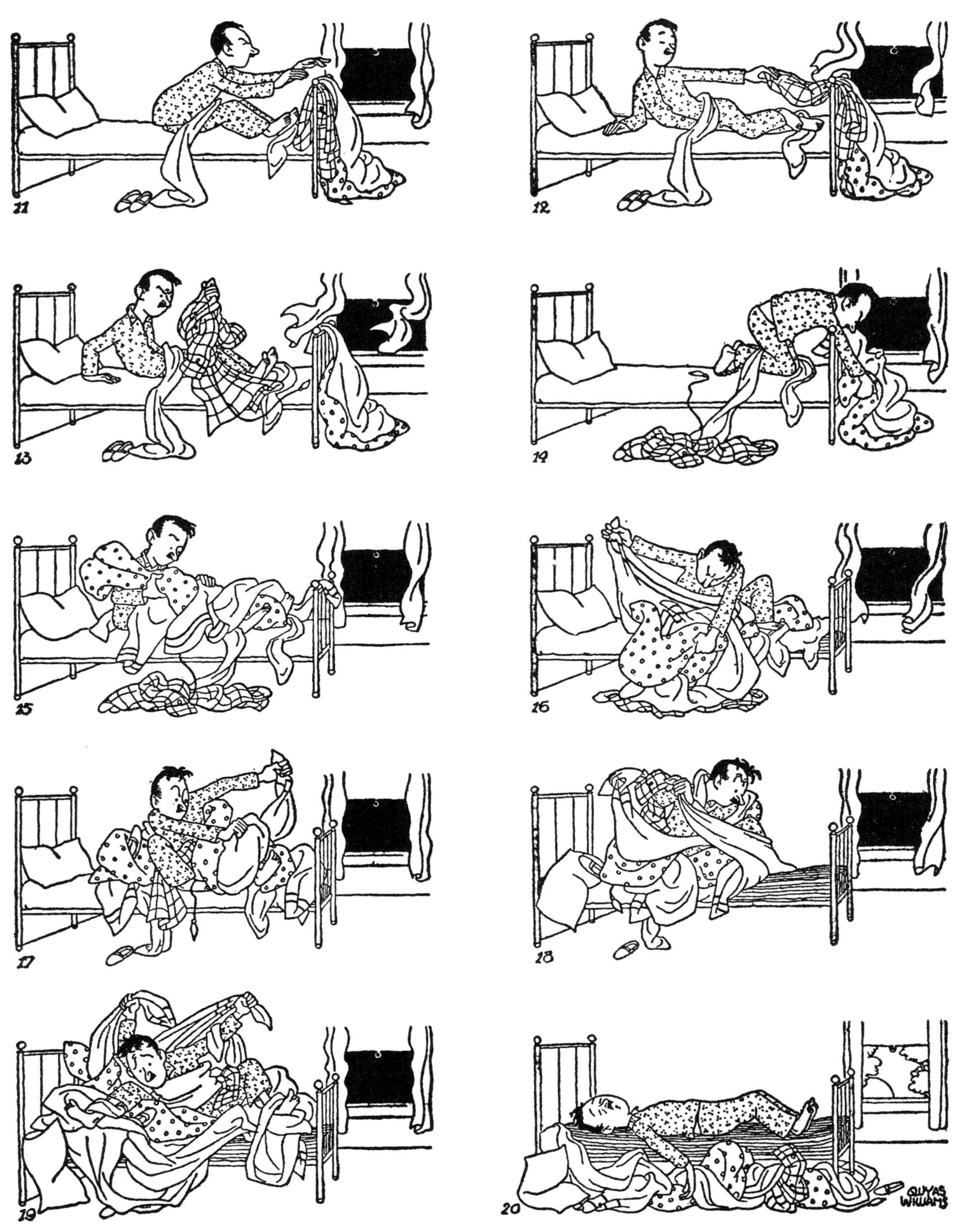

SUMMER BEDCLOTHES—II

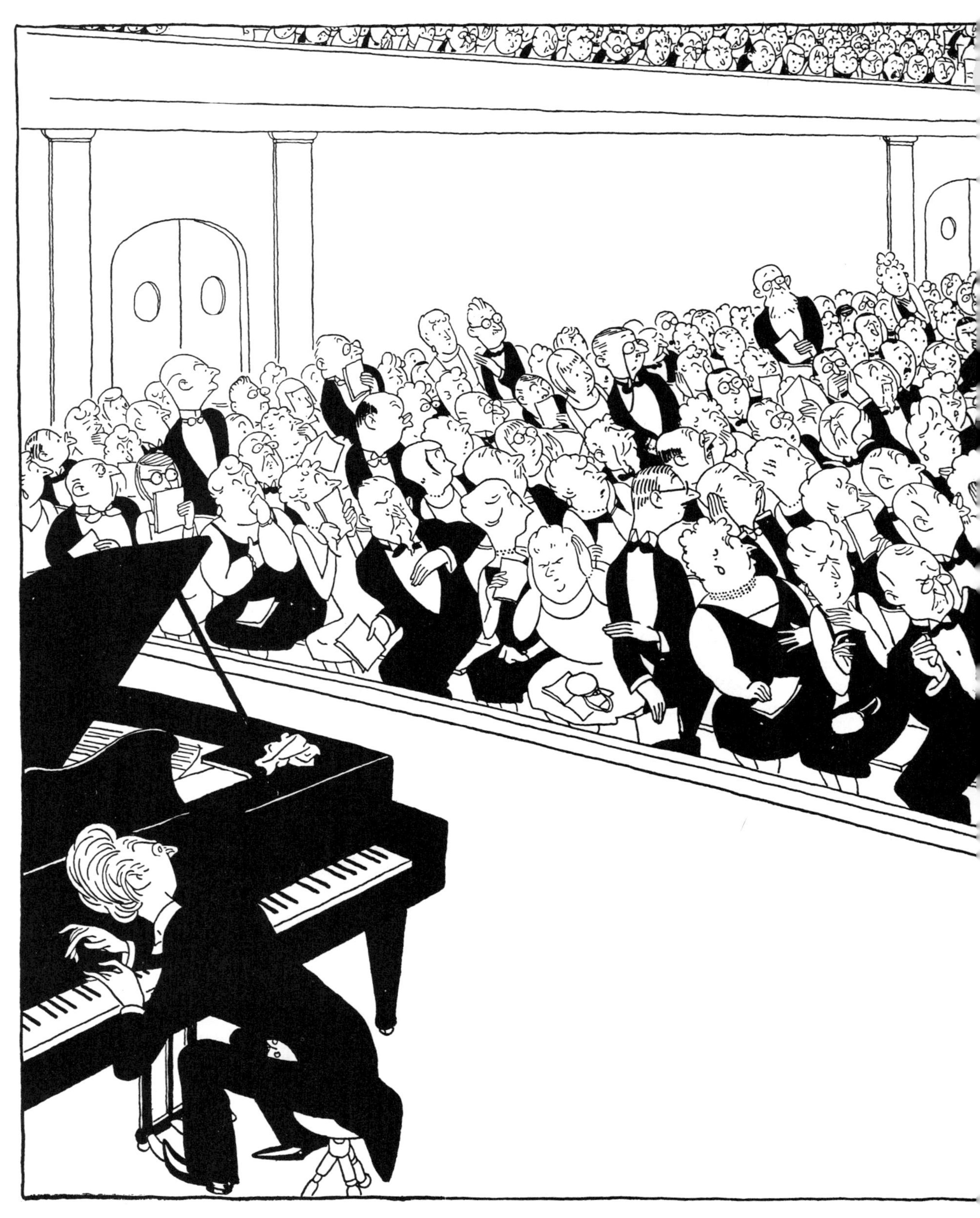

THE WOMAN WHO SNAPPED HEI

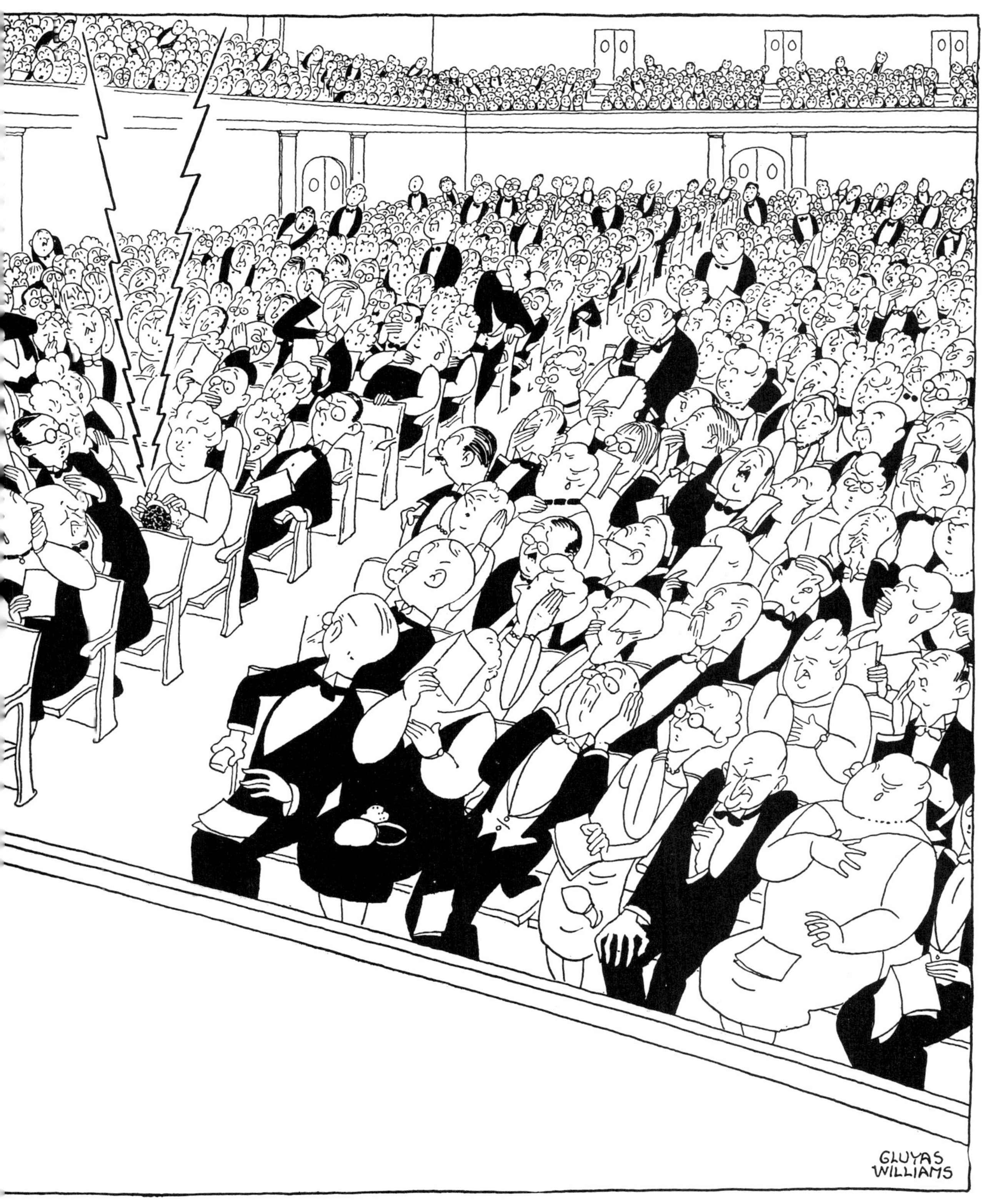

PURSE DURING A PIANISSIMO

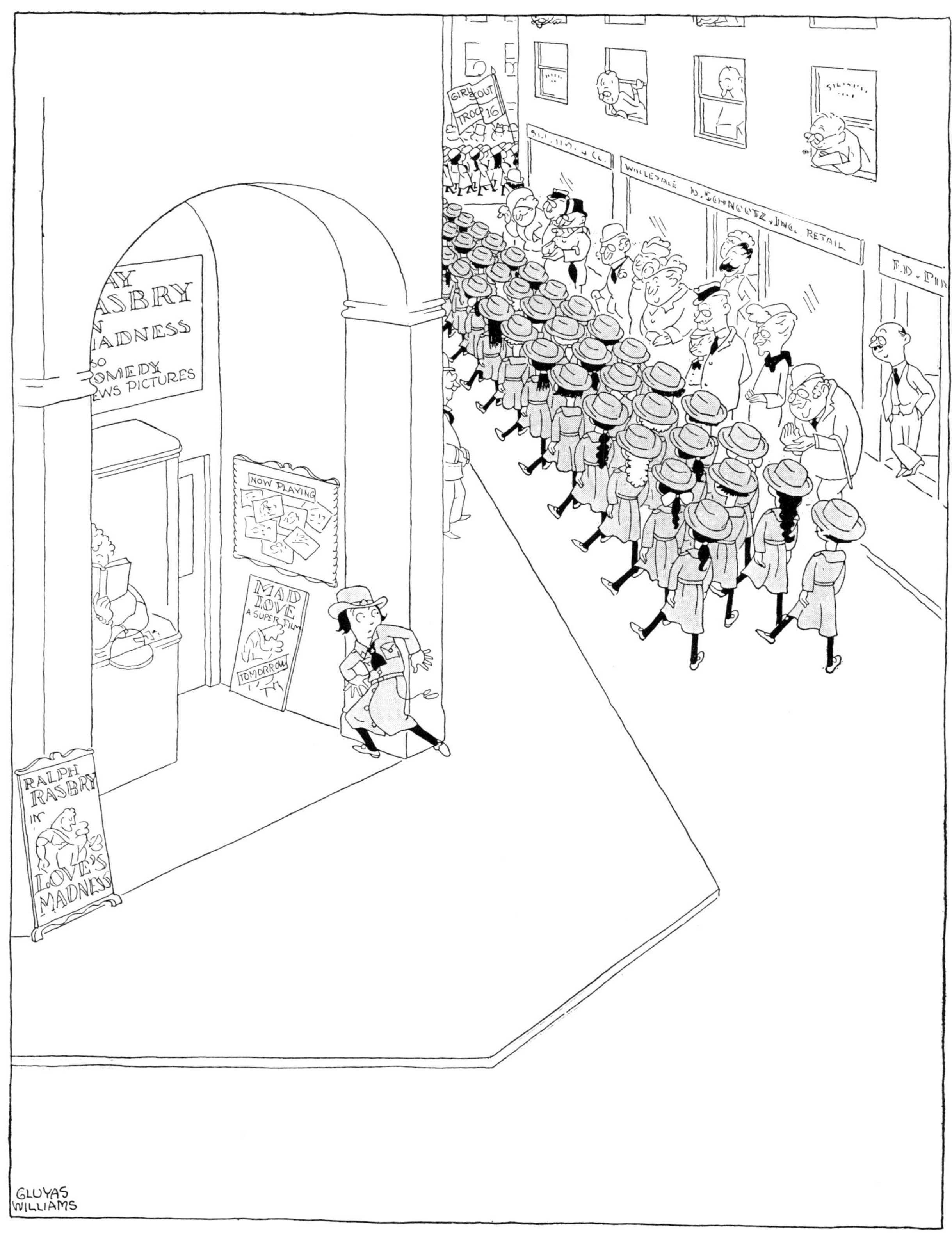

THE DESERTER

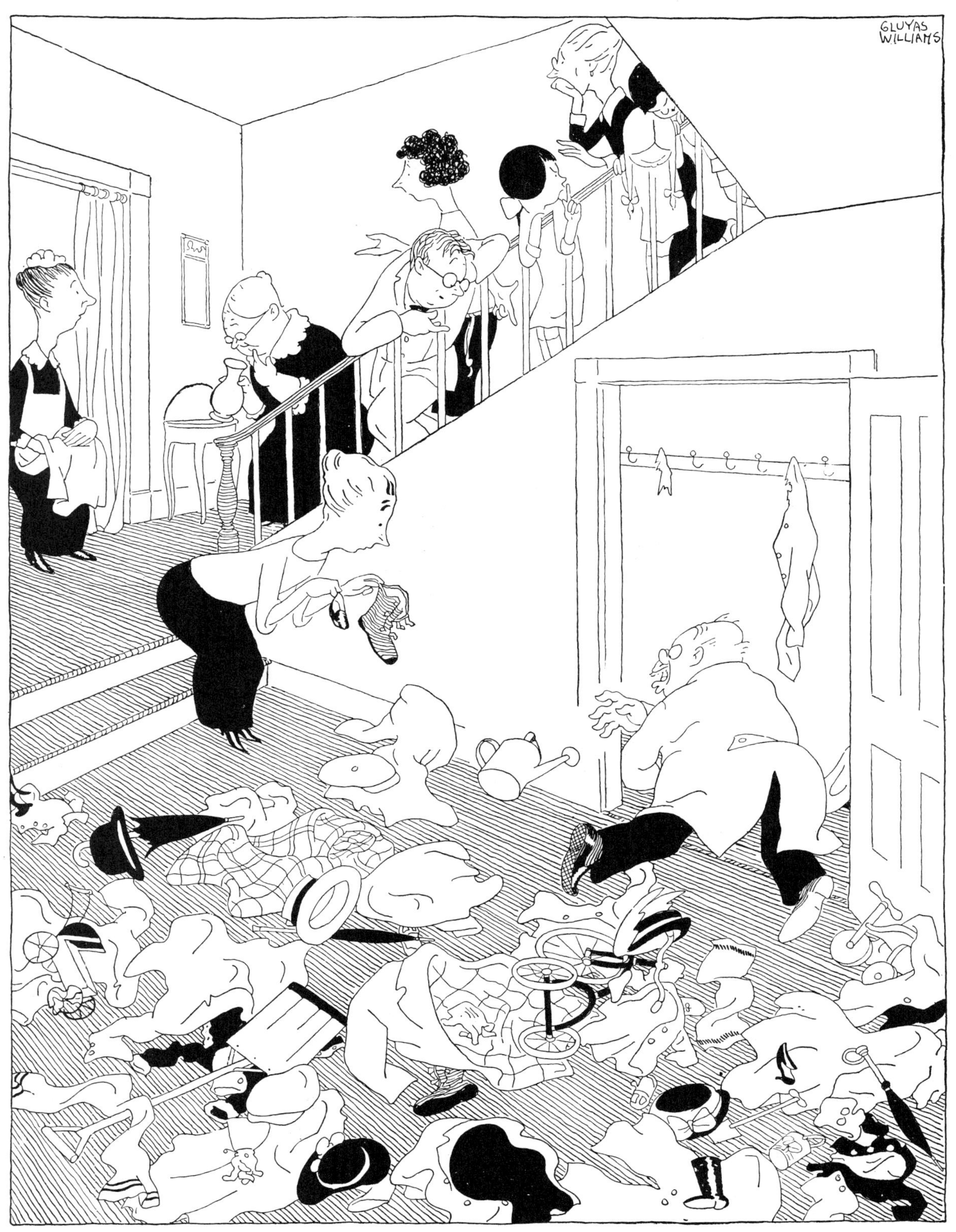

THE MISSING RUBBER

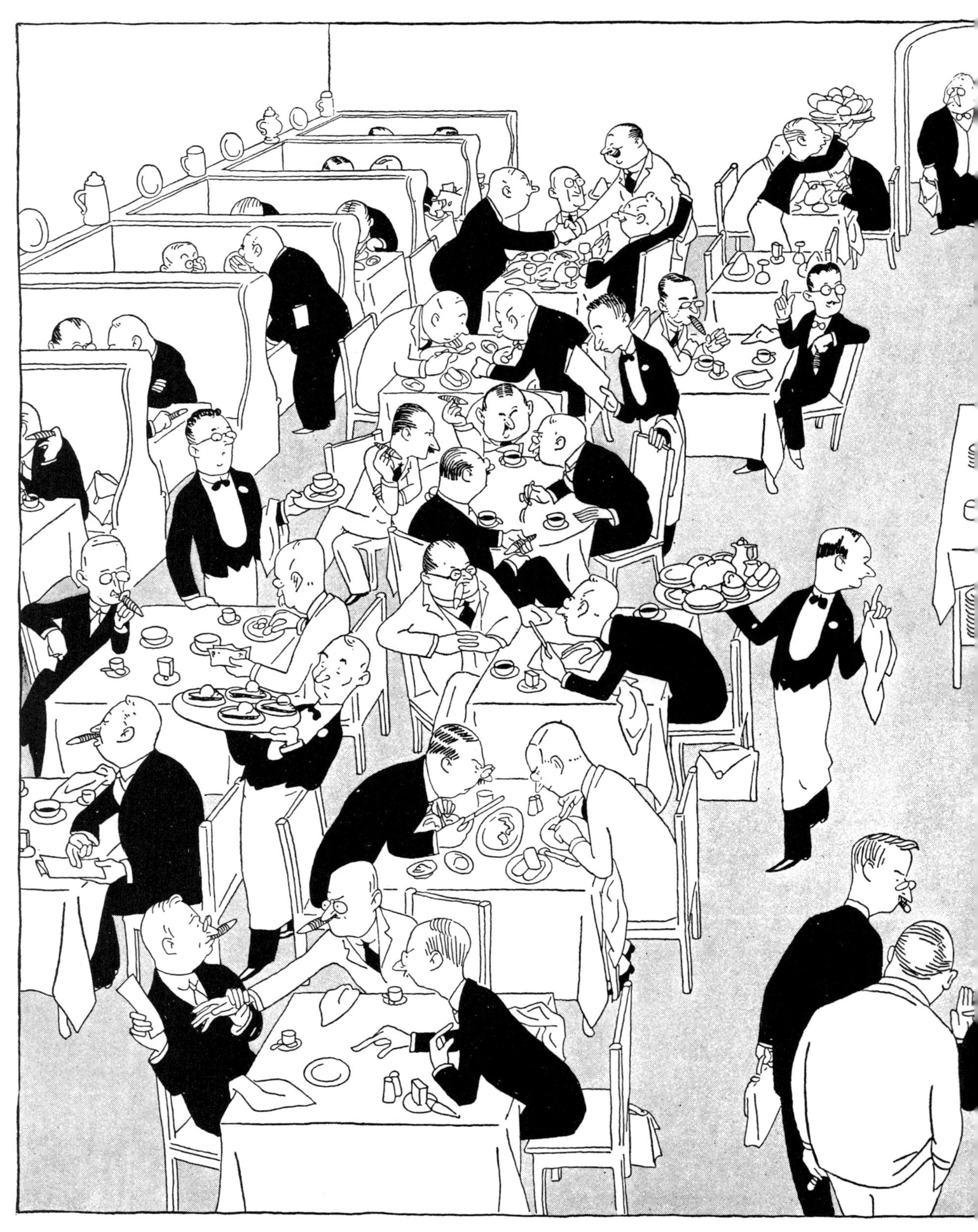

THE BUSINESS

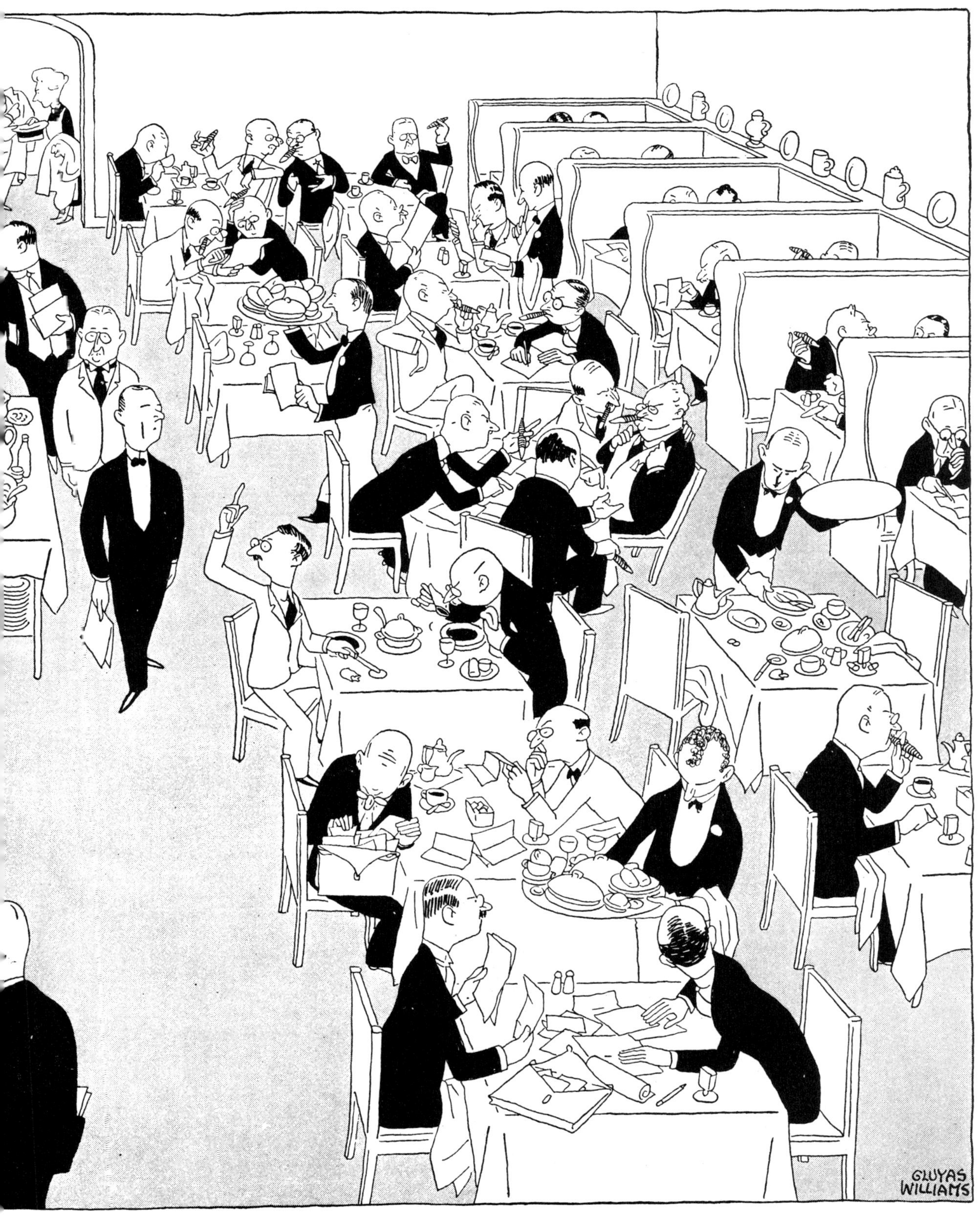

MEN'S LUNCH

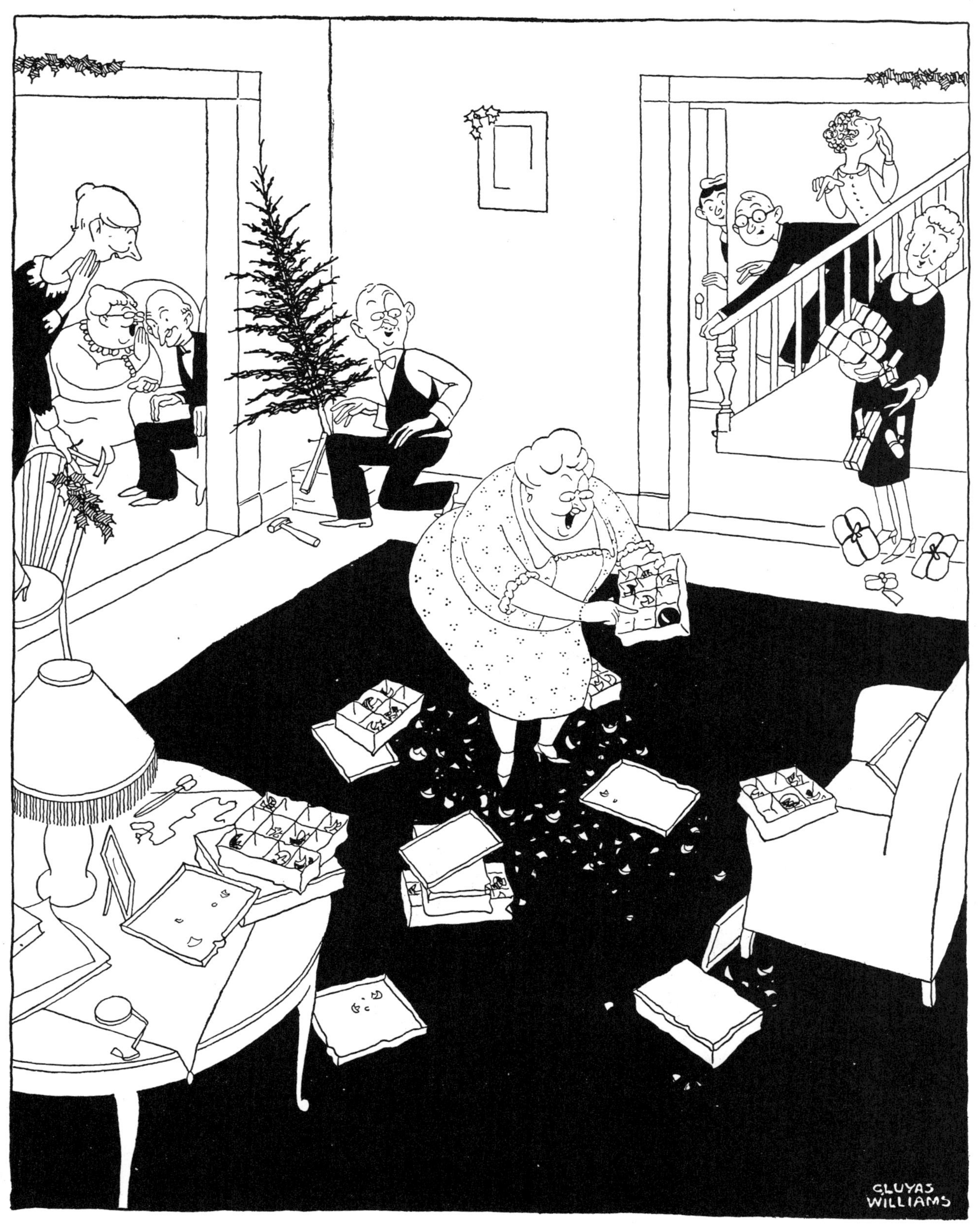

MIRACLE!

Mother finds one of last year's Christmas tree balls unbroken

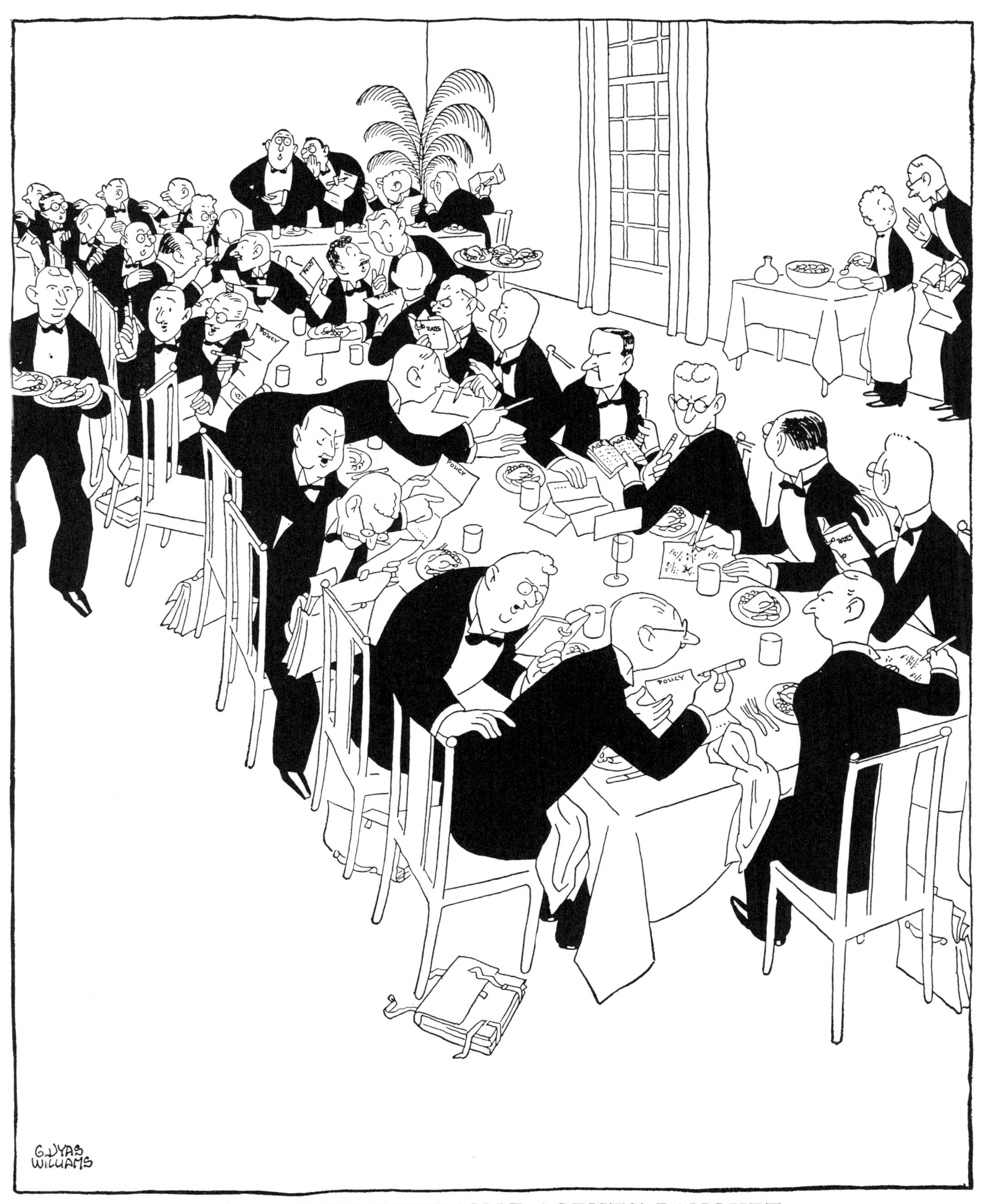

AT THE LIFE INSURANCE AGENTS' BANQUET

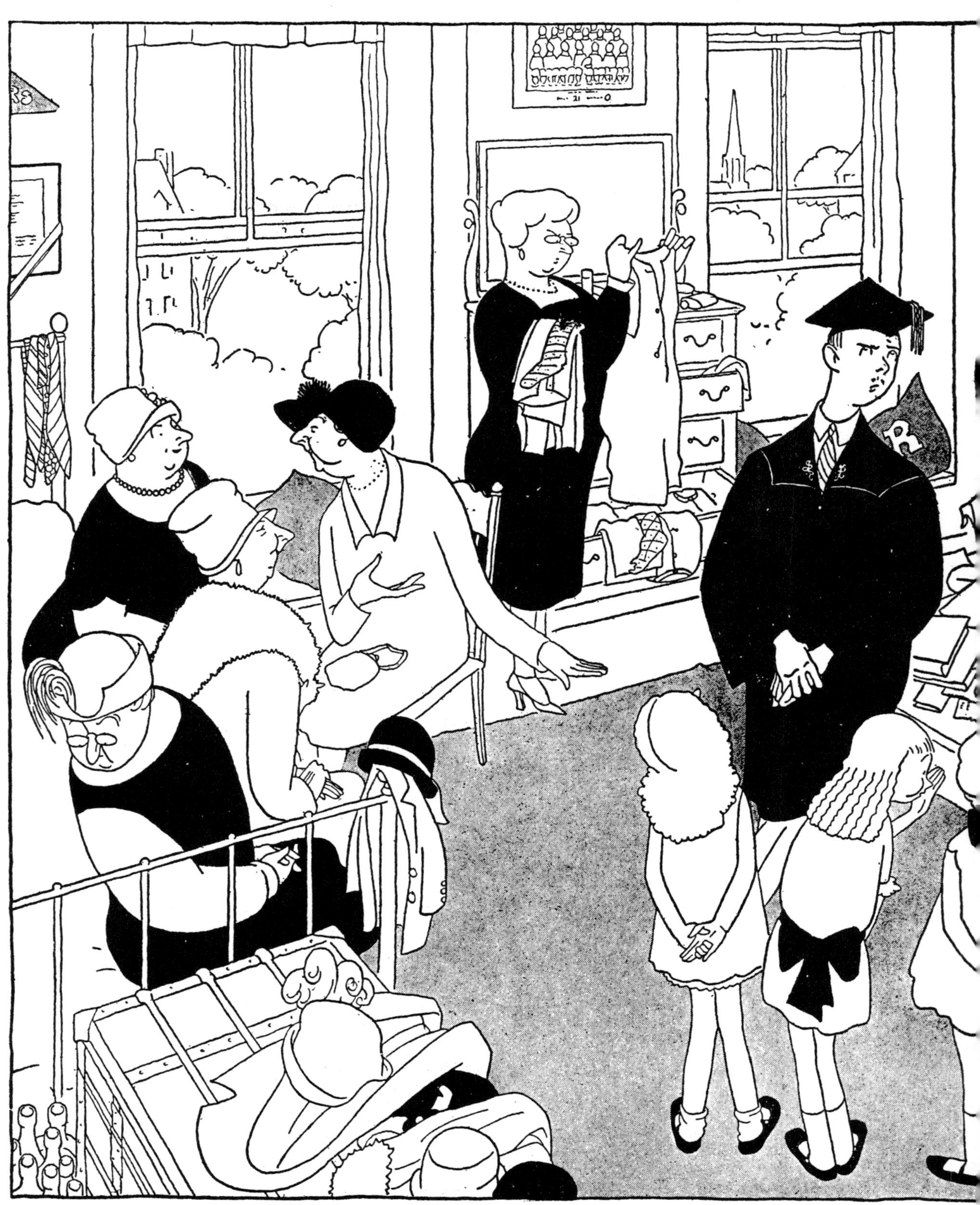

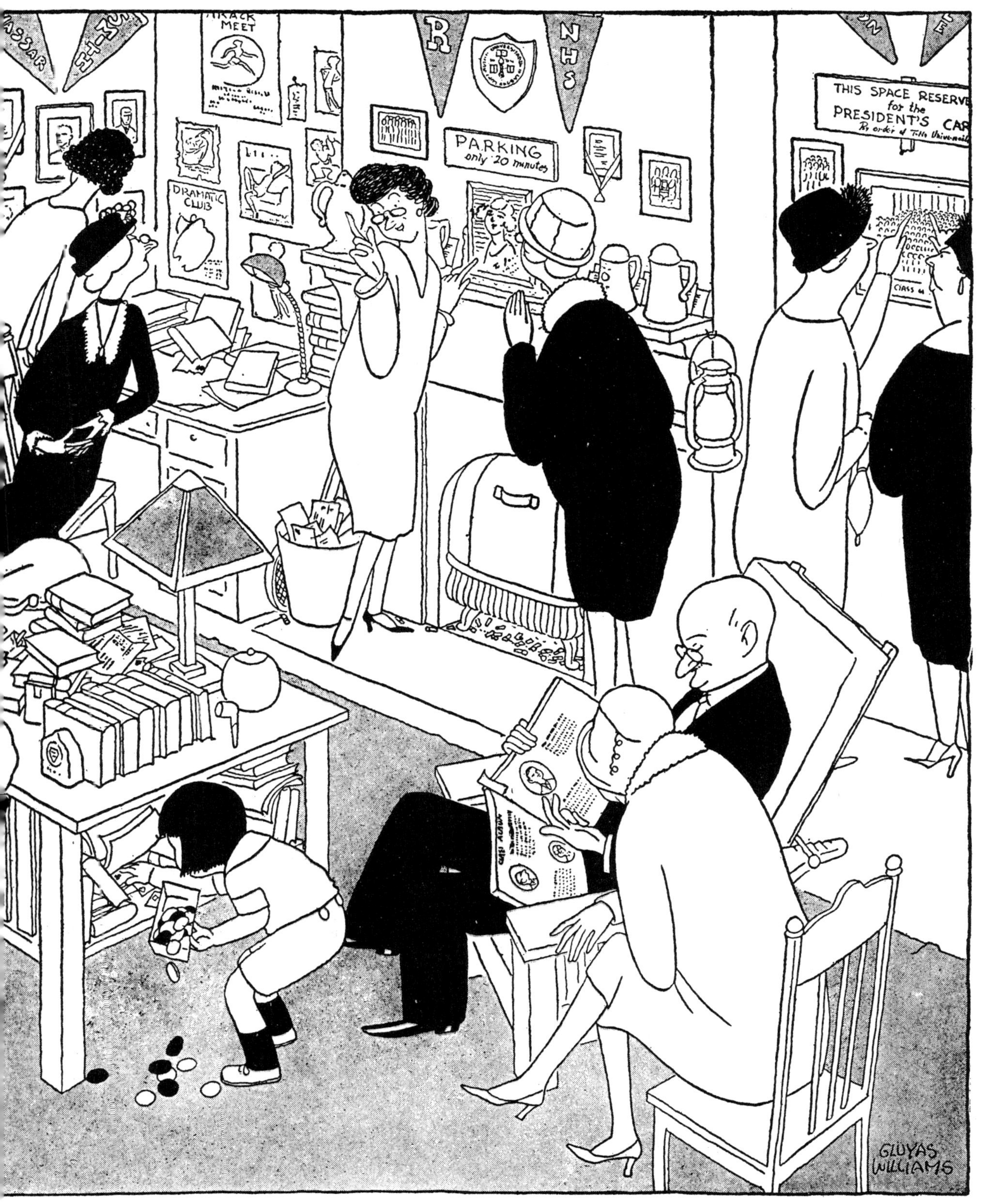

THE RELATIVES AT COMMENCEMENT

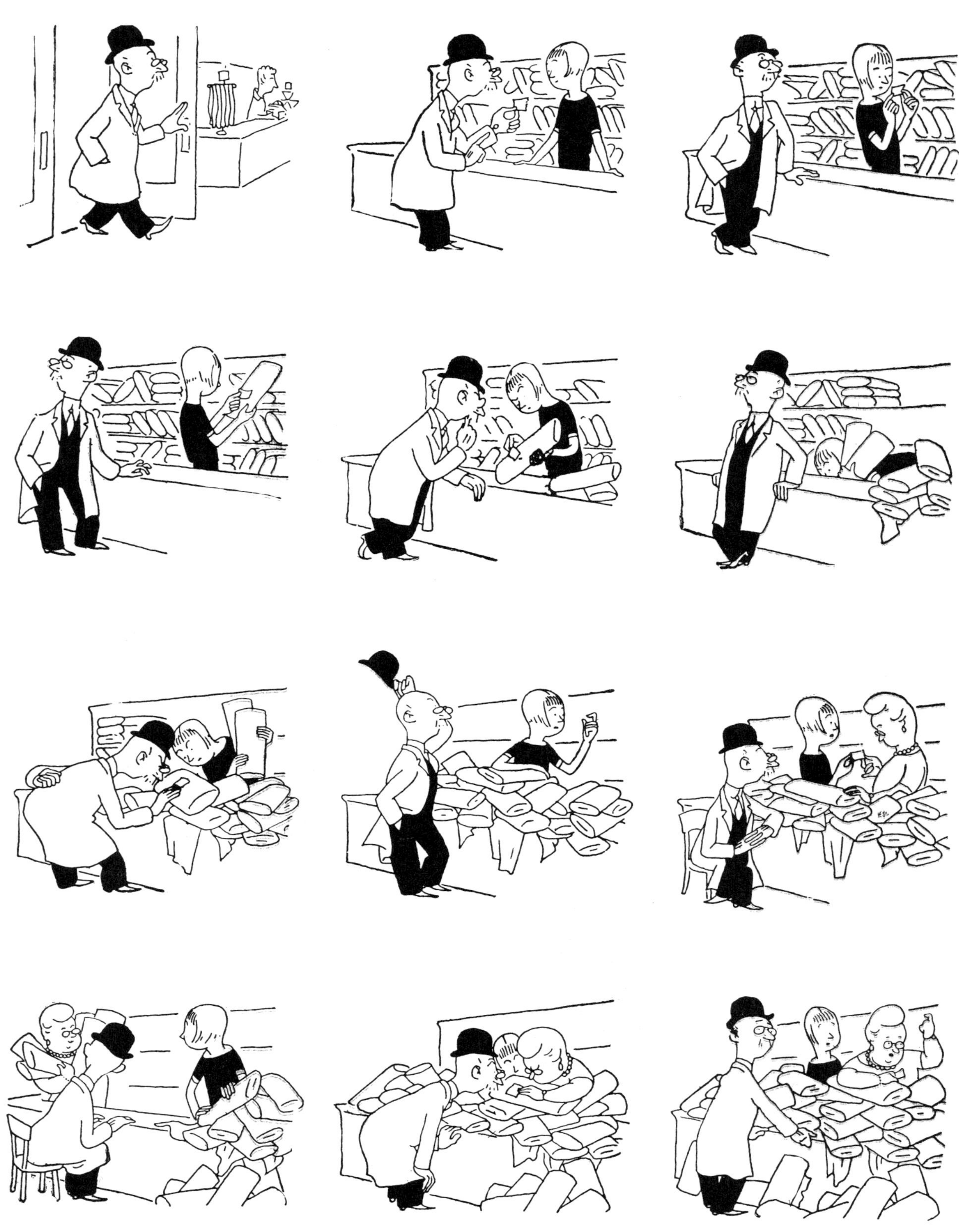

THE DIFFICULT MATCH—I

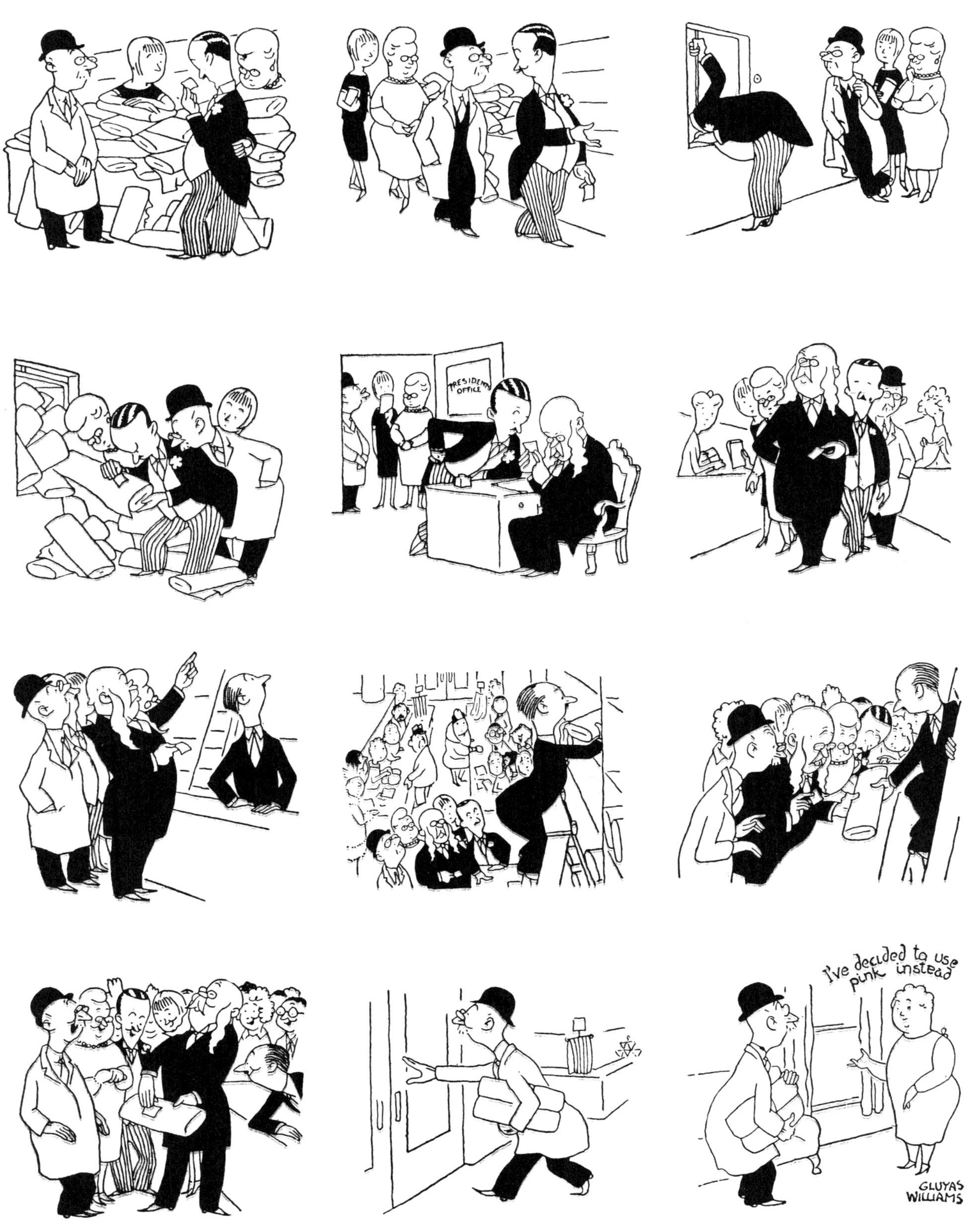

THE DIFFICULT MATCH—II

TIT

ACME
TAXI
CO

for

GAIETY
THEATRE
TAXI
TAXI
CO.
1123450
GLUYAS
WILLIAMS

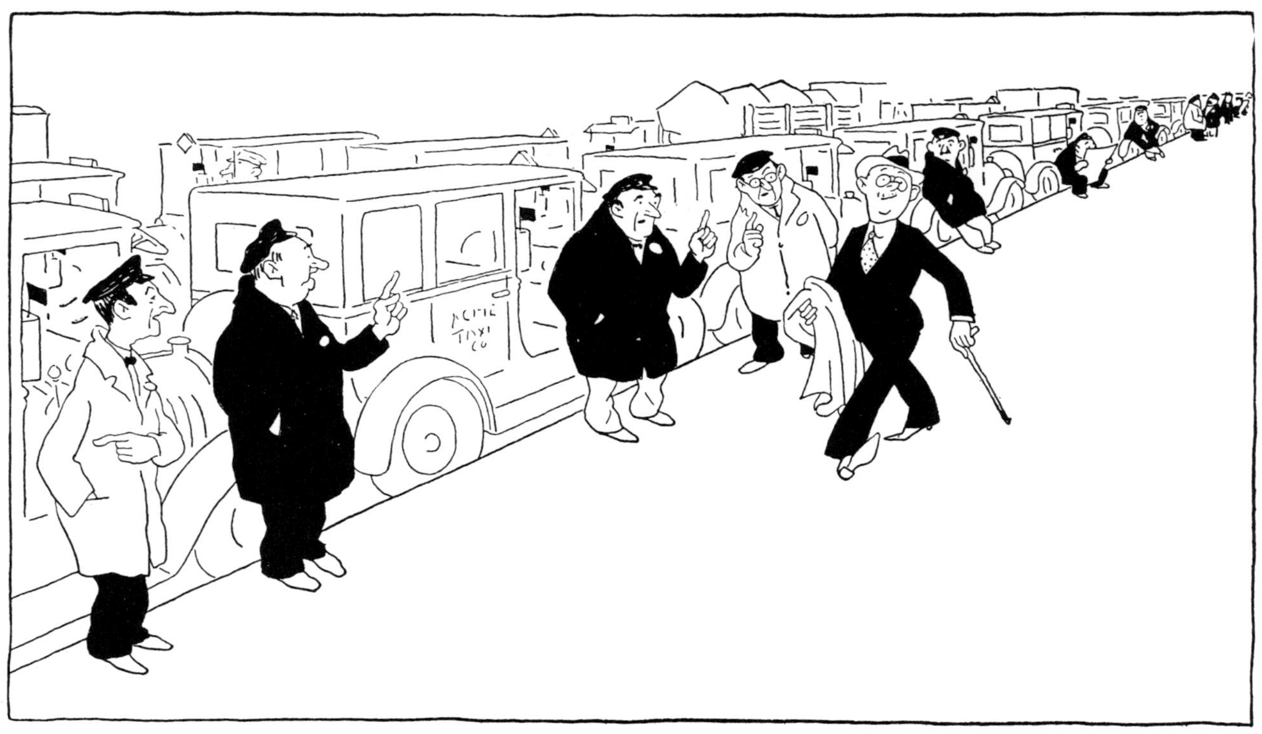

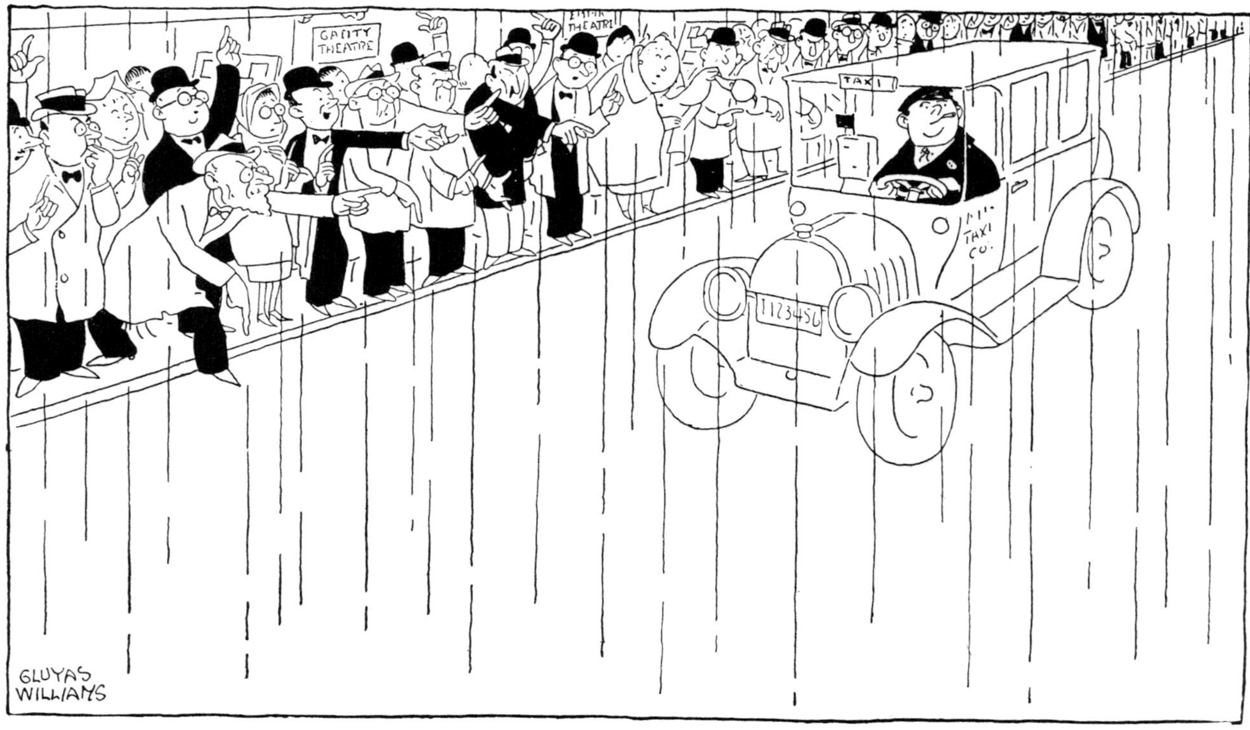

TAT

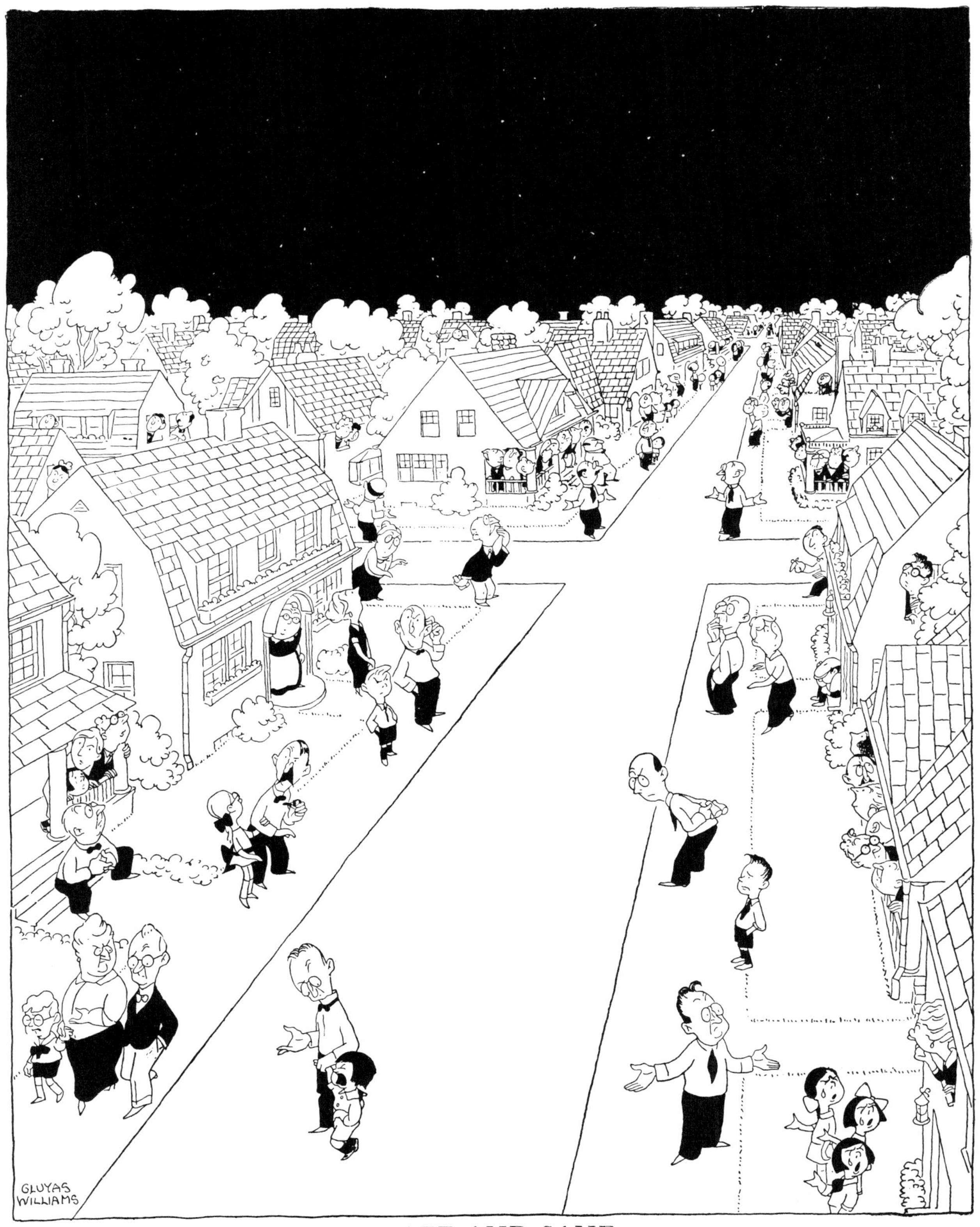

SAFE AND SANE

The night of the fourth was a dismal failure in suburbia this year because in a spirit of thrift each resident decided to dispense with his own fireworks and enjoy his neighbor's

PUZZLE
10¢
10¢
CAN YOU GET
THE RINGS
APART
?
BUY ONE FOR
THE KIDDIES
GLUYAS
WILLIAMS

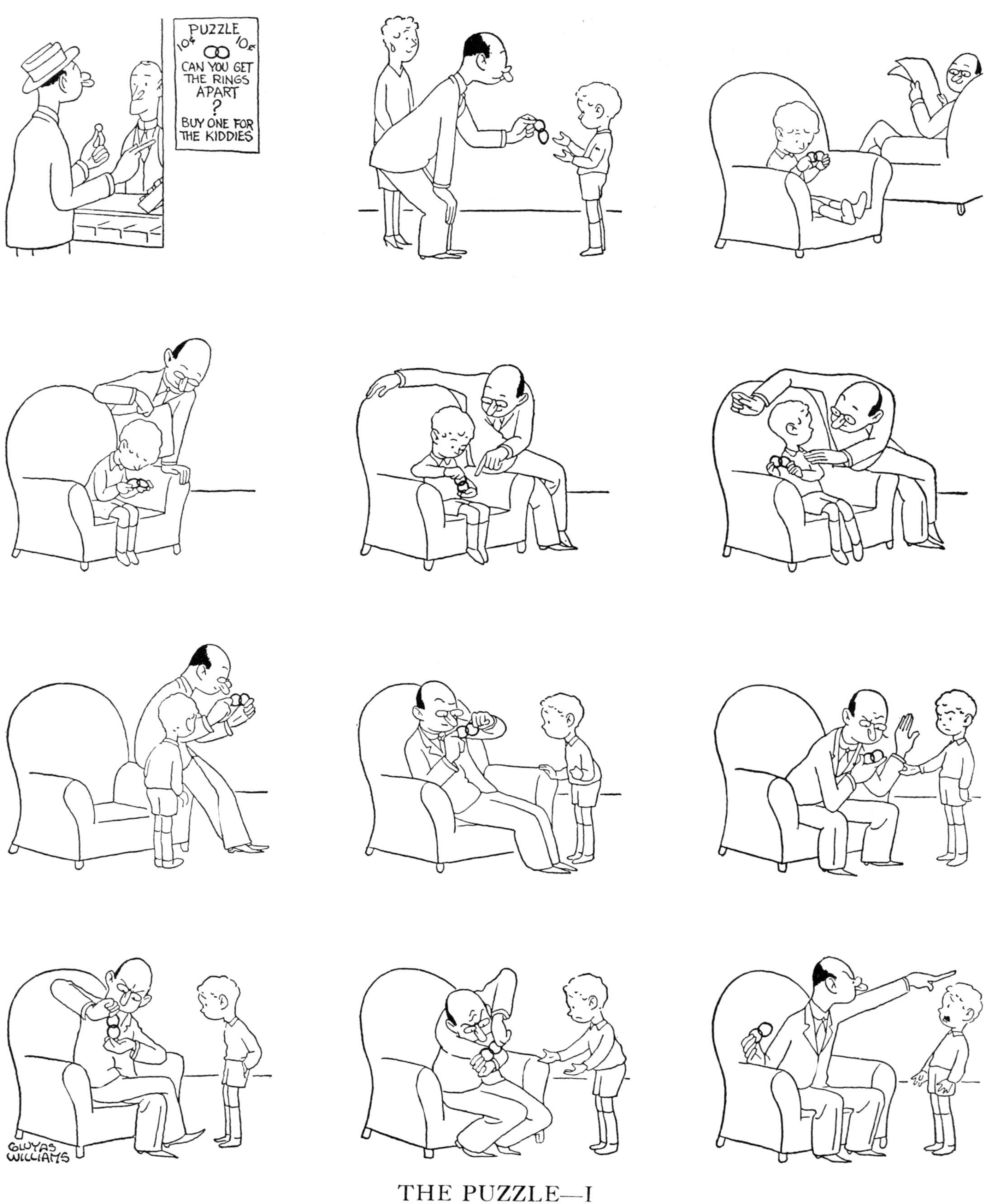

THE PUZZLE—I

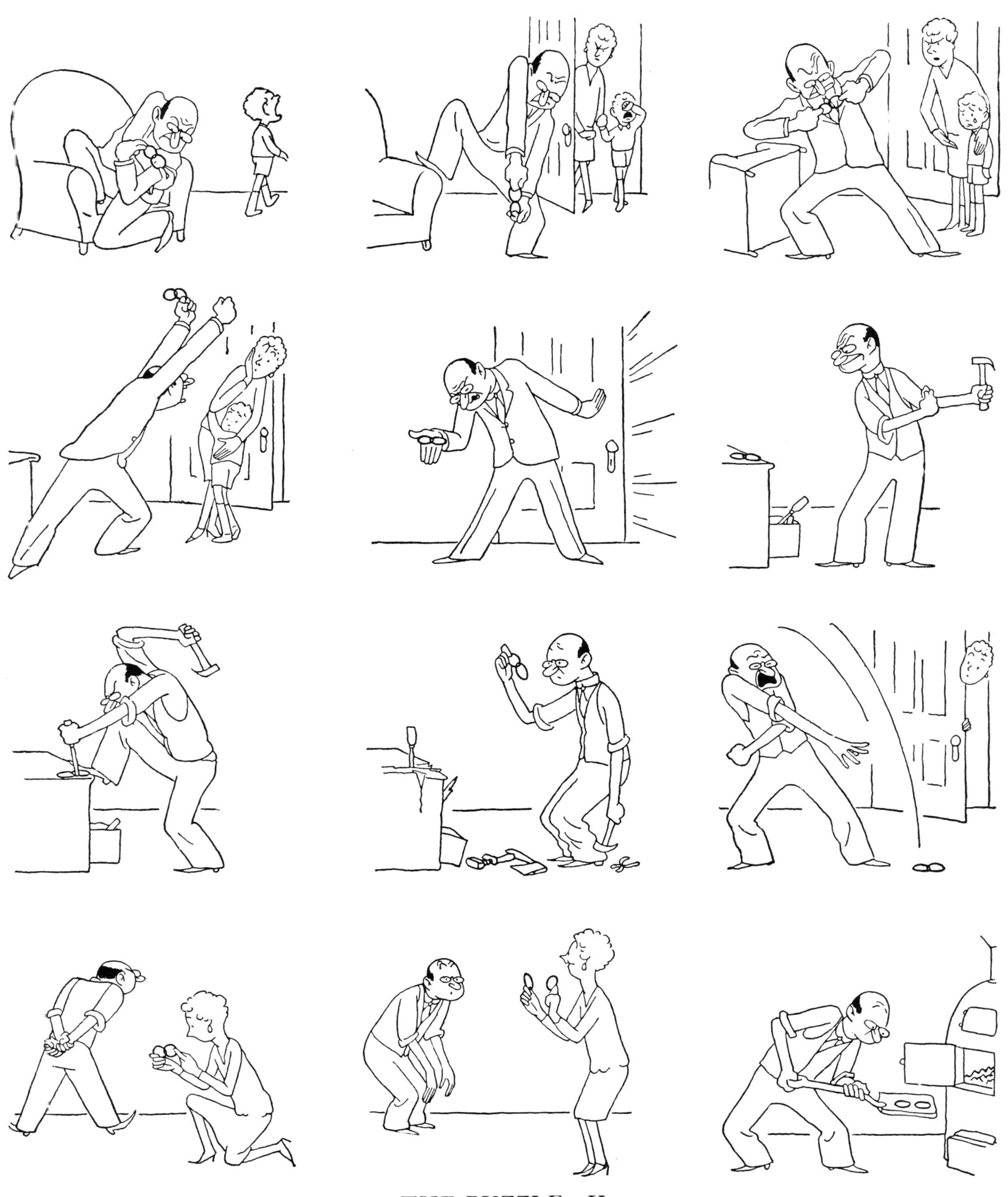

THE PUZZLE—II

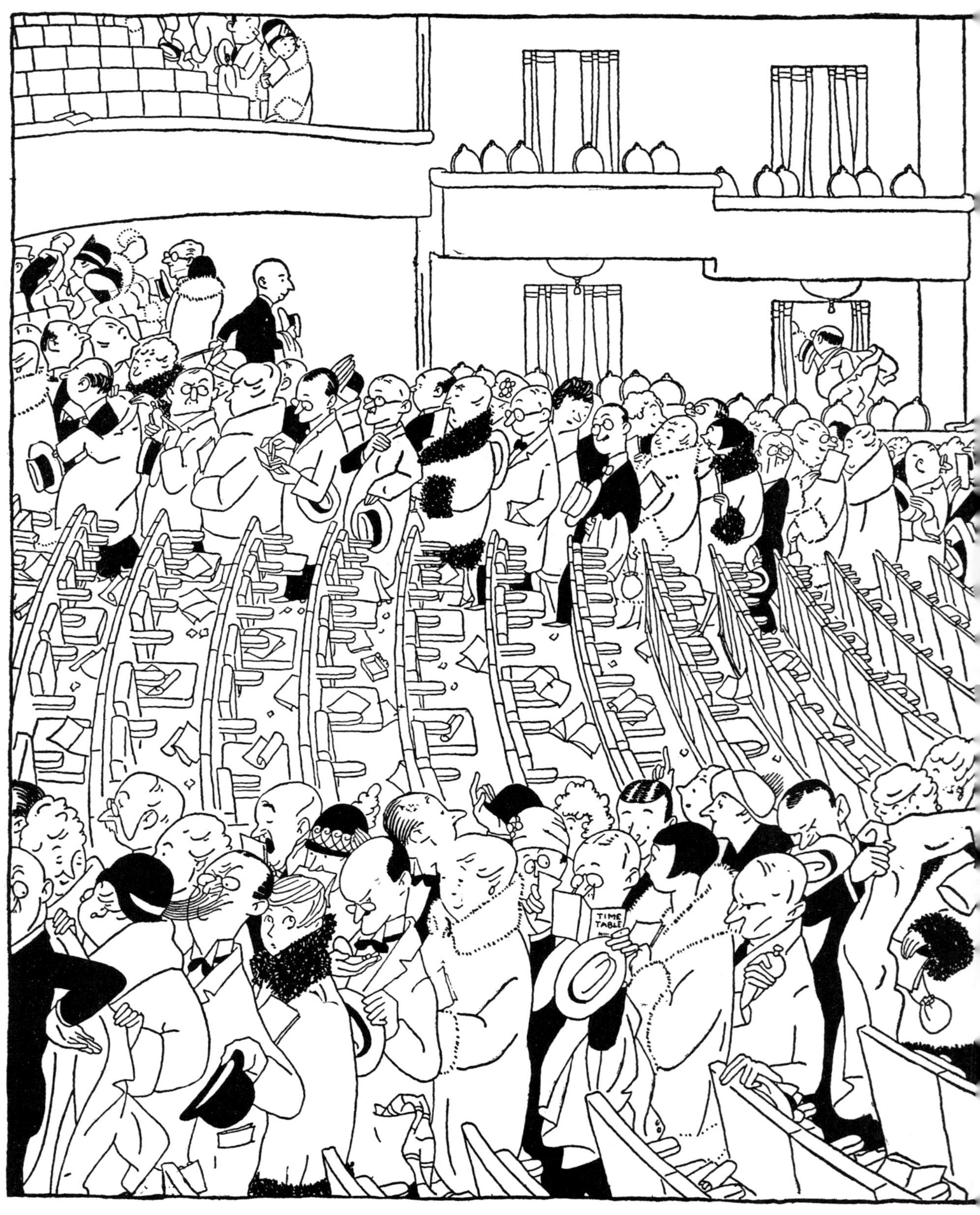
TIME
TABLE

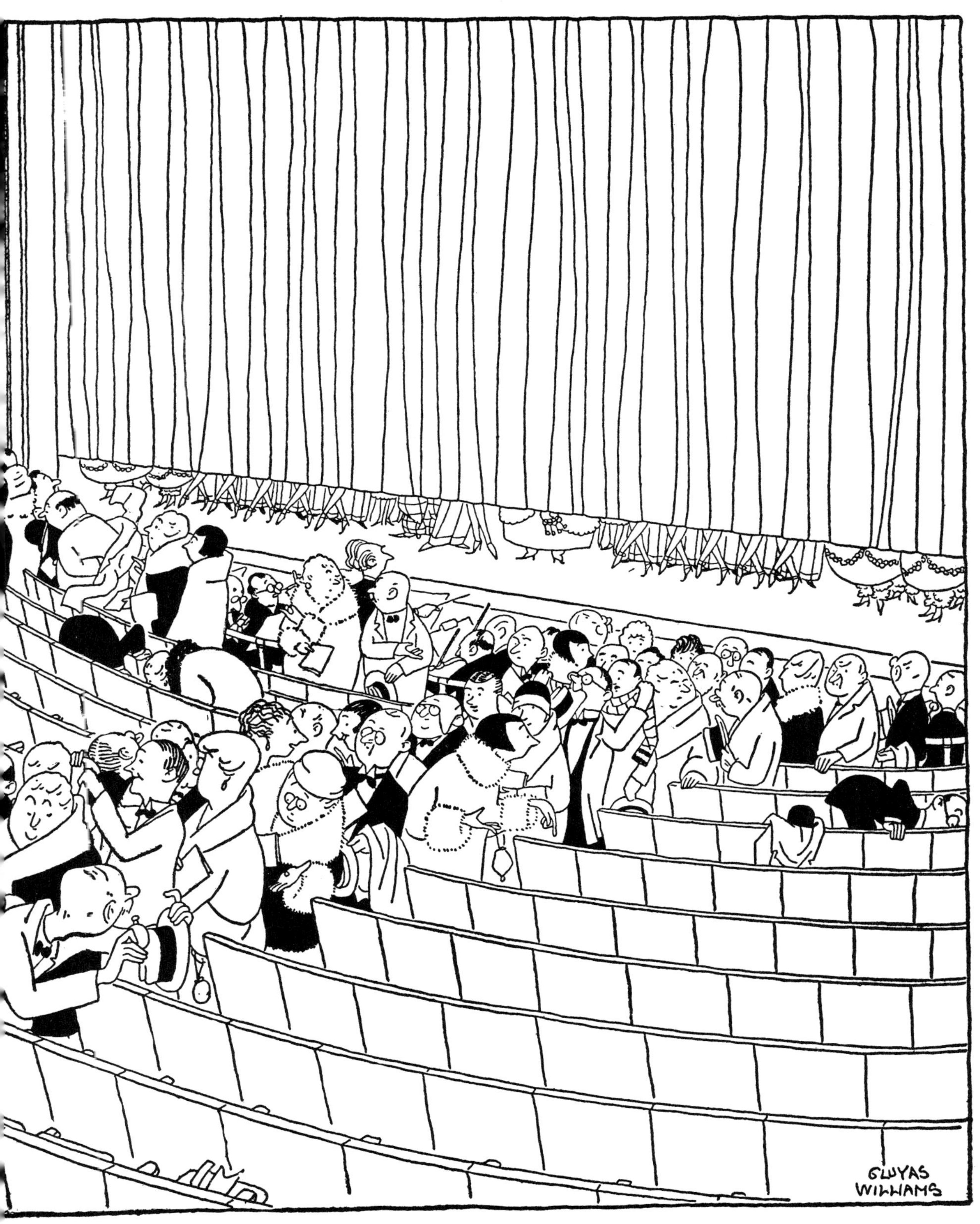

THE FINAL CURTAIN

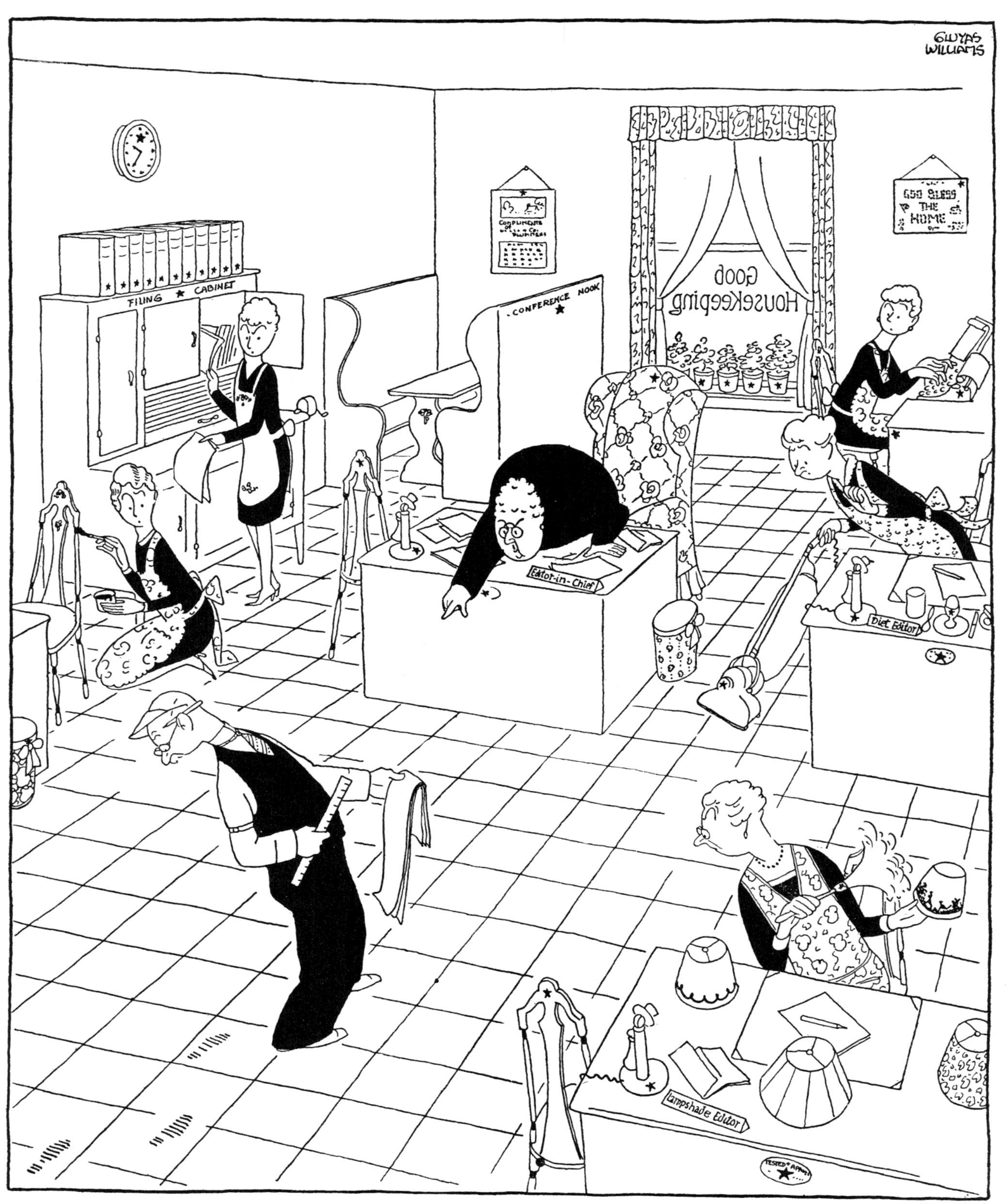

IMPRESSIONS OF MAGAZINE OFFICES—*Good Housekeeping*

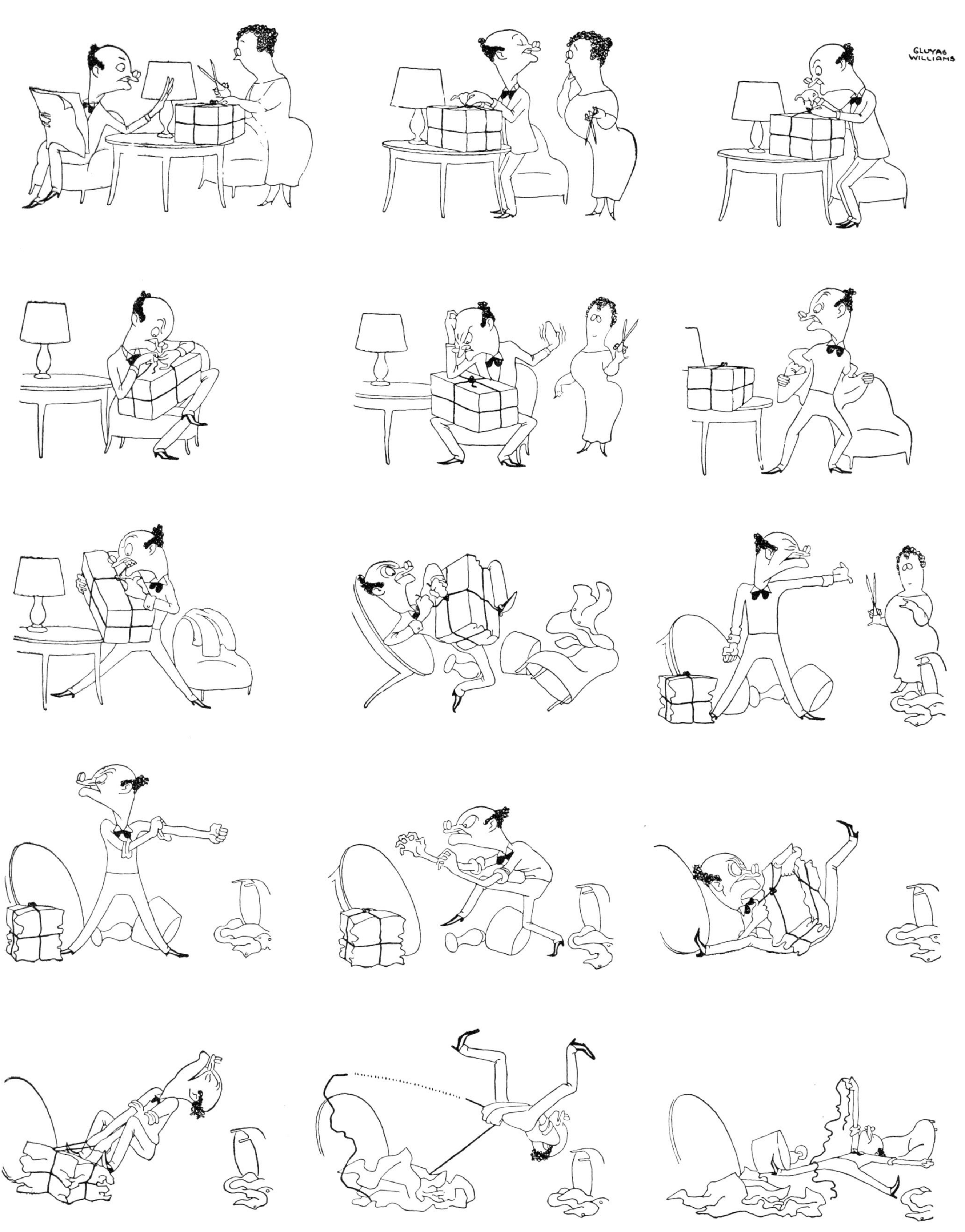

THE PASSION FOR UNTYING KNOTS

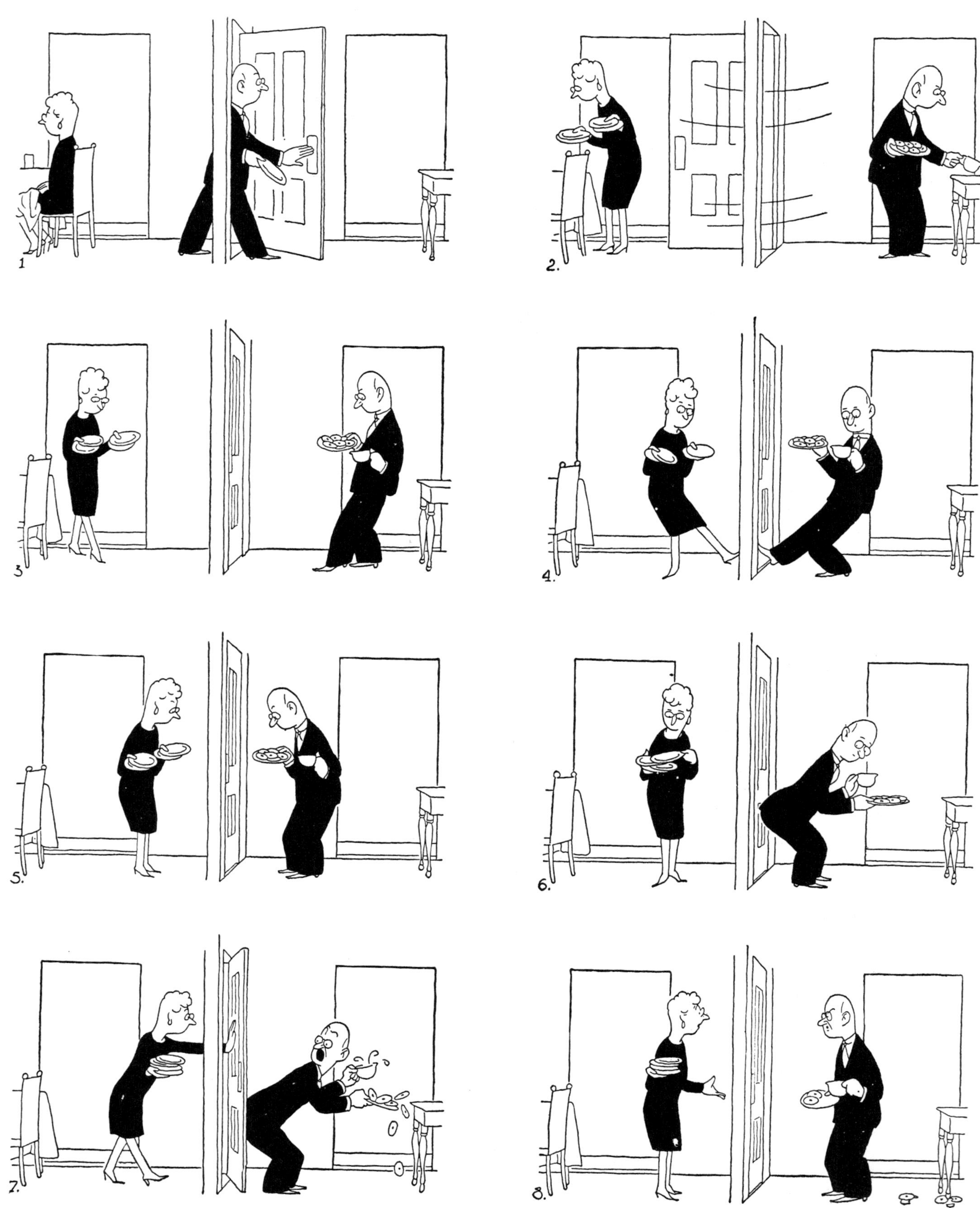

THE SWING DOOR—I

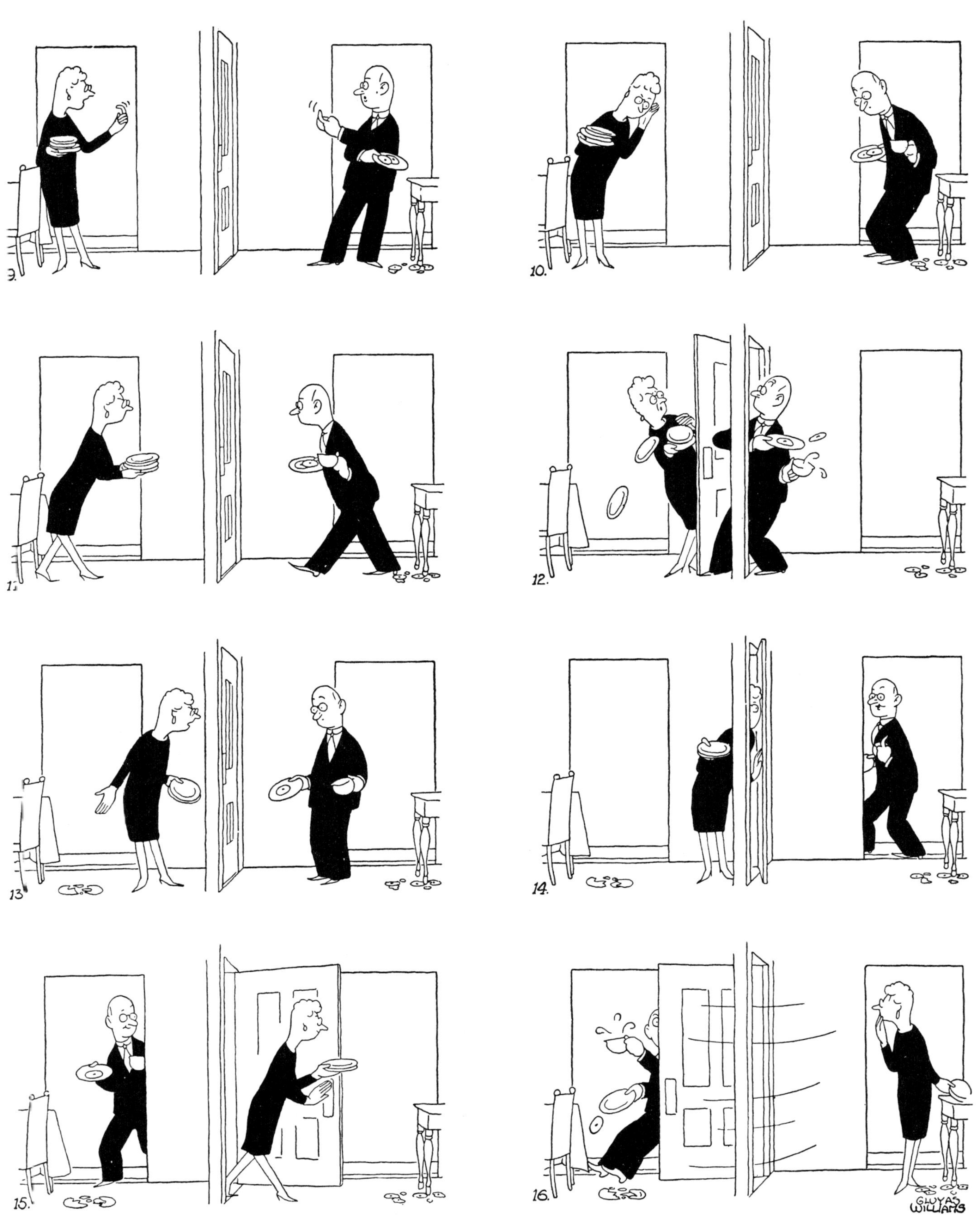

THE SWING DOOR—II